THE PATH OF PEACE

Also by Anthony Seldon

Churchill's Indian Summer: The 1951–55 Conservative Government
By Word of Mouth: Elite Oral History
Ruling Performance: Governments since 1945 (ed. with Peter Hennessy)
Political Parties Since 1945 (ed.)
The Thatcher Effect (ed. with Dennis Kavanagh)
Politics UK (Joint author)
Conservative Century (ed. with Stuart Ball)
The Major Effect (ed. with Dennis Kavanagh)
The Heath Government 1970–1974 (ed. with Stuart Ball)
The Contemporary History Handbook (ed. with Brian Brivati etc.)
The Ideas That Shaped Post-War Britain (ed. with David Marquand)
How Tory Governments Fall (ed.)
Major: A Political Life
10 Downing Street: An Illustrated History
The Powers Behind the Prime Minister (with Dennis Kavanagh)
Britain under Thatcher (with Daniel Collings)
The Foreign Office: An Illustrated History
A New Conservative Century (with Peter Snowdon)
The Blair Effect 1997–2001 (ed.)
Public and Private Education: The Divide Must End
Partnership not Paternalism
Brave New City: Brighton & Hove, Past, Present, Future
The Conservative Party: An Illustrated History (with Peter Snowdon)
New Labour, Old Labour: The Wilson and Callaghan Governments, 1974–79
Blair
The Blair Effect 2001–5 (ed. with Dennis Kavanagh)
Recovering Power: The Conservatives in Opposition since 1867 (ed. with Stuart Ball)
Blair Unbound (with Peter Snowdon and Daniel Collings)
Blair's Britain 1997–2007 (ed.)
Trust: How We Lost it and How to Get It Back
An End to Factory Schools
Why Schools, Why Universities?
Brown at 10 (with Guy Lodge)
Public Schools and the Great War (with David Walsh)
Schools United
The Architecture of Diplomacy (with Daniel Collings)
Beyond Happiness: The Trap of Happiness and How to Find Deeper Meaning and Joy
The Coalition Effect, 2010–2015 (ed. with Mike Finn)
Cameron at 10 (with Peter Snowdon)
Teaching and Learning at British Universities
The Cabinet Office 1916–2016 – The Birth of Modern British Government (with Jonathan Meakin)
The Positive and Mindful University (with Alan Martin)
The Fourth Education Revolution (with Oladimeji Abidoye)
May at 10 (with Raymond Newell)
Public Schools and the Second World War (with David Walsh)
Fourth Education Revolution Reconsidered (with Oladimeji Abidoye and Timothy Metcalf)
The Impossible Office?: The History of the British Prime Minister (with Jonathan Meakin and Illias Thoms)
Johnson at 10: The Inside Story (with Raymond Newell)

THE PATH OF PEACE

WALKING THE WESTERN FRONT WAY

ANTHONY SELDON

Atlantic Books
London

First published in hardback in Great Britain in 2022 by Atlantic Books, an imprint of Atlantic Books Ltd.

This paperback edition first published in 2023 by Atlantic Books.

Map artwork by Bell Hutley.

10 9 8 7 6 5 4 3 2 1

A CIP catalogue record for this book is available from the British Library.

Paperback ISBN: 978 1 83895 742 1
E-book ISBN: 978 1 83895 741 4

Atlantic Books
An imprint of Atlantic Books Ltd
Ormond House
26–27 Boswell Street
London
WC1N 3JZ

www.atlantic-books.co.uk

Printed and bound by CPI (UK) Ltd, Croydon CR0 4YY

This book is dedicated with admiration and thanks to those who have worked hardest to see the Western Front Way/Via Sacra become a reality: Rory Forsyth, Kim Hay, Tom Heap, Peggy Heap, Lal Mills, Amanda Carpenter, Kitty-Buchanan Gregory, Charles Pike, Laura Lestoquoy and Andrew Gillespie. All profits from the book will go to the Western Front Way.

And all her paths are peace.

Proverbs 3

Contents

1

The Silent Witnesses

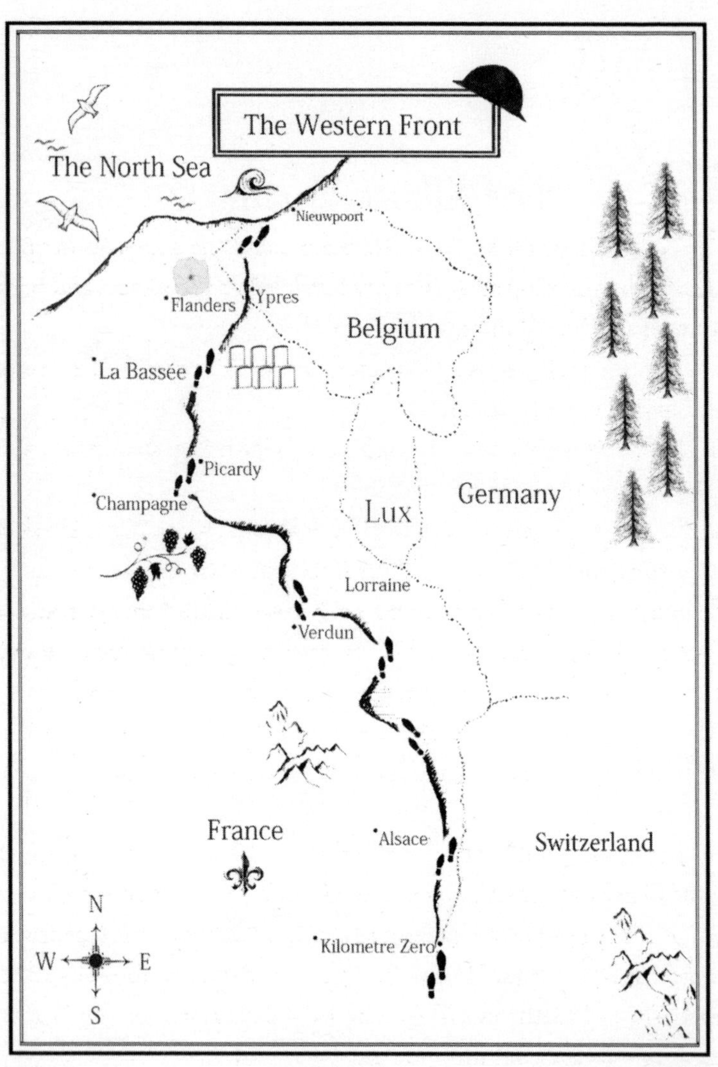

The Western Front
The North Sea
Nieuwpoort
Flanders
Ypres
Belgium
La Bassée
Picardy
Champagne
Lux
Germany
Lorraine
Verdun
France
Alsace
Switzerland
Kilometre Zero
N
W
E
S

DUM. *DUM. DUM. DUM.* It's 5 a.m., and the alarm on my phone is hammering away into my head. It has the tempo and bark of a Lewis machine gun, model 1915.

I drag myself up. I slept badly. I always do when I'm in a strange bed and have a big day ahead.

I creep quietly down the narrow staircase, put the kettle on, and take some tea in to Sarah's bedroom.

So much hinges on this day, Monday 9 August 2021. It's been a long time coming. A whole lifetime perhaps. But with the day now dawning, it seems to have come quickly, too quickly. I am not ready. The taxi is arriving at seven, and there is much to do. I pack and unpack my rucksack. I'm an innocent at this. I need more time to work through what I might need. I don't know what I'm doing. A hurried Covid test, debris left scattered on the sideboard, an even more rushed breakfast, and we're off.

Sarah and I don't talk much in the car. We are lost in thought. The radio blares out the half-remembered song 'Titanium' about a machine gun mowing people down mercilessly. Even here, we can't escape a long footprint of the First World War... I stare defiantly ahead as the taxi speeds into Heathrow's Terminal Two, disgorging us, our bags and dreams, into the cold morning air.

Confusion in all directions as we struggle to clear security and passport control. No one is listening to the announcements nor to the attendants. We're going to miss the plane – the whole plan is at risk – until the PA system tells us that Swiss Air Lines has pushed our departure time back eighty minutes.

Suddenly, we are in Row 34 at the rear of the fuselage. I'd been imagining we'd be almost alone. Fat chance. Full plane. Why on earth are so many flying to Zürich on a Monday morning? Haven't they heard about the pandemic?

Sarah squeezes my hand as we rattle down the runway, turns to me, and smiles, probing. This is it. No turning back now.

When did the plan to undertake this journey first come to me? I can no longer precisely remember. A decade ago, I was researching a book on the First World War and my co-author pointed to a letter written by a young officer, Douglas Gillespie, to his former headmaster at Winchester College. I'd worked in schools all my life so it caught my attention. Former students don't often write back to their schools, least of all to their heads. Who was Gillespie? I wondered as I gazed at his portrait. A sensitive face, proud perhaps, looking back at us in his crisp Second Lieutenant uniform, ready for the front. I had to find out about him.

Douglas Gillespie, newly enlisted in the Argyll and Sutherland Highlanders, 1915.

He was posted to the front between Vimy Ridge in northern France and the Belgian border. A dangerous part of the line. By coincidence, his beloved younger and only brother, Tom, had fought at La Bassée, just a kilometre or two away. Soon after reaching the trenches, Douglas wrote a letter to his parents in Linlithgow, Scotland, with an ingenious idea for establishing a path along No Man's Land from Switzerland to the English Channel after the war was over. I was immediately captivated, still more so by the expanded vision of the idea he wrote about to his old headmaster.

'I wish that when peace comes, our government might combine with the French government to make one long Avenue between the lines from the Vosges to the sea. The ground is so pitted, and scarred, and torn with shells, and tangled with wire, that it will take years to bring it back to use again, but I would make a fine broad road in the "No Man's Land" between the lines, with paths for pilgrims on foot, and plant trees for shade, and fruit trees, so the soil should not be altogether waste. Then I would like to send every man [woman] and child in Western Europe on pilgrimage along that Via Sacra, so that they might think and learn what war means from the silent witnesses on either side.'[1]

The silent witnesses…

These are the words that propelled me on my mission today. The words that could change history. If all goes well.

Douglas loved nature, as did many of his fellow soldiers. 'The Briton on service on the western front lived inside nature… [It] gave men a psychological, spiritual and religious uplift,' wrote John Lewis-Stempel.[2] Douglas grieved desperately at nature's destruction all around him, as he did at the destruction of human beings, never more than when his brother Tom became one of those silent witnesses, killed in action that first autumn, in October 1914. The loss changed his older brother as he toiled on month after bloody month at the front. His letters home on the surface remained stoical and cheerful, but the impact was very

LETTERS
FROM FLANDERS

WRITTEN BY 2ND LIEUT. A. D. GILLESPIE
ARGYLL AND SUTHERLAND HIGHLANDERS
TO HIS HOME PEOPLE

WITH AN APPRECIATION
OF TWO BROTHERS
BY THE RIGHT REV.
THE BISHOP OF SOUTHWARK

WITH PORTRAITS

THIRD EDITION
WITH AN APPENDIX

LONDON
SMITH, ELDER & CO
15 WATERLOO PLACE
1916

[*All rights reserved*]

The frontispiece of Letters from Flanders, *with a photo of Douglas Gillespie in 1911.*

evident, as when he wrote this, on 24 September 1915: 'My dear daddy, before long I think we should be in the thick of it. I have no forebodings, for... Tom himself will be here to help me, and give me courage and resource and that cool head which will be needed most of all to make the attack a success.'[3]

Twelve hours later, Douglas too was dead, killed in the opening hours of the catastrophic Battle of Loos. His body, mashed and mulched into the mud of northern France, was not recovered.

His distraught parents never recovered from the loss of their two sons, on whom they had pinned such hopes. To try to soothe their pain, in 1916 they published an edition of the letters Tom and Douglas wrote home: *Letters from Flanders*. A subsequent volume, pictured here, included an appendix with the seminal letter to his Winchester headmaster, Montague Rendall.

Douglas's audacious proposal for the Via Sacra, though considered idealistic in an increasingly jingoistic country, aroused some interest.

A review in the *Spectator* described his 'great Memorial Road idea' as a 'brilliant suggestion'. But it was soon swallowed up in the rip tides of the Somme in 1916 and Passchendaele in 1917, and after the war ended in 1918, neither the British nor the French governments had time or appetite to realize the vision.

Thus it was that his genius of an idea for a Western Front path lay dormant for a hundred years. When I first read the letter in 2012, with interest in the Great War surging as the centenary approached, I sensed something substantial and potent. Had the time now come to revive the proposal, to make it a reality?

I needed to find out why Douglas, uniquely it would appear among the millions of combatants, dreamt up this vision of a Via Sacra. What exactly was in his head? I started living with him for months looking for answers.

It was a moment of great joy when I discovered that Douglas's niece, great-nephews and great-nieces were alive, and proved as passionate about his vision as me. We met up to explore if his pathway might even now be established. The project began to snowball, with well-wishers joining us, not least Rory Forsyth, who became chief executive of the Western Front Way, the charity we formed to promote it. We knew we had an uphill struggle. If the project was indeed brilliant, why had no one created it in the hundred years since the armistice?

We decided we had to walk sections of the front to explore if a continuous path along its entire length was remotely realistic. It was a sobering experience. Far less than 1 per cent of the lines of trenches remained, with the rest ploughed over to restore working farmland. We struggled to find any kind of track to walk. Scattered paths close to the old front existed in places, but they were not joined up. Creating Gillespie's vision now would be seriously hard work. So it was we found ourselves out in France in the summer of 2016, Brexit-referendum summer, retreat-from-continental-partner summer. My wife Joanna's final summer.

I had not found life at all easy since Joanna's diagnosis of cancer in the summer of 2011, but her death in December 2016 shook me far more than I imagined possible. We had met at Oxford in the mid-1970s, had three dearly-loved children, and grew ever closer. She was dark-eyed and beautiful, preternaturally clever and knowing. I had lost sight of where I finished and where she began. Her death ripped me in two.

Work became my salvation. I toiled away harder than ever before, but with less success. I had been running a small university since 2015, Buckingham, which my father had helped set up in 1976, but without Joanna I had lost my touch. I always knew what I was doing with her beside me: I could make the weather. But now, almost overnight, nothing seemed to work out as I would have liked. On the surface it looked OK – numbers, profile and new buildings – and we were achieving a model of a caring, free-thinking and humane university where students and their mental health would be looked after; an exciting community with festivals galore; and innovative, with emotional and artificial intelligence. But my love for the job and ability to inspire colleagues had evaporated; my keeping one step ahead of the board, shot. Very early on, one high-up asked how it was going. Quite difficult, I replied. Why? Well, my wife is dying. You better get over it, came the reply. Fair enough, I thought. That's the way things are here. I have always needed people in the past to believe in me, to dream dreams with me. I was now on my own.

Work was making me ill, and in late 2019, I went down with shingles and almost certainly pneumonia. One icy night in Trafalgar Square on a charity sleepover with our students' union, and unable to stop coughing, I realized things had to change. I couldn't transact my magic, be the transformative leader I needed to be, and was becoming frustrated and angry. In the summer of 2020, I walked away after five years. I can't do things by half-measures. I felt a failure.

So here I found myself in 2021, without a job. Suddenly stopping work after many years of intense activity is a huge shock. I had always come alive in the company and stimulus of students: our houses at Brighton, Wellington and Buckingham were always full of young people, having meals with us, listening to brilliant speakers in front of the fire, or just chewing the cud. All gone. On top of that, I was without a tied house that for twenty-five years went with a succession of jobs running schools and then the university. New waves of realization of losing Joanna hit home in the echoing empty chambers of the free time I now had. No job, no home, no wife. No knowing what to do with the rest of my life. I better take action, quickly.

I would walk.

I would walk all the way from Switzerland to the English Channel, just as the young Douglas Gillespie had envisaged. And I would shout about it and lobby everyone I knew to ensure that his idea for the path came into being.

I had always loved walking – as a student, with the children and close friends. As head at Brighton College, I led walks with the parents from Eastbourne to Winchester along the Pilgrims' Way; at Wellington College, along the Thames from Oxford to Tower Bridge. I had entertained thoughts at job transitions of undertaking a long hike, John o'Groats to Land's End perhaps. But Gillespie's vision seemed to be more purposeful. And personal. I realized it was a long way, and I was sixty-eight, but by spreading it out with rest days, and some support, I reckoned I could manage it.

Foolishly, maybe, given I'd never been on a walk that lasted more than two days. This would need several weeks, cover 1,000 kilometres, and take over 1 million steps, through soil where up to 10 million soldiers and civilians had spilt their blood.

Which end should I start at? At first I thought west to east. But walking back from the Vosges mountains to the sea soon seemed more appealing because I would have a sense of walking home as well as towards the areas of greatest British involvement in the war, rather than away. I was due to leave in May, then on 9 June, but Covid restrictions kept upending my plans. Departure was pushed later and later. With reports that the virus was running rife in northern France, the walk began to look bleak. Hotels and restaurants were closing up. For three miserable weeks in July, it looked as if my plans would collapse, at least for 2021.

Then out of the blue, in early August, restrictions were lifted. Had I left it too late? September was approaching; the window was shutting. It was mad to go – the walk would be compressed, with rest days now ruled out because of time, and gone too any margins for error or mishap. The delays meant I would have to lose plans for a regular support team. I would have to move at pace and on my own, finding my own route and rest places in a country almost closed because of Covid. I knew the risks, but I knew I had to go.

Because this was to be more than a walk. It was to be a pilgrimage. Helping achieve Gillespie's dream of a permanent 1,000-kilometre path was certainly a powerful motivation; but it was not enough.

Gillespie wanted it to be more than a pleasant walk through nature. He had a deadly serious intent in that letter to his headmaster. He wanted it to be a path of peace and a walk of remembrance. It should be an encounter, a life-changing experience for all who travelled the path, a challenge to find greater peace within, peace with fellow human beings and with the natural world.

With my life as it was, I needed this pilgrimage as much as anyone. But could I myself manage to achieve the inner transition I would need to make? Despite a frenetic practice of meditation and yoga, and arguing for the teaching of happiness, enduring peace had so far eluded me. As long as I was busy, I got by. The swirl of activity kept me from introspection, from confronting my demons. Fear had been my constant companion. Fear of just about everything. Fear of failure. Fear that no one would want me. As now seemed to be the case.

I knew I was no different to the millions of others who yearn for peace in their lives. Like many alive across the world today, the First

World War had shaped my life profoundly. The war had been fought in Europe, Asia and Africa, with some 65 million mobilized, of whom approaching 10 million were killed.[4] Its scars are still buried deeply in the collective unconscious and a profound fascination with the conflict endures.

I had noticed as a teacher how gripped my students were by the First World War – far more so than they were by the Second. But I had never understood the hold the war had on me. Could it be to do with the experience of my four grandparents? I needed to find out more about them too as part of my pilgrimage, to probe the murky myths that all families pass on.

Confronting parts of myself that I had long suppressed was what frightened me most on the journey out to Switzerland. The physical challenge of the walk would be demanding, certainly, but nothing compared to the psychological challenge. Could I let go of my own ghosts, reconcile myself to disappointments, make peace with those who had damaged me? Could I move on from Joanna and find new love, enduring peace and happiness within? Could I change to a less manic gear? Writing a book on Boris Johnson, as planned, if I was to keep up my rhythm of books on recently departed prime ministers, would hardly help me do this. Could I find peace in places where numinous spirits floated just above the soil in which the millions died, ten silent witnesses for each pace I would be treading along the walk?

If the Western Front Way came into being, with my life broken as never before, I could pave the way to greater peace, as Gillespie envisaged, for all who walked along it.

What a time to be walking too, with so many mourning loved ones lost in the pandemic, Britain wrestling with its own sense of identity, and Russian threats towards Ukraine intensifying and Europe teetering on the brink of war. One hundred years earlier my grandparents had fled west from near Kyiv in search of peace. Now their descendants beat the same path.

So today I would start walking Gillespie's path of peace. I would walk it to see, a century on, if I could help it to be built; to help the Via Sacra become the Via Pax.

Now, all roads led to Kilometre Zero.

2

Kilometre Zero

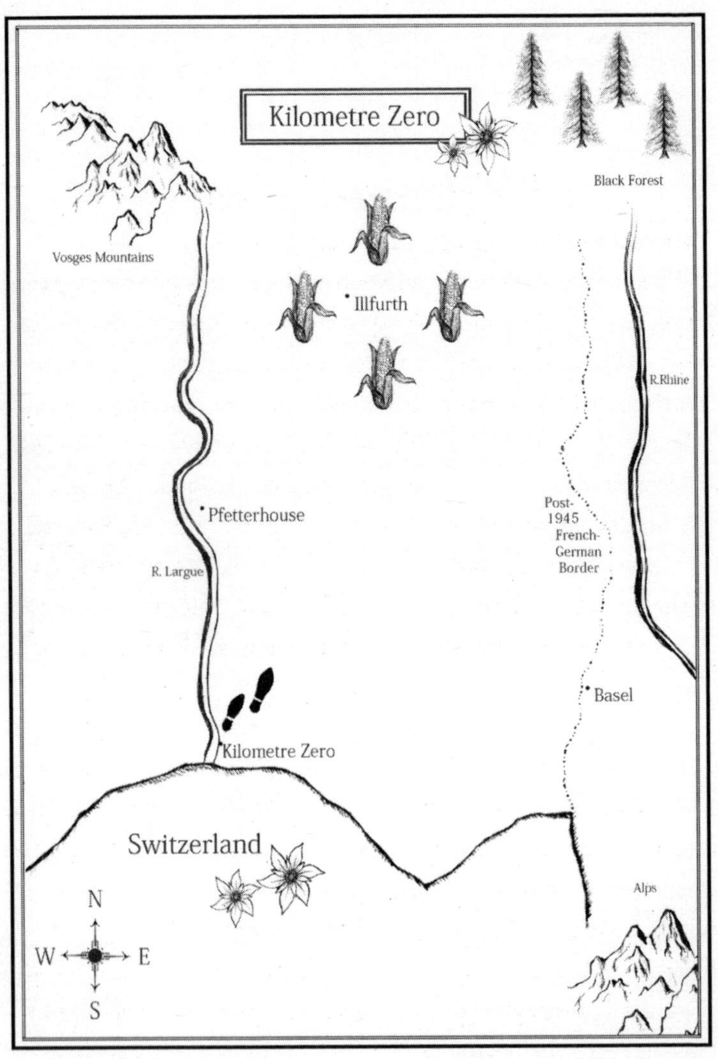

Kilometre Zero
Black Forest
Vosges Mountains
Illfurth
R.Rhine
Pfetterhouse
Post-
1945
French-
German
Border
R. Largue
Basel
Kilometre Zero
Switzerland
Alps
N
W
E
S

'CAN YOU REMIND ME why I'm doing this?'

'Because you said you must,' Sarah replies, returning to her magazine.

I look out of the window, as the sun rises over a carpet of cloud.

An hour later, we are at Zürich airport queueing at passport control. 'There should be two separate lines: one for those who voted remain, the other for Brexit,' I say testily. 'It wouldn't have made any difference,' she responds. 'Why?' 'Because Switzerland was never in the EU.'

We find ourselves last in a long queue for our hire car. On either side of us, the kiosks for other hire companies are empty. We find our car in the lot easily: it's the only one left. A long time after setting off, we pass Basle airport, the intended destination but for the delays. By mid-afternoon, we arrive at our destination.

After all the noise of the journey – the crowds, the flight, the two-hour car trip – we've made it to Kilometre Zero. Elated and exhausted, I am desperate to look around, but it is already late, 4 p.m., and I had planned to walk four or five hours that day. So, there is little time to explore beyond a hurried photograph taken by Sarah, my foot self-consciously positioned on a trench emplacement.

Kilometre Zero is where the Western Front trenches, which began their winding journey on the Belgian coast, came to an abrupt end. But, in this story, the beginning.

The beginning of my walk, and the beginning of the fighting in the First World War; the site where the first witnesses were silenced. The beginning of the front.

'The marker of three states', with a Swiss soldier to the left, and two Frenchmen on the right. *© Swiss Federal Archives*

Nearby Kilometre Zero is the spot where the Swiss, French and German borders converged. 'The marker of three states', as it was known in 1914, commemorates the exact spot with three stones, two clearly visible in the photograph above. The third, the oldest, is just visible at an angle at the bottom right. Although the Franco-German border now lies on the River Rhine 40 kilometres to the east, the stones still stand here innocently today.

A Swiss stream flows north from here to become the Largue river. Though barely 10 metres wide, it served as No Man's Land in this most southerly sector of the front. The French hunkered down on the west bank, the Germans facing them on the east. The Swiss army's task was to prevent them trying to steal round behind the other via their sovereign soil to the south. They meant it, in appearances at least.

They stationed a garrison on the border to ensure that the French and Germans, long versed in killing each other, played by the rules.[1]

The combatants understood that they could neither shell nor fire on or even over the Swiss trenches. The Swiss soldiers demanded cover nevertheless from stray bullets and shrapnel that would occasionally come their way. They remained to the end proudly neutral, resolutely above the fighting and slaughter afflicting their neighbours on all sides. Lapses were rare, and caused great consternation when they occurred.

Easter Sunday 1917 saw one such diplomatic embarrassment when a Swiss military band was playing, to the evident delight of the German troops who began to sing and dance extravagantly in the open air. As the Swiss territory jutted into French and German land, the German soldiers, though within comfortable range of the French, assumed they were safe as any bullet would have had to travel over Swiss land. Suddenly a shot rang out. A Portuguese soldier fighting with the French had not been apprised of the rules of etiquette. His bullet hit an unsuspecting German clean in the stomach. It was widely considered a very poor show. The innocent soldier, whose only sin was to become entranced, later died and is buried at the most southerly German burial ground on the front, just north of Altkirch, at Illfurth.

German soldiers were only too happy to serve in this peaceful sector. At the very end of their front line, they erected a wooden box for a sentry. Its signboard read: 'Final stop of the underground train from Ostend to Switzerland' (or in German, *Endstation der Untergrundbahn Ostende–Schweiz*). All very amusing, if not entirely accurate. As we shall see, the Western Front ended not at Ostend, but 15 kilometres south-west, at the coastal town of Nieuwpoort.[2]

If you had travelled the other way during the war, westwards towards the English Channel, you'd have encountered a multi-kilometre labyrinth of interconnected trenches which moved barely at all from late 1914 to March 1918. There was nothing quite like it in earlier wars, nor indeed during the Second World War nor since.

The afternoon is going, and I am desperate to set out on the walk. But before I do so, for those less familiar with the story, let me sketch out why the Western Front remained static in trenches for so long, despite the hope among all major European armies that rapid movement would characterize the war. This is the key to understanding the entire caboodle.

Field Marshal Alfred von Schlieffen was the dramatist responsible for penning the script for the Western Front. The Schlieffen Plan of 1905–6 envisaged that, in the event of a simultaneous war against France and Russia, the German army would quickly invade France through the Low Countries, rather than on their shared border further to the east. Having knocked out France at pace, Germany would turn its attention to fighting Russia on their Eastern Front.

In the early days of the war, his plan seemed a brilliant success. Though Belgium put up spirited resistance, its fortresses, including Liège and Antwerp, were pulverized by heavy German artillery. The French attempt to halt the Germans at the Battle of the Frontiers saw them thrown back with horrifying losses, while the British Expeditionary Force (BEF) with French support was sent into retreat after bloody fighting at the Battles of Mons and Le Cateau. In early September 1914, German forces were so close to Paris that their patrols glimpsed the Eiffel Tower.[3] France teetered on the brink.

As Germany prepared to defeat the French army once and for all, the Allies marshalled their forces in the First Battle of the Marne, shattering the German expectation of a quick knockout blow. The Marne saw half a million casualties on both sides in just one week, as the largest armies in history collided for the first time.[4]

The German forces pulled back, digging the war's first trenches by the River Aisne. In the ensuing 'race to the sea', both sides tried to outflank the other north-westwards up to the English Channel, while in the other direction, the front line edged south-eastwards down towards the Alps. With winter approaching, exhausted troops dug trenches to hold their positions, with the Germans often on the higher ground. Even if they had not yet knocked France out of the war, most of Belgium, and much of northern France, was in their hands. They were perfectly happy to dig in and defend.

Now, let's take a moment to consider trenches. Battlefields of the past, whether Agincourt, Ramillies or Waterloo – all incidentally fought close to the Western Front – left little tangible evidence behind. They were brief affairs, and if part of a longer conflict, the fighting moved on to fresh killing grounds. As war became mechanized from the nineteenth century, with rapid-fire rifles, machine guns and long-range artillery, troops needed better protection.

Survival rates on both sides proved many times higher when soldiers were able to find shelter below the direct sight of the enemy. Urban areas provided cover in buildings, but the First World War was a rural affair mostly. Hence trenches dug in farmers' fields, woods and open land. At first, they were thought to be a temporary expedient. But as the days turned to weeks, and weeks to months, and the line remained resolutely fixed with neither side able to break through, the system became permanent. The truth slowly dawned that it was much easier to defend than to attack trenches, at least until the arrival of tanks from 1916 helped the conflict to become the war of movement its scriptwriters had envisaged.

Early trenches in 1914 were primitive. Douglas Gillespie wrote in August 1915 that 'it was through this part of the country that Tom marched and fought during his last few days', remarking how better constructed the trenches already were by then.[5] Along the front, concrete, wood, brick, corrugated iron and steel, anything that was solid, was dragged into service. New trenches were constructed either from the surface down, allowing many soldiers to work at the same time but exposing them to enemy fire, or by sapping, where they extended the trenches at each end out of enemy sight, but with smaller numbers able to dig at one time. The soil removed was shovelled into sandbags, piled on top of the trenches at the front facing the enemy, known as parapets, and behind, known as parados. Trenches could be more than 2 metres deep, with a raised fire-step at the front on which soldiers could stand to see over the top. They were zigzagged, called traverses, to limit the impact of direct hits by shells or the risk in a successful raid of an enemy firing the length of a trench. Up to five or more parallel lines of trenches would face the enemy, with No Man's Land (controlled by neither side) between 10 metres to 0.8 kilometres wide, depending on terrain, separating both sides, and rows of barbed wire erected there for extra protection. The front-line trenches would have gently rising saps jutting out into it, from which wiring and raiding parties could sortie. Behind the front lines were support trenches; behind them, lines of reserve trenches. Linking them all were communication trenches. Dugouts which afforded protection from shrapnel were usually located in support trenches; the Germans dug them deeper, while the French and British dugouts had to be shallower because they were on lower ground more liable to flooding, and were rarely more than 5 metres below the earth.

To one side of Kilometre Zero lay these trenches and 1,000 kilometres of war. To the other, up to 1,000 kilometres of comparative peace, until the Eastern Front offered its own concoction of twisted flesh and steel. Because of the Germans' failure to stifle France quickly, they had no option but to fight on the two fronts Schlieffen had planned to avoid. The designation the 'Western Front' was thus coined by the Germans; to the British, the Western Front lay way to its east.

But which Western Front would I follow? There is no single Western Front. So the route I decided to take over the next five weeks is the line from late 1914 until the German breakout through the front in their great offensive of March 1918. With almost all the trenches long since disappeared, I needed all the help I could get from colleagues in our new Western Front Way team. We identified the closest tracks and roads to where the front lay in those thirty-nine months – sticking as close to the trench line as possible – at least until I reached Belgium, where the path by the summer of 2021 had been already marked out. I've never been any kind of pathfinder, let alone over such a long distance, and to be honest, I don't know how good I would be at doing it. Booking places to stay en route was extremely tricky as only larger towns seemed to have places still open. Walking through a plague was not making my task any easier. I only hoped I could rely on taxis to ferry me at the end of each day to a new abode – if I could find one.

My alertness to daily-changing Covid constraints was mirrored by my middle child, Susie, whose wedding had been long planned and most eagerly awaited by her for the end of August at our house in a village north of the Dordogne, the house I bought for her mother in 2015 on almost her last visit to our beloved France. Somehow, if it was to happen, I would need to break off my walk for a couple of days and find my way south. The timing of the wedding I could see would be significant for my journey.

The Western Front is not a clear line like the coastline of Devon and Cornwall. I envied author Raynor Winn walking a similar distance along that coastal path as recounted in her inspiring book, *The Salt Path*. If she and her husband Moth deviated from their track one way, they were in gorse bushes; the other, and they were over the cliff edge into the sea. Their journey was full of test and challenge, but they at least knew their route. Nor would this be like the Camino de Santiago, the 1,000-year-old pilgrim path across northern Spain to the Cathedral of Santiago de Compostela. In time, our hope is the Western Front Way might attract walkers with similar intent and in similar numbers. But as long as the route is not marked, it will lack the company of fellow travellers which is one of the Camino's great joys.

No, my journey would be more like that of Patrick Leigh Fermor, the legendary writer who walked from the Hook of Holland to the Danube across Germany and Austria as Nazism was taking hold in 1933–4, as recounted in his revered book, *A Time of Gifts*. He had to puzzle out his route as he went along, as I would too. He had to rely on the kindness of strangers, as I would. He was walking alone, as I would. The seeds of the Europe through which I would walk were sown by the Europe through which he walked. The seeds of the Europe through which he walked was flowering its blood-dimmed tide in Eastern Europe with increasing menace as I walked.

I could never forget Gillespie's dream was to create not just a walking route along the front, but a path of peace. I would be walking in part to explore what he meant by that elusive word 'peace'. What had it meant to those who fought in the war and survived? What did it mean to those whose livelihoods had depended on the millions of hectares ravaged by war?

Fighting, as we know, ceased with the armistice at 11 a.m. on 11 November 1918, a truce which required the cessation of all hostilities along the Western Front, and the withdrawal of German forces east of the Rhine. While the Germans had to surrender most of their army's weapons, warships and aircraft, and release Allied prisoners of war, the blockade of Germany was to remain in place. The armistice had been signed at 5.45 a.m. at Compiègne, but fighting continued until 11 a.m. An estimated 2,738 unfortunate soldiers were killed in those final hours.[6]

Work began almost at once on a peace treaty, requiring the armistice to be extended three times. Representatives of thirty-two nations met in Paris from January 1919, though the proceedings were dominated by just three: France, Britain and the United States. The Treaty of Versailles, which dealt with Germany, was signed on 28 June 1919, five years to the day after the assassination of the Archduke Franz Ferdinand in Sarajevo. The final of the five peace treaties – Lausanne, focusing on the Ottoman Empire – was not signed until July 1923.

Five peace treaties.

Did they bring peace? Not to the millions suffering from what we now call post-traumatic stress disorder. The guns might have fallen silent, but not the guns still raging in the heads of those poor souls.

The poet and composer Ivor Gurney, who spent the last fifteen years of his life in psychiatric hospitals before his death in December 1937, is one of the better-known 'long' casualties of the war. What of those millions of unknowns who woke screaming night after night in terror? Where too was the bounty of peace for the children, the women and the parents, like Douglas and Tom's family, deprived forever more of those they most loved and needed?

On the very western tip of Europe, there was no peace in Ireland. Nor for the 'cornermen', returning soldiers, damaged in body and mind, without jobs or hope, begging on street corners year after year. Nor on the eastern frontiers of Europe was there peace for the Jews, victims of the collapsing Russian Empire. Pogroms – rampages by locals whipped up at Easter by anti-Semitic clergy – had been commonplace for centuries before 1914, leaving behind them a trail of death and rape. But from 1917, the perpetrators included the upper classes. To the Bolsheviks, the Jews were bourgeois swine; to the White Russians, they were dirty revolutionaries, kinsmen of Bolshevik Trotsky. Some 150,000 Jews are estimated to have been murdered in 1918–21.[7] The depravity and cruelty of the Russian Civil War at large, and the 'Red Terror' unleashed by the Soviet Union's first head, Lenin, which left many times that number dead, has rarely been matched in history. So much for 'the war to end wars', as, following the title of a 1914 H. G. Wells book, the First World War came to be known.

'Peace', at least at a national level, held in Europe for twenty years after the armistice before forces, unleashed by the war and its aftermath, propelled the world into an even greater conflagration after September 1939. Before 1914, Europe's great powers had been at peace, mostly, for a hundred years since the Battle of Waterloo in 1815 had brought the last great continental war to an end. Is peace, then, merely the absence of war? Or is it something altogether deeper?

The walk would for the first time ever give me the prolonged chance to reflect on how my life, like that of hundreds of millions alive today, has been affected by what happened between 1914 and 1918. I have been captivated by the Great War for as long as I can remember. I have been at my happiest when conducting trips around the trenches. Before departure, I encouraged those joining to research their family and the war, something almost all are eager to do, making connections and reaching new understandings.

This walk would give me a taste of my own medicine. I knew some facts, but not the emotions nor the deep way that the experience shaped my parents, and hence me. My grandfather Wilfred Willett, a Cambridge graduate training to be a doctor at London Hospital, enlisted in the London Rifle Brigade as soon as war was declared. By October, he was out at the front, taking part in fighting to the south of the Belgian town of Ypres on what was called 'the salient' (an area jutting out into enemy territory). On 13 December 1914, one of his men was wounded in No Man's Land. He slithered out over the top and, utilizing the basic medical knowledge he had acquired, tended the man's wounds. While doing so, a sniper's bullet glided into the side of his head. But for his wife Eileen badgering the War Office to let her travel across the Channel to France to bring him back home when all had given up hope, he would have died.

Eileen's twenty-first birthday had fallen on the day Britain entered the war, 4 August. Joanna shared the same birthday, a fact my mother always thought significant. The story of Eileen's journey to France and Wilfred's partial recovery thereafter is retold in Jonathan Smith's novel, *Wilfred and Eileen*, and in a BBC 1 television series.[8] So it had become, in my head, a sepia-tinted story of romantic love and heroism. I had to plumb much deeper.

For Wilfred, there was no peace after 1918. Deprived by injuries of his vocation of becoming a doctor, he sought solace in writing and politics. His close friend, author Henry Williamson, based his character Phillip Maddison on him in his *A Chronicle of Ancient Sunlight* series of books. But when disillusion with peace struck in the 1920s and Williamson turned sharply right, Wilfred turned left, becoming a Communist, and selling copies of the party's newspaper, the *Daily Worker*, on the railway bridge by Tunbridge Wells station. His daughter, my mother, crossed the street every publication day to avoid him on her journey home from her private school. She too knew little of peace in her family home, her father suffering violent mood swings and at war with her brother. Once she jerked a Lee Enfield rifle away from her brother taking aim at their father in the garden. Her childhood made her anxious, giving her a sense of foreboding which I inherited. Unexamined, I have lived with it all my life. I too am a child of the war.

My father too was sculpted by the war. When the *Sunday Times* some years ago wanted to conduct a joint interview, he couldn't face talking about his own childhood. He later told me the reason was 'there was so much death'. The facts I knew. His parents, Jewish émigrés from Pereiaslav near Kyiv, found safety from pogroms in London's East End. But not from the Spanish flu spread by the war, which killed them within a week of each other in July 1918. My father, adopted by a cobbler in the East End, didn't know till he was twelve that he had brothers and sisters. They found out where he lived and wrote in chalk on the street cobbles outside: 'Abraham is our brother.' The shock was said to have given him his lifelong stammer.

The First World War has preoccupied me throughout my life. No sooner had I become a schoolteacher than I bundled the cast of R. C. Sherriff's play *Journey's End* that I was directing into a minibus heading to the trenches. More recently, I was executive producer of the film of the play, directed by Saul Dibb. In between these came the sixty or so trips I led to the trenches, for students, staff and, most recently, parents. Every time, the experience is fresh, fresh as the hopes of the young men marching off to war. What keeps drawing me back, again and again? Telling the stories to different groups, noticing how they all, sooner or later, become engaged emotionally, clearly fulfilled a need. Helping others make deep connections spared me from travelling deep inside for myself. We are all children of that war.

The plays, the trips, my family's experiences, were all pointing me to this day, the day I begin my pilgrimage.

Here I am at Kilometre Zero on Day 1. My face looks anxious. Gillespie had no real idea what he had let himself in for when his photograph was taken. Neither, a hundred years later, did I.

Kilometre Zero, Day 1, 9 August 2021.

3

Alsace

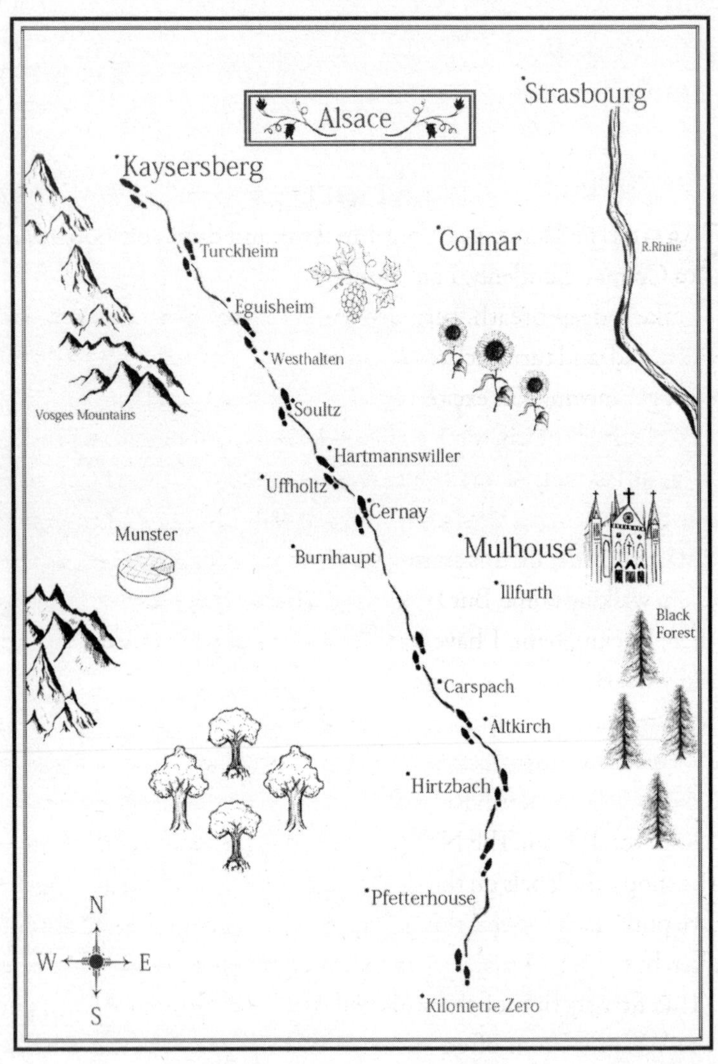
Alsace
Strasbourg
Kaysersberg
Colmar
R.Rhine
Turckheim
Eguisheim
Westhalten
Vosges Mountains
Soultz
Hartmannswiller
Uffholtz
Cernay
Munster
Mulhouse
Burnhaupt
Illfurth
Black
Forest
Carspach
Altkirch
Hirtzbach
Pfetterhouse
N
W
E
S
Kilometre Zero

SARAH STEPS BACK INTO our hired car and drives off northwards to Colmar. Suddenly, I am alone.

I take a deep breath, turn around one final time and look into Switzerland, and turn back to commit that first step, the most difficult. Once I get moving I'm excited and happy.

I feel a rush of joy, after so many anxious months of waiting, to be here at last, on the eastern tip of the Western Front. I don't care about the difficulties that may lie ahead. I'm just thrilled to be alive and starting the walk this summer afternoon, walking to the Channel.

I am walking home. But I don't have a home. Since leaving Ondaatje Hall at Buckingham, I have lived in a succession of rented flats, my worldly possessions in storage. So what!

The walking kit on which I will rely is feeling good. My IsoGrip boots (£200, reduced to £150) came from Mountain Warehouse in Brighton, and my long-sleeve North Ridge top, cowboy hat and waterproof trousers (£250 in total) from The North Face in Bath. The portentous names of the shops, the labels on the clothes and the expense reassure me that I have purchased the real thing. I may not be a genuine long-distance walker, but at least I make a passable impression of looking like one.

This first section of the walk will take me through Alsace, part of the Western Front often left off British maps of the war. Neither British nor Commonwealth forces fought here. But the region through which I will be walking saw intense fighting in 1914, with three battles between the French and Germans.

In the opening days of the war, Joseph Joffre, commander-in-chief of the French forces, saw the area as ripe for a *coup de théâtre* by seizing Alsace back from the Germans. On 7 August, the French First Army thus advanced eastwards across the German frontier to the city of Mulhouse (Mülhausen in German), which the surprised Germans rapidly quit. But then reinforcements arrived, and the French withdrew themselves back towards the Vosges. There, they mustered, and attacked again on 14 August as part of a vast military advance along their entire frontier, inspired by Napoleonic zest. For a second time, they seized the city, only to withdraw again when it became clear that the plan was collapsing in the face of superior German strength. On 24 August, Joffre accepted that his cunning scheme had failed, and with German forces breaking through in Belgium, he ordered a retreat.[1]

Now it was the Germans' turn to attack, deploying their Sixth and Seventh Armies, mainly Bavarian soldiers, under the command of Rupprecht, Crown Prince of Bavaria. They made more progress to the north-west, in Lorraine and the Vosges, than in Alsace, where the French forces held out, and by mid-September, with 66,000 German casualties, he called off the attack. For the next four years till the armistice, Alsace was one of the war's quiet sectors.[2]

I'm only dimly aware of this history as I start, so am having to gen up on it as I go. More immediate concerns than Rupprecht, though, fill my thoughts. How will I possibly recall everything I see? Details of Kilometre Zero are already confused in my mind. Realizing how easily I will forget thoughts and details of my journey, I decide then and there to dictate a diary into my phone as I strut along, snapping periodic photos at will. It proved a happy decision.

'So, that first step I took ten minutes ago from Kilometre Zero has been trodden,' was my opening comment. 'The emotion and tension towards the first day built and built, but now it has happened, it's happening in prose, not poetry. I am climbing a hill a little too steep for comfort coming away from Kilometre Zero towards Pfetterhouse, the first community on the long route.'

Looking back at my walking diary from the tranquillity of my writing desk, I had forgotten how I saw the task at the time. 'I'll be undertaking two walks in parallel,' I recorded, 'one in the present moment, through Covid-affected villages, with flies and sweat, while trying to puzzle out the route; the other will see me walking a hundred years ago following the old front line, missing the flies and the sweat, the fear and noise.'

This book is written in two tenses: the present for the walk and what I see during it, the past tense when writing about the war and its aftermath.

What I failed to understand on that first day was the walk would be taking place in a further dimension, neither in colour nor in black and white, nor indeed in physical time, but in the depths of the subconscious. The physical walk, and the sights I would see, shone a light on suppressed chasms of thought and emotion which continued long after the walk was over. In that churning liminal space, I find it difficult to tell dreams from reality.

Back to the diary: 'The first afternoon is still warm. My plan is to be walking north-west along the front in the first half of the day, which means the sun will be mostly on my back. But walking today north and starting out at 4 p.m., the sun is on the left side of my face.'

To my west lies the low mountain range of the Vosges; to the north, the flat plains of Alsace; and to my east, the southern tip of the Black Forest. Cradling it, the mighty Rhine, the first of the seven rivers that will be my touchstones on the walk. My route never allows me to see it, but for my first hundred kilometres, the Rhine is a constant companion. I can sense it, can smell it almost, and can never forget its pulsing urgency. The Rhine indeed was the ever-present unconscious shadow of the Western Front. For four and a half years, it was never within sight of the fighting, but never beyond its sounds. It mirrors the front's length: 1,036 kilometres from the Old Rhine Bridge at Constance in the Alps till, at the Hook of Holland, it expires into the dark oblivion of the North Sea. As the Western Front runs north through Alsace, it mimics it flowing north from Basle; then, as the front wheels north-westwards, so too does the Rhine, both travelling urgently onwards in search of the sea. I am never happier on the walk than when I am beside a river, always on the move, always lifting my spirits and urging me on.

'Now I'm thirty minutes in. Cars whistle periodically by on the country lane into Pfetterhouse,' I record. 'Lush green fields in every direction, the lane stretching straight ahead, here and there tractors at work in the fields. The air is full of the smell of manure and flowers.' Blue cornflowers, pink and white mallow and wild parsley! After all the planning and worries of the last year and more, suddenly here is deep peace. Messages from friends and well-wishers arrive regularly on my phone. *The Times* featured the walk today as its page-3 story, accompanied by an editorial in support of our Western Front Way. 'I can see keeping up with messages is going to be a challenge. And possibly dangerous if I'm going to be replying to them when I walk. As I will. Patrick Leigh Fermor didn't have to contend with this.'

I am pulled up short when I walk down into Pfetterhouse. I am not certain what I expected of the first community on my journey – an open café at least – but what I find is a ghost town. Not a car, not a person, not an open shop, a railway station closed years before, a reminder of a once flourishing community. Though only early August, the carefully tended gardens have an autumnal feeling, the smell of burning leaves and wood lingering in the still air. And despite the town's elegant timbered houses, *À VENDRE* signs are ubiquitous. Sudden dog barks enfilade the stillness, without sign of the hounds or their owners. Is this a foretaste of what I can expect?

With no time to tarry, I consult my map, and decide to take the road north to Seppois-le-Haut. 'One hour in exactly, it's 5 o'clock, and the first euphoria is wearing off,' I record. The path that will take shape doesn't exist this far east, and I gloomily envisage being forced to walk along busy roads with cars shooting past in both directions day after day. The honeymoon is over before it could begin. 'I've just had my first altercation with a mosquito, which results in me spraying on industrial quantities of insect repellent. After just one hour, my right knee is beginning to hurt, as it has done periodically over the years.'

In preparation, I had been to see Rupert Molloy, a physiotherapist in Henley-on-Thames, who told me the problem wasn't my knee, but my ankle. 'No, it's my knee hurting: it's my knee and I know it's my knee.' 'Have you ever twisted your ankle?' he replied gently to my tart response. 'When running, repeatedly,' I said. 'Well that's it,' he pronounced, as he took my ankle in his hand and showed me exactly where the pain was based, causing my kneecap to be misaligned. His solution was German 'instructional leggings' to re-educate my knee back into its right position. I'd been feeling very sorry for my knee. I meekly accepted his advice that it needed re-educating.

I press on through Seppois-le-Haut and le-Bas to the village of Largitzen. Already I'm fretting about the time. It's nearly 6 p.m., and my target for today is Altkirch (*Alte Kirchen* in German, old church). But at current rate of progress, I won't arrive there till 8 p.m., too late to have dinner in Colmar, a good seventy-five minutes away by taxi. I'm not good at admitting failure, least of all on Day 1. Torn between trying to make my first day objective, and a convivial dinner in Colmar with Sarah, I decide the latter is much the preferable. So, I summon a local taxi to meet me in Hirtzbach, 5 kilometres north. Feeling a little downcast, I press on. I haven't even the excuse of heavy baggage to blame for slowing me down; my rucksack contains only water: Sarah has taken all my heavy equipment, which I will have to carry with me after she leaves. The prospect is not an encouraging one.

The German place names remind me that I'm emphatically not starting out on my walk in mainstream France. For this is Alsace, which, along with Lorraine, had for centuries been contested territory with the German states. From the end of the Roman

La Tache Noire (The Black Spot) by Albert Bettannier (1877).

Empire in the fifth century for over a millennium, Alsace was part of the German world. I see echoes of this repeatedly. The half-timber architecture with flat roof tiles has more in common with German buildings. The cookery is Germanic, with pork and sauerkraut favoured dishes. Even the drinks – schnapps, lagers and distinctive Alsatian white wines – are closer to what can be found over on the east bank of the Rhine than to France.

France annexed Alsace in 1648 at the end of the bloody Thirty Years War until Germany grabbed it after crushing Napoleon III's forces in the Franco-Prussian War of 1870–71. The culture of the territory was truly hybrid: during the 220 years of Catholic French control from 1648, German-speaking was common, as was toleration of Protestantism (unsurprising given the leading role Strasbourg played in the Lutheran reformation). Now, thanks to migration, French is the common language.

The 1871 German annexation of most of Alsace-Lorraine, including its biggest city Strasbourg, had been a source of enduring bitterness in France and inspired strong feelings of revanchism. The statue depicting the City of Strasbourg in Paris's Place de la Concorde was draped in black fabric and wreaths for decades afterwards. The simmering resentment was never better captured than in the painting opposite, with the teacher pointing a stick at the map to show his schoolchildren the region lost to their beloved country.

By 1914, Alsace was part of the German province of Elsaß-Lothringen. Germany clung on to the province on the west bank of the Rhine for strategic protection. The First World War proved how prescient Germany was: it gave it an initial springboard against France, and both Lorraine and Alsace would remain mostly under German control.

I am thus starting my walk in the only part of the Western Front to be fought on German soil. Nearly 380,000 soldiers from Alsace and Lorraine were drafted into fighting for Germany.[3] Viewed with suspicion by the German High Command, it was decided in March 1915, after a spate of desertions, that soldiers from Alsace-Lorraine would be drafted elsewhere, to the German interior, the Eastern Front or the navy.

Germany, I remind myself, had in 1914 only been united as a nation for a little over forty years. Its troops fighting under Rupprecht in Alsace saw themselves as both Bavarian and German. Similarly, French-speaking troops dragooned into fighting didn't see themselves as 'German'. With desertion rates soaring, many fled into Switzerland, and some 17,500 escaped over the border to volunteer in the French Army.[4]

War memorials in Alsace reflect this painful divide. Statues of a soldier in German uniform would not have been palatable post-1918, so memorials often feature a bereaved woman carrying a child and dressed in Alsatian costume, an allegory for Alsace mourning her lost sons. Alsace-Lorraine suffered terrible hardships during the war, akin to those communities in northern France that found themselves in late 1914 trapped behind German lines. Thousands of refugees from the fighting fled to Strasbourg in search of food. The destruction of farms and property led to shortages, and factories were transferred to the German interior. To combat growing dissent, draconian Germanization policies were introduced, with Governor Johann von Dallwitz declaring in 1914 that an 'iron broom' would expunge anti-German sentiment. The French language was banned, thousands were imprisoned for singing the Marseillaise, or wearing a cockade, or providing intelligence to the enemy. Thousands more who were considered pro-French were placed in 'preventative detention' camps.

After the war was over, French anger welled up, with some 100,000 Germans who had settled since 1871 in Alsace, or who were believed to have collaborated, summarily deported. Yet within twenty years, Alsace and parts of Lorraine were back in German hands.[5]

Over the next hill, with the sun lowering in the sky, I walk into Hirtzbach (Hirtz, a local name, *bach* German for stream). 'The church bell has just tolled seven. Hirtzbach is such a charming place, with a brook running through the middle between the timbered houses, like an Alsatian Lavenham.' My taxi meets me on cue outside the Restaurant Munzenberger at the bottom of the village. The good hour of the journey gives me time to reflect on the first day. 'I refuse to feel bad about missing my target because of the late start. The main downside has been the lack of any pavement and constantly having to get into the ditch to avoid traffic.' That night I record a list of possible reasons for not completing the walk: 'Number one, being hit by a car; two, twisting an ankle or similar injury; three, catching Covid or another illness. Whatever the obstacles, I know that I have to finish this walk. I have to finish.'

The Hôtel Saint-Martin in the middle of old Colmar is charming, if idiosyncratic. No time to explore it before we rush out to dinner in the last restaurant still open, in the Place de la Cathédrale, and drink Gewürztraminer, white wine made from the popular local grape: 'I can see drink helping evenings ahead,' I later record.

Sarah in Colmar, helping me plan Day 2.

I am wrong about the drink. It sends me to sleep immediately in my attic bedroom, more beams than walls, more bed than floor, then wakes me at 3 a.m. feeling alert and in a cold sweat about the walk. The article in *The Times* looms large: nice to have yesterday, but in the middle of the night, it has cranked up the pressure. How could I possibly live with myself if I flunked it? Feeling fraudulent, I go back to sleep fitfully.

I wake to find that my plan to take only one set of clothes and to wash them overnight has fallen flat at the first fence. My socks and underpants are still sopping wet. The dryer in the hotel room whines into life in a bid to make the latter wearable, though my special walking socks remain impervious to its spluttered gusts, so I carry them round my neck all morning hoping the fresh air will complete the task. At least one thing has gone to plan: the re-education of my right knee, with no pain evident that day. Conscious of the taxi hovering outside to carry me south, I pass the dining room and stuff a couple of rolls with cheese for later, and, garlanded by flying socks, career out of the Saint-Martin into the awaiting street.

Making up the distance is my primary imperative that second morning. Finding visible remains of the First World War and hugging closely to the front line are, I am ashamed to admit, far from my mind as I am dropped at the exact spot in Hirtzbach I ceased walking the previous night (I become obsessive about this routine). My planned route to Altkirch will entail more road-walking and evading traffic. But my map suggests that a deviation due west along the line of the old railway track will keep me away from cars. I'll grab it.

I thus just miss out seeing the German cemetery at Illfurth. Blast. It's the first of many occasions when I agonize over whether to make a detour. This site is of particular significance – it contains the body of the first German to be killed, even before France and Germany officially went to war on 3 August. But if I make the detour, after the debacle of yesterday, I could seriously lose control of my timetable. So the walk, not the history, wins out. This time, anyway.

On 2 August at about 6 a.m., a German cavalry patrol led by Lieutenant Albert Mayer crossed the border into France about 15 kilometres to the west of where I now stand. Mayer galloped up to a French sentry and brazenly attacked him with his sword, but succeeded only in ripping his billowing blue jacket (in contrast to the khaki-coloured uniforms of the British, and the Germans' field grey, French soldiers began the war sporting flamboyant blue jackets and red trousers). A French patrol, led by Corporal Jules-André Peugeot, was alerted to the incursion. He and fellow soldiers ran towards the Germans ordering them to '*halte-là*'. Mayer's response was to take out his revolver and fire three times, hitting Peugeot in the shoulder. French soldiers returned the fire at Mayer, who tumbled off his horse, stone dead. The time was 9.59 a.m. Peugeot, who died of his wound at 10.37, became equally the first French soldier to be killed in the war. Mayer's body was later dug up to be reburied at Illfurth after the fighting was finally over.[6]

I really am beginning my walk at the beginning of the war.

After a couple of kilometres on the rail track, I pick up a country lane to go through to the sylvan Alsatian community of Carspach, before diving deep into a track through woods. 'This is what the Via Sacra can and should be.' Soon after recording this, my path disappears to almost nothing. Without Google Maps, I realize, I would be going in circles; but now, as the path diverges, I lose Google Maps. Radio coverage has clean disappeared and, for half an hour, I am totally lost.

More through luck than design, I find my way out of the woods into glorious open farmland to see the Vosges mountains close by to the west, the Black Forest beyond the Rhine off to the east, and the flat wide valley in between ahead of me. I have a blissful morning walking along farm tracks and lanes, through sleepy hamlets, serenaded by red admiral and cabbage white butterflies. Lunch sitting on a garden wall coming out of the village of Eglingen, a delicious feast of bananas and cashew nuts complementing my squashed cheese rolls. 'Tastes like very heaven,' I note, 'as I listen to the cocks crowing in the village, the only sound.' As I leave, I notice a nest perilously perched on top of a chimney, with two white storks, the legendary Alsatian bird, undertaking an even more precarious love dance around the nest's rim.

Ping. A message from writer Michael Morpurgo arrives on my phone. 'We just saw that you are walking the whole length of the Path of Peace. In awe of your legs and feet... We should love to emulate you next year, the fortieth anniversary of the publication of *War Horse*,' he writes. Many years before, in his local pub in Iddesleigh in central Devon, he had met locals whose stories sparked the idea for a novel about the war from the perspective of a horse. Thus was born the tale of Joey, a Devon horse bought by the army, who saw action on the front, and the attempts by fifteen-year-old Albert to bring him safely home.

I have never been very successful on horses, but have always loved them. The British army had requisitioned 120,000 from their owners in the first months of the war; by 1918, it had purchased over 460,000 in Britain, and still more from abroad.[7] The Germans rapidly mobilized 700,000 at the start of the war, as did France.[8] Horses had always been central to war, and they had always suffered cruelly in it. By the time of the American Civil War in the 1860s, the effectiveness of cavalry was being called into question because of the deadly accuracy of musket and rifle fire. Yet it remained fundamental to the Boer War at the turn of the century, and all major powers envisaged a key role for it in 1914. In the first few months of the conflict, it was deployed for scouting actions and skirmishes, with the riders using their swords and firing rifles from their saddles. But while cavalry continued to make appearances thereafter, as in September 1916 on the Somme, their day had passed, due to their vulnerability to bullet and shrapnel, and the progressive arrival of the tank, the armoured cavalry.[9]

Horses remained in demand for a variety of other purposes in the war: moving artillery guns, transporting supplies from railhead to the front line, couriering messages, and pulling ambulances. But motorized transport was becoming more robust and numerous during the war, with the British and French each having some 90,000 road military vehicles in France. The animals too were expensive to feed, requiring ten times as much food as a soldier. Even in November 1918, though, some 80 per cent of artillery remained horse-drawn.[10]

The British Veterinary Corps worked hard to care for the animals, those with light wounds being given the chance to recuperate. But up to 9,000,000 horses are believed to have been killed during the war, many more through malnutrition, disease and exhaustion than by enemy action. At the end of the conflict, the British army found it had to sell some half a million horses, with 61,000 sold 'for meat'.[11]

I can't help reflecting that a horse would have been a huge boon this afternoon as I travel along roads, mostly without pavements, through a string of endless 'le Bas' and 'le Haut' villages – Ammertzwiller, Burnhaupt and Aspach. I find zero local interest or awareness of my walk, but every hour or so, a farmer stops their tractor and asks if I want a lift. I explain '*Je marche à la côte belge*', and am met by looks of sympathy or incomprehension. I will ask Sarah to teach me what to say so at least I can reduce the latter reaction.

* * *

Now I'm back on a quiet disused country lane going north in the cool of the evening and it feels good. I've just walked past a dead badger: beginning to smell, very bulbous, seemingly out of place. I stop for the day south of the town of Cernay, having walked just short of my daily target of 30 kilometres. I allow myself a brief moment of achievement before the doubts flood back in. Supposing I can't finish? Supposing I do finish? What then?

Sarah meets me in a lay-by full of Alsatian zest and whisks me back to Colmar for dinner at a plush restaurant she's booked on the river in the old town. I won't be able to sustain this lifestyle when she leaves. I drink too much, fail to notice I'm being bitten by mosquitoes, and remember nothing of the walk back to the hotel. My lack of preparation comes home when I am woken in the night by painful toes. I tend to think I'm above bodily worries, but my toenails have become too long, have been rubbing into my shoes, and they hurt. I rummage around and find some clippers at the bottom of my bag and cut them right back, too far in one case. I return to sleep wondering how the soldiers managed with their much less forgiving boots. For the nth time, I remind myself how petty are my concerns compared to theirs.

A taxi takes me at 9 a.m. to the lay-by near Cernay for the third day, so I can start from the exact finishing spot again. I walk north into the town past a café belching out its odours. I am reminded when younger how much I loved the sweet back-of-the-throat pain of Gauloises and Gitanes cigarettes, the tang of thick French coffee and the fug of crowded Parisian cafés. I don't regret smoking twenty or thirty cigarettes every day at Oxford, nor my deeply unhealthy daily diet washed down by never less than two pints of Wadworth 6X bitter after the libraries closed at 10 p.m. No less unhealthy, though, than the vitamin-free food the soldiers consumed, nor the cigarettes that they were encouraged to smoke. French soldiers received 20 grams of tobacco a day in their rations, less than half their British comrades, beneficiaries of the booming domestic cigarette industry. To boost morale, the British government even organized fundraising 'fag days', as did the Red Cross and YMCA, to raise money so the soldiers could smoke even more.[12]

At last, I arrive at the cemeteries. First up is German, with 7,085 buried from the First World War and a further 1,479 from the Second. Nearby, the SS had an 'ideology school' at which soldiers were taught race theory. A short walk to the north, in Uffholtz, is a French military cemetery, laid out in 1920. It contains bodies of French soldiers killed nearby in the summer of 1914, as well as those of Russian and Czech soldiers reburied in the 1930s, and the bones of French soldiers among the 25,000 killed in the Battle of Hartmannswillerkopf. One solitary British grave stands amidst the crosses, the most south and easterly burial of the war. Driver G. F. Bond was in the 94th Battalion of the Royal Field Artillery, and died on 10 December 1918, a full month after the armistice. Here, if one is needed, is a reminder that peace did not come on 11 November 1918. Why on earth was he here so far away from the British forces? I determine to find out more about soldier Bond.

I contact George Hay, historian at the Commonwealth War Graves Commission, who tells me that Bond had been a prisoner of war, captured near Ypres in 1916, who died of influenza in December 1918. The wonders of mobile phones.

Mid-morning, and I'm walking the route gently rising towards the Vosges, brown cows swishing their tails urgently. I walk through village after village, Hartmannswiller, Wuenheim and Soultz, with hotels closed, restaurants and cafés shut, even shops boarded up, which makes finding water difficult. My initial plan to move from village to village each night, staying in small hotels, as I would have loved to have done, seems hopelessly naive. Coronavirus is dictating my entire strategy of making for larger towns where the hotels are still open, and relying on a mixture of Sarah and taxis to take me to drop-off points. The taxi bills on the first two days are astronomic, but I don't know how else to make it work.

Sarah joins me for lunch in Soultz, once terminus of the German light railway which took provisions to soldiers fighting 10 kilometres away in the hills to the west. We sit by a pool in the square in 30-degree heat and consume crudités, lentil crisps, fresh fruit and smoothies. 'Absolutely delicious,' I record, 'though the 20 kilometres this morning leaves me semi-exhausted – the sun is intense, and my blue hat absorbs the heat. It feels like a nuclear reactor underneath.'

After lunch, Sarah puts on her trainers and we walk on past Bergholtz, taking the high route through farms on the slopes of the Vosges, wending

My path through Alsace, with the Vosges in the distance.

our way in and out of endless vineyards. This is our first time walking together since I set out. She finds my single-mindedness a challenge, but we are edging closer. When Michaela from British Forces Television calls me for an interview about the walk, though, I become distracted, and wander way off our course while chatting away. Sarah, I can see, is not impressed by either call or sense of direction, but says nothing. We arrive at Westhalten, another vineyard village, and though late in the afternoon, we decide to press on for Pfaffenheim, which means one more hill to climb before the end of the day. Though the sun is going down, the heat is still intense.

I've walked 32 kilometres today, but rather than elation, I feel drained. Looking back, it seems obvious that I was letting myself become dehydrated, but I didn't notice at the time. Sarah says I was all but hallucinating at one point. Instead of watching my water intake, I am obsessed by the thought that I'll only succeed if I push myself very hard. I have yet to clock that if I push myself too hard, I won't succeed. How hard, though, is too hard?

This is a warning. When we arrive back in Colmar, we discover that our hire-car doors won't lock. Hours are spent on the phone to the hire company, to no avail. I am not thinking clearly, and little things are looming large. I feel too exhausted to sleep, until 3 a.m. when I take a slug of sickly-sweet warm Gerwürztraminer to lull myself off for a few hours.

4

The Vosges

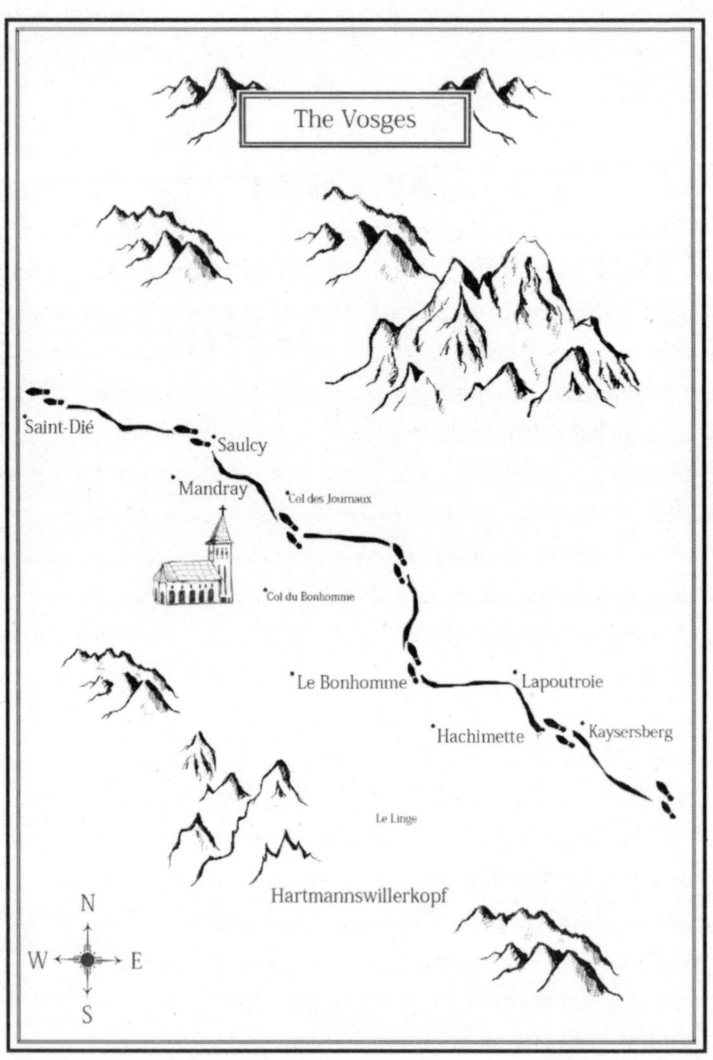
The Vosges
Saint-Dié
Saulcy
Mandray
Col des Journaux
Col du Bonhomme
Le Bonhomme
Lapoutroie
Hachimette
Kaysersberg
Le Linge
Hartmannswillerkopf
N
W
E
S

THE VOSGES MOUNTAINS TO the west of the Rhine basin stretch 120 kilometres from north to south and, from 1871 to 1918, formed the frontier between Germany and France. By Alpine standards, these are pygmies. The highest point, the Grand Ballon, is a mere 1,420 metres, barely 100 metres taller than Ben Nevis in Scotland. But they have an enchantment and menace all of their own.

I have been dreading crossing them, the more so as each day passes and the mountains draw nearer. It is hardly the height of the range, nor their width to traverse (a mere 30 to 40 kilometres). But I know it will be a demanding shunt uphill with my load, and I'm not sure how much water to take and whether shops will be open for fresh supplies, or whether my phone will drop out of range. I keep changing my mind between mountain crossings: do I go for tracks that will be beautiful and wild, or roads that will be noisy and dull?

But I'm excited too, not least because the serious fighting in the First World War began right here. Virtually unknown in Britain compared to the iconic battles of the Marne, Verdun, the Somme and Ypres, the Vosges saw brutal and sustained fighting from late 1914 to late 1915. Uniquely on the Western Front, the soldiers were fighting in mountains and on exposed rocks or in extensive pine forests, all of which made protection from enemy fire much harder.

Crown Prince Rupprecht's Seventh Army attacked the French on the then border on 23 August 1914. Disenchantment with the hostile environment was quick to set in. Lieutenant Karl Gruber, fresh from his architect practice in Freiburg, recorded how his Bavarian soldiers kept badgering him with questions: 'Lieutenant, will we be in Paris soon?' and 'Lieutenant, will the murdering stop soon?' Adolf Hartner, a Bavarian telegraph specialist, recalled that the artillery took little time in reducing the forest trees to matchsticks, while littering body parts far and wide. 'Here a torn-off foot, there an arm, a leg, then another body part torn apart to the point of non-recognition; one was missing half his face and both hands.'[1] Conditions would worsen for the soldiers in the mountains when winter arrived, with icy wind, driving snow and the constant freezing temperatures.

Unlike the French with their famous crack troops, the *chasseurs alpins*, the Germans started without soldiers specially trained in mountain warfare. Nor did they have the high-angle artillery necessary to fire shells in the mountains. Both sides suffered from the dense fog in that first autumn, which meant soldiers were often killed by their own fire. Difficulty in digging trenches into bare mountain rock meant fighting was often close, with bayonet charges and hand-to-hand killing. Witnesses recorded how the creeks of the Vosges ran red with blood, while the screams of wounded soldiers thrashing about on the ground ricocheted off the rocks, blending with the drums and bugles to make a sound from hell they could never dispel.[2]

Yesterday, as I walked through Hartmannswiller, I was too distracted to register my passing due east of Hartmannswillerkopf, and under the shadow of the Grand Ballon. Few vantage points in the Vosges offer a clearer view of the Alsace plain, the Rhine and the Black Forest than this pyramidal rocky spur (956 metres). The French had captured it by the end of August 1914 and clung tenaciously on to their strategic gain, repelling wave after wave of attacks. By the end of the year, the Germans had all but surrounded the forces on the summit, and on 19 January 1915 launched a ferocious attack, aided by a *Minenwerfer* (a trench mortar) lugged to the top over several days by forty men, which lobbed 50-kilo bombs repeatedly and with far greater accuracy than distant artillery on to the French stronghold at the peak. The position became hopeless, and the surviving three French officers and 127 men surrendered. The Germans immediately began blasting trenches, dugouts and infirmaries into the summit's rock face, as did the French within spitting distance to the west.

Throughout 1915, fighting raged back and forth at Hartmannswillerkopf (*kopf*, which appears regularly as a suffix in local place names, is German for head or top). On 26 March, the French regained the summit, only to lose it on 25 April. New technologies began to be deployed, including poison gas and flamethrowers, which helped the Germans retain their ascendancy. But on 21 December, they were hit by a surprise barrage from 300 French mortars and field guns: shells rained down continuously for five hours, driving their soldiers deep down into the dugouts and destroying communications. The *chasseurs alpins* stormed the German positions and dugouts. The following day, they counter-attacked, and yet again, the French were pushed off the mountaintop.[3]

On 26 December 1915, Captain Ferdinand Belmont wrote a lyrical letter to his parents: 'We are… among the pines of a little valley south of the Hartman… From the lines I went over yesterday and this morning, one has a view of the plain of Alsace… At night, one can see quite well the twinkling of the thousand lights of Mulhausen [Mulhouse], and further off those of Basel… the lights appear quite near.' Two days later, as described by Belmont's senior officer in a letter to his parents: 'During the engagement of December 28 last, at 4 a.m., your son, with a few *agents de liaison* and myself, surprised by a violent bombardment, was crouching under a shelter when a wretched shell splinter struck my unfortunate captain on the right arm… he saw that he was fatally wounded. His arm was almost severed above the elbow… He charged me to tell you, sir, that his last thought was for his parents.'[4] Ferdinand was buried next to his brother Jean, killed in the Vosges in August 1914, in the cemetery at nearby Moosch.

As 1915 drew to a close, the French parliament witnessed bitter debates over the sacrifices that year, culminating in the Minister of War forbidding all future fighting in that area serving no wider strategic purpose as such actions were just inexorably increasing casualties.[5] From 1916, the Vosges thus joined Alsace in becoming a 'quiet' part of the front line, used by the Germans and the French to allow units to recuperate after strenuous service on the front further north. The High Commands in both countries acknowledged that the terrain on either side of the Rhine – the Black Forest and Vosges – was so treacherous to cross that any attempt to try would be folly. The Vosges and Alsace thus became the only places on the front where, even after the 1918 Spring Offensive, the line never moved. Nowhere else on the entire Western Front illustrates more perfectly the futility of the fighting than the Vosges.

It is a testament to its terrible losses that Hartmannswillerkopf itself became one of just four 'National Monuments' the French built after the war, opened by French President Lebrun in 1932 (I will visit the other three, at Verdun, the Marne, and Notre Dame de Lorette, north of Arras in Artois).

It's Day 4; the air is warm and sweet. The landscape of the Vosges, with its profusion of flowers – harebells and foxgloves, wild anemones and yellow gentians – appears unimaginably different to how it must have looked during the war. I wake up in Colmar with my head lost in sleep and dreams, but my body in one piece. After the heat of yesterday, I decide I need a hat that repels the sun. The receptionist directs me to a Millets store, which sounds promising, on the other side of town. Twenty minutes later, I arrive at Milex, a computer store on Rue Rapp. Cursing my inadequate French pronunciation, I run back to find an outdoor shop less than one minute from the hotel, grab a light brown hat, and dash into the taxi waiting to take me back to Pfaffenheim.

I can't get the dead badger I saw yesterday out of my head, not helped by macabre morning reading as the driver wends me up to the

The Hartmannswillerkopf battlefield in 1915.

hills. A French soldier fighting in the Vosges wrote of how 'the bodies of infantrymen who have fallen in the course of successive attacks and the bodies of Germans killed by our guns in recent counter-attacks lie stretched in all positions amidst twisted barbed wire and felled pine trees.' He concluded: 'At certain times, the air is tainted with an abominable smell.'[6] I start wondering whether human bodies decompose more quickly in the heat than the badger.

Inside our intestines are microorganisms, disloyally at the ready for a new life, advance guards of decomposition should we die and lose our ability to keep them under control. Once the heart is no longer beating, and blood no longer circulates, bodies start to decompose rapidly, especially if the weather is hot, the ground damp, and bountiful animals and insects are present to feed on the flesh. In the first hours after death, body temperature falls to the ambient temperature, then the body stiffens (rigor mortis), before the blood collects in the area nearest to the ground.

The soldiers in the trenches had to live side by side with the changing sight, smell and sounds of their decomposing comrades. Smell begins to emanate as the microorganisms in the gut digest the body's tissues, excreting gases that cause the torso and limbs to bloat. As the intestines decompose, 'purge fluid' is forced by the gas pressure in the gut out through the nose and mouth. The top layer of skin begins to fall away, giving the corpse an awful appearance. As tissues liquefy, the skin blackens, and bluebottles, beetles and mites attracted by the smell lay eggs in orifices and open wounds. Maggots proliferate. As tissue cells completely break down, putrefaction occurs, and chemicals are released into the soil which can be detected for many years afterwards, helping to identify the presence of the dead.[7]

At the end of the decay process, depending on the condition of the trenches' soil, all that is left are the bones, which skeletonize. I can never forget that the walk is leading me to tread over the bones and long-putrefied bodies of millions upon millions of dead soldiers.

These biological facts are unsettling. It makes me wonder how the minds of the living soldiers, young and old, could possibly maintain equilibrium under the physical assault on their senses and sensibilities, all the more so if the decomposing flesh had once belonged to a friend. Earlier wars had been wars of movement. For better or worse, dead soldiers, like sailors who died at sea, were left behind. Out of sight, out of mind. Perhaps. But the First World War saw life and death intertwined with each other. Even today, we find it hard to forget shocking images in a novel or film, or for the unlucky few, in real life. Why did even more Great War soldiers not crumple, not least when so many of their domestic reference points which gave them mental stability had been stripped away from them?

I'm walking alone along a quiet lane which shadows the busy D83 from Cernay to Colmar. The land is gently rising, as I walk past fields growing maize, changing to vines once enriched by decomposing flesh as I approach Obermorschwihr. My phone buzzes and it is David Moore, my head at St Dunstan's College in Catford when I was first a deputy. He's seen the article in *The Times* and wants to know the story. 'So what on earth are you up to?' he asks in his typically kind way. For four years in the mid-1990s, Joanna and I lived in an Alpine-style house a short distance from the school. The children were young, and it was one of the most carefree periods of our lives: in many ways, I was happier as a deputy than as a head. Now, exactly twenty-five years on, it's no longer me but my children in charge. They told me very clearly last night that I shouldn't push myself too hard today, and they are insisting I stop at 4 p.m. Not that they can check up.

My phone conversation makes me reflect on the two heads I had when a schoolboy myself, both of whom went out of their way to know every pupil in the school. The first was strict, tall and formidable, beat me eight times, and went on to become the vice chancellor of Cambridge. The second, a former Oxford don, befriended me and I stayed with him at his retreat in Scotland after I'd been in severe trouble at school for organizing a demonstration. He took his life five years after leaving the school but he left an enduring mark on me, not least my trying as a head always to seek out and support those having difficulties.

My highlight of the day is walking through Eguisheim, renowned as one of the most bewitching villages not only in the region but in all of France. The Romans developed the community as a centre of the wine trade, and in the eleventh century, the Dukes of Alsace built a castle here, around which the substantial number of surviving half-timbered houses were erected. Walking around the cool medieval streets, I find that here, at last, the restaurants, cafés and hotels are open, more than on my entire route to date. I sit down in a small square by a cattle trough bursting with geraniums to munch my bread and cheese, almost disconcerted to have people walking past me after the deserted communities so far.

Conscious of my early stop time, I press on through yet more beautiful villages, Wintzenheim and Turckheim (*heim* being German for home), until I reach my destination for the day, Ammerschwihr. Shortly before arriving, I come across a concrete bunker hidden amidst the vines, a rare reminder of war among the bucolic gently sloping hills.

Sarah meets me and we drive up a valley to the town of Munster, named after the monastery where the strong-smelling soft cheese, for which the place is famous, was first produced. Here Sarah spent a year as the English *assistante* in a school while an undergraduate at Durham. Munster is much bigger than she remembers, and as she walks around its winding streets, she is lost in memories too personal to share.

Rising above the town to the south-west is the small peak of Reichsackerkopf (792 metres). Its strategic importance is due to it marking where the Munster Valley splits, south to Petit Ballon and west to the Col de la Schlucht. On Sunday 21 February 1915, the Germans attacked here. In places, the trenches were only 10 metres apart, too close for the German artillery to be able to bombard the French front line before the onslaught. At 5 a.m., the German guns opened fire on the French rear lines. The combat that followed was fierce. One German recalled how an officer came down the trench, apparently wounded and insane, shouting, 'Follow me!' Then he jumped out into the open, to be hit before taking one pace. 'Suddenly I felt a burning on my right arm,' said one soldier, 'next to me a comrade was hit in the mouth. Any further attempt to leave the trench would've been suicide.' Nevertheless, the Germans won the day.[8]

How shallow is my own complaint which I notice only as we wander through the Munster Valley in search of the battlefield. Just four days in, the first blister has appeared on my right ankle bone. I blame my heavy socks, so I buy thinner, lighter substitutes. It's alarmingly early into the walk to be developing problems, and I start fretting, not without cause, about how my feet will bear up over the thirty remaining days. So over dinner in a Eguisheim restaurant courtyard, soothed by Riesling from grapes grown on the hills through which I'd walked, we decide to move our base camp tomorrow from Colmar further west, to up the pace. On the first four days, I have walked just 85 kilometres. I have 900 to go. Whatever the children and blisters are saying, I'll never finish unless I speed up.

Determined to keep the pressure on, I pack before going to bed, and by 7.30 the next morning have left the 'highly rated for cleanliness' (as

Booking.com boasts) Saint-Martin for the final time. An irrational fear of heights suddenly and unhelpfully grips my mind. This is the day of the climb, as I switch from walking north to walking due west. Will I find myself having to walk across the Vosges equivalent of Striding Edge in the Lake District, with its vertiginous drops on either side? The day begins with a perilous 3 kilometres along the busy D415 to Kaysersberg, facing oncoming traffic, and jumping into the verge every time heavy lorries lurch towards me. In opting for a safe crossing, I have put myself in greater danger. I'd have been a lot safer on Striding Edge. I try listening to music to stop the unsettling thoughts rising into my mind.

The First World War lifted the lid on the unconscious mind. Last night, I dreamt I was in a large stone mansion. Shadowy people I knew but couldn't place lined the corridors. I was drawn to steps going down and down into a cellar or dungeon. I wanted to descend into it, but was terrified. Whatever was down there scared me in the deepest core of my being. 'Please write down your memory of your dreams first thing in the morning, so we can reflect on them,' said a therapist I saw in my thirties when I realized that my fears were not going to simply dissolve with the passing years. Joanna, though unable to find the answer, had been supportive. She herself was named after Anna Freud, the psychoanalyst daughter of Sigmund, who had analysed her mother.

I had always been more drawn to Carl Jung than to Freud. Jung's memoirs, *Memories, Dreams, Reflections*, focus on dreams, which he saw as the psyche communicating with the conscious mind, offering opportunities for growth which might otherwise be overlooked. During the war, he lived in Switzerland, with the distant sound of gunfire. While Europe tore itself apart, he became commandant of an internment camp for British officers near Lausanne. Both sides sent their injured prisoners to Switzerland to recover: by 1918, 4,000 British servicemen were in the country. Jung's respect for the British, and his fascination with dreams and the unconscious, remained with him for life.[9] Siegfried Sassoon, in his poem 'Does It Matter?', writes of 'those dreams from the pit'. As the heavy lorries rattle past me like disturbing thoughts, I muse on how this war didn't put the lid back on the subconscious mind after it was over. The can had been knocked out of shape and the lid no longer fitted. I wonder afresh what my own dreams and fears might denote. *Kopf*, I am reminded, also translates as 'mind'.

I'm shaken back to reality by arriving in Kaysersberg, another striking Vosges village full of winding streets, fast-flowing streams and half-timbered houses. I fall in love with it, stop for a coffee if not long enough to enjoy it, and call in to the tourist office. 'We do not see the English any more since Covid,' the forthright lady behind the counter tells me. 'Germans of course, and Dutch, though less of them too.' I commiserate with her, and ask what is the best route to walk over the top; animated, she sells me an expensive local map, pointing out a track through the woods. I am thrilled as I locate the path along a stream through the trees, which takes me to Hachimette and then on to Lapoutroie where I shelter in the porch of the church, built in 1912 just in time for the war. The cemetery boasts one of many monuments to the illustrious *chasseurs*.

Once I've stopped for my bread and cheese, I correct proofs for the *Spectator*. When headmaster of Brighton College in 2004, I was working one afternoon in my study when Boris Johnson, then its editor, called to ask me to write on how exams were destroying independent and scholarly learning. My PA rushed in agitated, not knowing who was on the line, but convinced that it was somebody of consequence. He sounded as if he was just back in from a good lunch, and his head was buzzing with the idea. Sixteen years on, I am updating the article. I wish I could now report that overly prescriptive exams and tests no longer throttle our schools, squeezing out the creativity and imagination from student and teacher alike. But in truth, the blight has got worse. Presided over for three years by Mr Johnson.

After lunch, I follow a cycle track up the mountainside. When it peters out into the undergrowth, I see no option but to rejoin the main road up to Le Bonhomme, facing again into the oncoming traffic on the dreaded D415. Here, the road cut into the mountain leaves little margin for pedestrians between carriageway and barrier. I distinguish two kinds of drivers. Those – walkers themselves, perhaps – who give a wide berth and an occasional wave, and others, who seem irritated by us, or by life, and head directly at us, leaving a margin of half a metre or less. At times I have to press myself hard into the barrier.

Up in the Vosges above the tourist villages, the cafés and hotels are closed, some permanently, with *À VENDRE* signs all too common. 'The pandemic is ripping the heart out of Alsace-Lorraine', I record in my diary, 'and only the biggest towns and prettiest tourist villages are surviving.' By mid-afternoon, I arrive at Le Bonhomme (height 670 metres). A sign tells me that I have reached what was the border from 1871 to 1918, and I read about the customs post: '*Un poste de douane est installé dans la maison voisine de la Grotte de Lourdes.*' Another 130 metres further on and I have at last crossed the old German–French frontier. It feels like a moment of real importance on my journey.

A monument was unveiled here on 12 August 1939 to Frenchmen killed in a German artillery bombardment on 8 September 1914. Ironically, within a month of the ceremony, on the twenty-fifth anniversary of that bombardment, both countries were back at each other's throats. How often both world wars intertwine on my route. I take a byroad due north from here up to the Col des Bagenelles which winds up and up through the sweet-smelling pine trees to the pass at the top at 900 metres. Exhausted, I sit on a wooden picnic bench looking out in all directions, to find it is infested with ants. It is a relief to get into the insect-free car with Sarah, and to drink the cool water she has brought.

We drive a short distance back through Le Bonhomme to see the historic Le Linge battlefield. Only now do I understand why there was nothing to see after Hartmannswillerkopf. In April 1923, the French parliament had taken the massive, if flawed, decision to remove almost all traces of the First World War, levelling the trenches and returning

The memorial at Le Linge, with the stone-supported trenches on either side.

them to farmland, and reforesting all areas that had been stripped of their trees. Remarkably few sites were designated in the 'red zone', including Le Linge and Verdun, to be preserved as sites for memorials and remembrance and spared the bulldozer and plough. The latter, given its unique historic importance to France, was always awarded far more national prominence.

Not till 1968, on the fiftieth anniversary of the armistice, did volunteers begin work to restore Le Linge, capped by a twisted flame-shaped memorial dedicated to the 11,000 French soldiers who died here. In the 1970s, work began on a museum, near to the cemetery whose cross, above, bears the word which lies at the heart of my pilgrimage, '*Pax*'. A small wooden cross enclosed beneath it was carved by a French soldier in 1915 from local pinewood. At its base, below the words '*Aux morts du Linge*', lies a sculpture of a prostrate French *chasseur*. We walk around the cemetery with its 2,200 crosses, wander into the closing museum, and then up into the extensive preserved and reconstructed trenches. Sarah is stunned to see how vivid and well maintained the battlefield is: when she had been teaching at Munster just 5 kilometres away, the school took regular trips to Verdun; no one ever thought of visiting Le Linge on their doorstep.

Fighting in these Lingekopf trenches was intense.[10] The front lines were close enough for the troops to throw taunting messages at each other. In October 1915, a projectile landed in the French trenches with the words: '*Hast du kein Kugel mehr?*' ('Have you no more bullets?'). The French responded with a small box with newspapers recounting recent Allied victories in Champagne, to which a note was appended – 'Just come and you'll see whether the French have any more bullets for Germans!', and underneath '*Vive la France!*'.[11] A French soldier wrote in less jocular mood that November: 'Mud, snow, fog – that is what we found this morning... The shattered trunks of the pines, seen through the fog, evoke a necropolis. That terrible Lingekopf is indeed a cemetery; and no one will ever know how many sleep there under the stones.'[12] By Christmas 1915, the line had stabilized, with the Germans in control of Lingekopf as all other summits, and the French lines to the west in close proximity. So much suffering for so little.

We have found an Airbnb in Sainte-Marguerite, close to Saint-Dié, on the west side of the Vosges. Sarah drives as I collect my thoughts after Day 5, moved and uplifted by Le Linge, and sensing that I might just be able to bring this off. She has an uncanny gift for finding great places to stay. Once arrived, I can't wait to be free of my knee supports, and rip off my clothes and glory in the first ample shower of the trip. I can readily understand why the soldiers' greatest pleasure once out of the line was the opportunity to wash and have their clothes cleaned. The British army ensured communal baths were available for all soldiers by 1915, the men expecting a bath at least once a week.

I relax on the terrace looking out over the hills, cared for by our very attentive hosts, she a teacher, he a serving soldier home on leave. Dinner at a restaurant in the main square by the cathedral in Saint-Dié, named after goodly Saint Déodat (Le Bonhomme was named after him as well). Few towns suffered more than Saint-Dié, or illustrate better the livid wound of history through which I am walking. During the fifteenth, sixteenth and seventeenth centuries, the town was repeatedly sacked, and much of what remained was destroyed by fire in 1554 and 1757. Fighting raged in the streets too in the First World War, '... at Ste-Dié, all the houses were closed and the streets deserted,' wrote a French soldier in August 1914. 'We were ordered to erect barricades and take up positions to defend the streets of the town; and there we waited to resist... The weather was terrible. Everyone was dog-tired, silent, driven into corners against the walls, whilst the shells fell on the town.'[13]

Saint-Dié was rebuilt after 1918 only for it to be largely destroyed in the fighting between the Americans and Germans in late 1944. The Allied victory brought no reprieve. In 1945, Brutalist architect Le Corbusier's plans included erasing historic dwellings on the right-hand bank of the River Meurthe, relegating inhabitants to living in cabins in the woods for many years until his modernist ambitions were eventually abandoned. All along the front, as in other cities like London damaged in war, new building of various distinction and none can be seen. We take all this in as we walk around the red mock-sandstone buildings before returning to our new abode. What two wars didn't complete at Saint-Dié in terms of destroying historic city buildings, Le Corbusier did.

Day 6 sees me back at the Col des Bagenelles by 10.30 a.m. ready to go. I ascend to the Col du Pré de Raves, the highest point of the entire walk at 1,005 metres, according to my Gaia app. So here I am at the top of the Vosges. My fears of becoming lost or falling off cliff edges have come to nothing. I take a few moments to pause before heading north-west down a track. I have not gone a hundred metres before I encounter a sign telling me '10,000 men were killed on these hills.' To its side, one solitary grave with an inscription saying that this soldier is buried where he fell, close to the front line.

Who was this soldier? I wonder. I can find no name. I utter a silent prayer and pause before moving on. Now I am on a heavenly track through a conifer forest, gentle gradient downhill, wild flowers to either side – purple foxgloves, wood anemones and mountain pansies, sounds of a stream babbling away nearby, pine smell everywhere. I stop for a *pain au chocolat*, my morning treat, and drink half a litre of water straight down. I feel less energetic today, not surprising perhaps given the climb of yesterday, so I decide to take the rest of the day more slowly. Here and there, I notice long-ossified tree stumps beside the road, with bullet holes and shrapnel marks, as can be seen on the Somme and Ypres. These relics of war help me imagine amongst all this peace how it then looked. 'Here nature is disfigured by war,' wrote a soldier fighting here. 'There is not a tree trunk which does not bear the trace of shot or shell; the bark of the pines bears gashes either slight or deep; other trees are amputated halfway up or cut close to the ground. The largest have sometimes been broken off by shells as though they had been mere sticks.'[14] I am thinking about this as I pass by the Col des Journaux, a monument at Ville de Fraize bearing the legend '*En homage aux 400,000 morts de la grande bataille des Vosges 14–18*'. I reel at the numbers blithely written. These Arcadian hills saw bitter fighting too in the Second World War. I pass an American and French monument 'in commemoration of the valorous American soldiers who gave their lives to liberate Fraize'.

Soon after, I walk down a steep farm track into the village of Mandray. Above all so far, I have loved approaching villages along ancient byways, stealing upon them unawares. Even though it's Saturday afternoon, there's nobody about. The sun is beating down – perhaps they are sheltering from the heat? I take a swig of an energy drink – a new secret weapon – but I'm still weary, and yearn to be back at the farmhouse to take a cold shower. The 21-kilometre walk today should've taken just four hours but will end up taking six by the time I get home. I decide to abandon my planned route through the woods in favour of a straight road. The sun is relentless and the lane, dead straight for well over 2 kilometres, offers no trees under which to shelter.

Is the road Roman, I ponder, and how did the soldiers cope with the monotony day after day of walking on their irritatingly straight highways? I make a note to find out. Meanwhile, the Indians rather than the Romans, and cricket not marching, are claiming my attention. Every ten minutes I check in on my phone to see how the second Test is going at Lord's, specifically how Sam Curran is performing. After a long run of success, not very well this match, I fear. He's just been out for a golden duck, ameliorated by his taking the key wicket of Indian captain Virat Kohli. The Curran boys, Tom and Sam, joined me with their brother Ben in 2013 when I was head of Wellington College, after their father Kevin, a Zimbabwean cricketer, had died the previous October. Had that been 1913 rather than 2013, the brothers might have experienced the same fate as Douglas and Tom Gillespie.

* * *

England has one other obsession right now, A-level results. How far away all that world seems. Waiting for the A-level and GCSE results had always been my two most nervous days of the year, knowing how much it meant to pupils, their families, and, let's be honest, to the reputation of the school. I'm thrilled to be free of that, and to be free of comment on the stories about grade inflation and pressure on university spaces. I am glad to turn down media requests for interviews. But I still worry about individual students who I know personally, and I still want their results to be stellar.

The Roman road I am still walking is called the Rue du Mal de Lattre de Tassigny, named after the great French hero, five times wounded in the First World War, commander-in-chief of the French forces in Germany at the end of the Second World War, and overseer of the French war effort in Indo-China before his death from cancer in 1952, a loss that contributed to the ultimate French defeat in Vietnam at Dien Bien Phu in 1954. Just before the town of Saulcy-sur-Meurthe, I encounter a French National Cemetery, which contains the final resting place of 2,500 French soldiers. René Fonck, the French pilot known as 'the Ace of Aces', responsible for an incredible seventy-five German aircraft kills from 1915–18, was buried here when he eventually died in 1953.

One final push, a wasted half an hour when I take a wrong direction, and at 5 p.m. I am back home in the hills above Saint-Dié, drenched with sweat and exhausted. I collapse on the bed motionless for several minutes before starting to book fresh lodgings for the days ahead. Covid makes the task more complicated, but so too does moving out of the prosperous and tourist region of the Alsace and the Vosges for the depopulated open land through which I will be passing for the next few days. Sarah had been handling bookings to date, on top of innumerable phone calls in her eloquent French to help with daughter Susie's fast-approaching wedding in our home village of Saint-Jean-de-Côle. After constant stops and starts, it is to take place on 28 August. It's been touch and go for many weeks, and I am so happy for her.

To express my thanks to Sarah for helping Susie as well as me, I'm treating her to a five-course mini Michelin extravaganza dinner on my very own Airbnb terrace. What could possibly go wrong? I have been thinking through the menu all day, curtailed I have to say by the single gas ring and lack of raw materials. But I am quietly pleased with salade à Saint-Dié, cantaloupe melon with prosecco, smoked salmon with once-fresh baguette, a healthy full platter of Saint-Dié vegetables *chaud et froid*, rounded off by chocolate mousse in colourful tubs. Wild flowers in a coffee mug decorate the table centre. The cloudburst doesn't help the smooth running, nor does my inability to find a corkscrew for the inevitable Gewürztraminer. But Sarah sits through the procession of courses stoically and, I feel, with some pleasure. The bottle of prosecco, which poses no cork problems, no doubt helps proceedings.

When walking in the long afternoons, I have found myself looking forward to the prospect of alcohol at dinner. I'm not very good with drink normally and can consume less and less. But local wines and beers in the evening have been a joy. Never much, I tell myself, but just enough to feel woozy and to help lull me off into sleep. But tonight, I didn't drink enough water on my return, and I'm awake again throughout the small hours. I worry ridiculously about sleep, so much so that it stops me sleeping. At times like this, I console myself by thinking that the soldiers survived for days on end with very little sleep. I am finding the Tommies are becoming a constant reference point. They did it. I can do it too. Discovering how they endured at the front has become my new quest.

The normal routine was four days in the front line, four days in reserve, and four days 'at rest'.[15] 'In reserve' meant serving in rear trenches or in villages and woods just behind the front line but within enemy artillery range. As the war went on, 'rest days' sometimes meant manual labour, just away from the front line. This afforded little opportunity for quiet unbroken rest, nor a horizontal bed on which to lay down their tired bodies. Uniform and boots had to remain on throughout, however wet, infested and stinking. Sleeping was even more difficult during the four days of high alert. While officers had dugouts with makeshift flat beds, ordinary soldiers had to make do with holes hollowed out from the side of trenches in which insects would nestle. Shells and other projectiles falling throughout the night, sentry duty and working parties sent out into No Man's Land to repair wire or scout the enemy, all eroded any sleep time. Sentries had a particular fear of going to sleep, a capital offence: 449 death sentences were passed on British soldiers for sleeping on watch, but only two were carried out, both in Mesopotamia. So they adopted a habit of resting the soft flesh under their chin on the sharpened point of their fixed bayonet, 'a device guaranteed to keep the sleepiest sentries awake'.[16] Only in the four 'at rest' days were the men safely behind the front lines where they could hope to sleep – until nightmares or vermin awoke them.

An extraordinary 346 British soldiers were court-martialled and 'shot at dawn' for various crimes, including cowardice, disobedience to lawful command, and two for 'casting away arms'.[17] The vast majority, though – 266 – were shot for 'desertion'. Executions were carried out at first light by soldiers of the victim's unit, with an officer giving the order and finishing off the task if the victim showed signs of life after the opening volley. After the execution, the news was widely distributed as a stern warning of the consequences of defying military law.[18]

One chaplain, Julian Bickersteth, wrote of his anguish when accompanying a soldier sentenced to be shot in December 1917: 'Once again it is my duty to spend the last hours on earth with a condemned prisoner. I have, I hope, learnt much from the simple heroism of this mere lad of nineteen, who has been out at the front since 1914... As they bound him, I held his arm tight to reassure him and then he turned his blindfolded face to mine and said in a voice which wrung my heart, "Kiss me, sir, kiss me", and with my kiss on his lips, and "God has you in his keeping" whispered in his ear, he passed on into the Great Unseen.'[19]

I contemplate their final exchange as I gaze out near dawn into the valley of the River Meurthe to the lights of Saint-Dié. No, I have nothing to complain about. Besides, I have made it across the Vosges.

5

Lorraine

Lorraine
Verdun
Hattonchâtel
Heudicourt
Seicheprey
Richecourt
Pompey
Nancy
Pont-à-Mousson
Lunéville
Baccarat
Raon-l'Etape
Étival-
Clairefontaine
Dombasle-
sur-Meurthe
St Mihiel
R. Moselle
R. Moselle
R. Meurthe
Saint-Dié
N
W
E
S

I SPEND SEVEN DAYS walking through Lorraine. I adapt to being on my own and carrying my luggage on my back, planning my route and stopovers, accepting that my Covid-squeezed timetable will brook absolutely no margin for delay nor error. Nor give me the time I wanted to reflect. If I'd had the euphoria in Alsace, Lorraine is where the walk turns to bloody graft.

Lorraine is three times the size of Alsace, stretching from Saint-Dié in the south-east to Verdun in the north-west. With borders on three countries – Germany, Belgium and Luxembourg – it had been at the epicentre of disputes and conflict since the Romans, and is criss-crossed with their roads. Called Lotharingia after Emperor Lothair, grandson of Charlemagne, it later morphed into the independent Duchy of Lorraine. The 'Spanish Road', established under Philip II of Spain in the latter sixteenth century, passed straight through it, the vital artery for Spanish troops en route north to repress the Dutch. The Duchy's inhabitants suffered savagely in the bloody Thirty Years War (1618–48), sandwiched as it was between France and the Holy Roman Empire, with massacres, lootings and executions commonplace at the hands of wandering soldiers and lawless mercenaries. It flourished in the eighteenth century, proud of its distinctive identity and culture until, in 1766, it was annexed by Louis XV's France. After 1871, Germany took over the predominantly German-speaking northern half till it returned to France after the First World War, bar annexation by Hitler from 1940–45. Lorraine is a restless place, as was my journey through its heart.

Lorraine is also central to our understanding of the First World War. Fighting was almost continuous here from August 1914, culminating in the Battle of Verdun in 1916. It reminds us that for the first half of the war until the Battle of the Somme, the Western Front fight was mostly a Franco-German affair, for all the understandable British focus on the narrow section at the north-western end on which its soldiers fought, and where the Gillespie brothers died. It was here too in Lorraine that for the first time in history the US army was deployed outside the American continent, accelerating the country's rise to superpower status after one of its shortest and most successful military interventions. As a mirror opposite, while I progress through Lorraine in August 2021, the US is leaving Afghanistan, after one of its longest and least successful interventions.

At last my route will take me along the front line, which I have been only skirting since leaving Kilometre Zero. The Frontiers Offensive in August 1914 saw the taciturn French commander Joffre's forces surge into the German-held areas of Lorraine in a bid to retake Alsace-Lorraine and then push on deep into German territory. The attack was a total debacle, with French forces crushed by strongly defended Germans. No fewer than 75,000 French soldiers were killed in action in August 1914, including 27,000 on one terrible day alone, 22 August, at the high point of the offensive.[1] By the end of the month, the stunned remaining soldiers had retreated back into the haven of French Lorraine.

Now it was the German turn to attack, which it did at the end of August in the Battle of the Trouée de Charmes, named after the 'gap of Charmes' between two towns through which I will be walking, Lunéville and Raon-l'Étape, unprotected by major fortresses. A German bulge was rapidly created deep into the French lines. Intense fighting between Nancy and Lunéville saw whole towns and villages razed to the ground: 'Completely reduced to ashes. Left and right nothing but smoking ruins,' recorded Fritz Burger, a German officer who had been a professor of art at Munich University. 'Pompeii must've looked like this after the violent upheaval.'[2]

Rupprecht decided to press the advantage by taking Nancy, the region's key city now in a French salient jutting into the German lines. In the Battle of Grand Couronné, formidable heavy artillery pounded the depleted French lines. But a triumphant entry into Nancy was denied the Germans as they suffered their first major setback of the war, some units losing as much as 60 per cent of their infantry strength.[3]

Attention now switched far to the west to the broad-fronted Battle of the Marne. Here, Joffre fared better. His forces halted the initial German Schlieffen Plan offensive aimed at speedily defeating France. Chief of General Staff Helmuth von Moltke, Schlieffen's successor, ordered a retreat to defensible positions. 'My God, how could this possibly have happened,' he protested to his staff on 11 September 1914. How indeed? Three days later, he was out of a job.[4]

Contemplating all this drama, into which I will be walking, I set out on Day 7, a day of contrasts. I'm on my way at 7.15 a.m., elated at how cool and tranquil my virgin route along the side of the hills is above the Meurthe Valley. I think I may have cracked pathfinding. As I descend into Saint-Dié, the cocks are crowing and the church bells tolling 8 a.m. It is Sunday. As the sun burns off the morning mist, figures scuttle into the churches and out of the *boulangeries*, baguettes under arm.

I sit down in the square for my first drink of the day and breakfast-sequestered *pain au chocolat*, and the world feels good. Then reality dawns. I've been stung by mosquitoes on my tranquil path, I've left my money, credit card and extra water back in the room, and my new sun-busting light-brown hat from Colmar has fallen off in the undergrowth through which I clambered. At a stroke the world looks much less promising. Sarah is not impressed when I call her. 'What will you do after I leave in two days?' What indeed. We arrange a meeting point later in the morning for her to replenish and reprimand me.

To pick up my spirits I decide to abandon my carefully planned route in favour of walking by the side of the Meurthe, the second of my seven rivers. Its source is just below the Lingekopf in the Vosges before it wends its 160-kilometre way through Saint-Dié and on to Nancy then Pompey, where it merges into the Moselle. I am utterly enchanted as I walk along the south bank of the river, leaving Saint-Dié behind me. But after a kilometre or two, the riverside path begins to fade away. Refusing to give in to obstacles, I press on, through harder and harder terrain, until I find myself battling relentless high undergrowth. When I reach an unfordable tributary, I am forced to admit defeat. I spotted a path some way back that led away at right angles from the river. I have no option but to take it, though it proves difficult to follow, and I notice no indication anyone has walked it for a long time. Turning a corner, I see why. It runs straight up against a high wire fence. Moments later, a Dobermann is jumping up the swaying barrier snarling furiously at me. This is not what I had expected.

I backtrack at pace, quicker than I've moved all day, and find another path that might lead out of the woods. My head frequently turns to check the hound hasn't climbed over the fence, as it threatened to do. Is this dog episode a harbinger? In the rush, I forget altogether to keep my bare skin away from possible ticks, another concern of the walk. Half an hour, tickless but many scratches later, I arrive on a road. I pause, take a long swig of water, and proceed westwards to the North Sea. This time, my way is barred by the 'Circuit Geoparc', a racetrack humming with souped-up Ferrari and BMW saloons being put through their paces.

Another day, it might have been a pleasant distraction. Not now. My scratches and bites are hurting. The blisters on my ankle are aching. My boots have at least twice prevented my ankle turning over when I stepped on uneven terrain, but the high sides are rubbing away at my ankle bones. I try walking round the racetrack on one side, but am blocked by a railway line, and on the other by the river. It's now mid-morning, and I've lost all the advantage from my early start; I have no option but to rewind my way on the road back almost to Saint-Dié, before picking up a country lane, feeling a complete failure. Sarah, who's been tracking my progress on her phone, finds me in the car, and dispenses extra water and, with some reluctance, the blue floppy hat of mine that she never liked. Fortified, I walk on through a series of villages, shadowing the south bank of the Meurthe, until I finish the day at Étival-Clairefontaine in late afternoon.

I take stock. The exact line of the front has constantly eluded me, and my pace remains too slow. My original plan had been to start early, walk six or so hours every day (30 kilometres), to finish at 1 or 2 p.m., have lunch with Sarah when with me, before exploring and reading in the afternoon. Another plan to bite the dust. Overnight, I decide to redouble my efforts. I have been lacking sufficient discipline. So this morning, I check my route and equipment three times before I leave at 6.30 sharp, and a taxi has me at Étival before the working day begins.

My route quickly takes me up into the woods, the Forêt Domaniale de la Côte de Répy. As part of my new Iron Man approach, I decide so early in the day to dispense with insect repellent. Big mistake. Before I even notice, I'm bitten in five places by mosquitoes. Clearly, no one briefed Lotharingia mosquitoes that they're not supposed to engage in combat until the evening.

I light up when I spy, some 200 metres ahead of me, a hiker, my very first of the trip (how, how different I yearn for that to be when the walk is properly established). He struts purposefully towards me with the whole professional kit, poles in each hand. A kindred spirit wells up as I say a few words in French. I'm suddenly emotional at the prospect of sharing walking yarns with another human. But he glides past, silently, without looking at me. Perhaps he doesn't acknowledge me as one of the genuine walker fraternity. More likely, he hadn't understood a word I muttered.

* * *

A message from Rory Forsyth, chief executive of the Western Front Way, sets off a new train of thought. A letter has appeared in *The Times* challenging what I had been quoted as saying about the pointlessness of the war in the story last Monday. Had I gone too far? Gillespie had wanted people on both sides of the conflict to walk the front 'as a reminder of where war leads'. I need to understand better what he was thinking. Certainly, he believed in the war, initially at least. They all did. But had the sheer scale of the slaughter, or Tom's death, caused him to think his path was needed as an ambulatory nudge to prevent the world descending into horror again? I struggle to see how the First World War served any useful purpose, certainly not commensurate with the 10 million soldiers killed and 20 million wounded, along with perhaps 13 million civilian fatalities.[5] Sure, it accelerated democratic, economic and scientific change. But what peace, what price? As every schoolchild learns, the punitive mentality of the victors, principally President Clemenceau of France, engendered bitterness in Germany that precipitated the Second World War.

I wend my way along the path pondering all this, the breeze in the branches the sole sound. I return again to what's been gnawing away at me – what did Gillespie mean by 'peace'? His hope, which is so well grounded, was in part that those who walk and form bonds are less likely to want to kill each other. Did it extend to walkers finding greater peace with those with whom they have fractured relations? Surely it must. I reflect on all those I myself have hurt, through my own egotism and misuse of power. I make a mental list. My parents, Joanna, friends, colleagues, people in my books, even ex prime ministers. It's painful. But walks, like prayerful silence, can change us within.

These are my thoughts as I hear that, overnight, Kabul has fallen to the Taliban. I listen transfixed to the news, radio another boon of my telephone, and it takes me straight back to the fall of Saigon in

1975 when I was at Oxford. Fresh from our elegant 1 May champagne breakfasts and listening to the choir on Magdalen Tower, we young revolutionaries knew which side to cheer. Whichever way you look at the Afghanistan exit now, it's a bloody mess.

A message pings in from Jessica, oldest daughter, just off for a much-needed holiday to Split in Croatia, another place bitterly fought over for years. She has finally left No. 10 after five years as an official, a stint longer than the entire length of the First World War. I was so proud of her there, and was glad she went on to become head of news at the Department of Health, where she continued to be on the front line. Soon after she joined, Covid took off again. I worry about the children far more than when Joanna was still alive, when she did the worrying for me. They spend a lot of time too worrying about me. Not least, during this walk. Susie messages that she is daily more excited about her wedding to Jonny in Saint-Jean-de-Côle in two weeks, now she has the all-clear. Adam, our youngest, sends me a photograph of dinner with partner Steph on their holiday in Annecy, near the French Alps, taking a circuitous way to the wedding to Jonny. As a family, I feel we are still regrouping, learning how to be without the person who held us all together.

I press on through the woods and cross the River Meurthe into Raon-l'Étape. The town thrived after the railway came in the 1860s, allowing timber from these woods to be transported quicker than by river, and tourism to grow. What a different era. Today, I see a depressed town with houses and shops boarded up. I pass a shop selling brightly coloured ribbons and wools, a local speciality. After the primary-colour palette of my walk, here is an explosion of sensation: emerald, sapphire, turquoise. Is anyone around to buy the sweet red ribbons? Later that afternoon, I walk through the glass-crystal-manufacturing Baccarat, another once-thriving town on the Meurthe. Before 1914, it had been home to the local barracks of the *chasseurs à pied* (light infantry), the buildings still standing proudly today. A smell of manure hangs in the air. I stop at the patisserie for a pear tart and try hard to admire the church rebuilt after the war with a concrete spire like the London Shard – in shape at least. I fail. The streets are empty. I contemplate the damage we have done to our communities by out-of-town retail outlets and by shopping online, speeded up by Covid. Businesses perish never to be reborn. I'm as bad as anyone – I will go to the supermarket rather than the local greengrocer.

Sarah is leaving tomorrow. She meets me in the afternoon as I finish at the village of Ménil-Flin by the Meurthe. We had planned to have a late picnic together on the riverbank. But it starts to rain, and a bus shelter is the only cover we can find. For her last night, I have booked what sounded like a promising small hotel overlooking the Église Saint-Jacques at the heart of Lunéville (German, Lünstadt). In the eighteenth century for a time, this was the capital of Lorraine, a centre of power, culture and tourism. The Duke of Lorraine rebuilt his *grand château* overlooking the river in 1702, which became known as the 'Versailles of Lorraine', with Voltaire and Rousseau among the visitors. But in 2021, we find the town a shadow of its former self. We cannot find anywhere open for dinner, and our accommodation won't let us in till 5.30.

Feeling disloyal, we decide to abandon Lunéville and drive west, splashing out on the Grand Hôtel de la Reine in the Place Stanislas in Nancy. After so many downtrodden places, it's a joy to be in a vibrant city. The hotel's graceful square was built during the 1750s in neoclassical style by Stanislaus, King of Poland (and the last Duke of independent Lorraine). Only on his death in 1766 did Louis XV of France annex Lorraine, retaining Nancy as its capital. It escaped the German occupation of northern Lorraine after 1871, but was captured by the Nazis in 1940, and renamed 'Nanzig'. Today, the magnificent Place Stanislas is a UNESCO World Heritage Site.[6]

My spirits rise once ensconced in a building that is spacious, elegant and clean. In my biggest hotel room of the trip, I sit on my bed for a couple of hours resting while catching up on messages. Time too for half an hour of overlooked yoga: I catch sight of a pale face staring back at me in the mirror. To thank Sarah for all her help, and make amends for my cooking, I book the Brasserie Excelsior, an art nouveau restaurant by the main station with interior pure Alphonse Mucha. No one seems worried about Covid here: we drink champagne, eat fresh white fish and toast everything that Sarah has contributed to the walk. Strolling back after, we find a *son et lumière* about to begin, projecting on to our hotel and three sides of the square. Powerful pinpoint images are accompanied by a pulsating soundtrack, a résumé of previous shows dating back to 2012. It's unusual for me on this walk to be out this late, and I have nothing warmer than my simple top, thin protection against the creeping cold as autumn draws nearer. Once in my bedroom, I fall into a dreamless sleep, nestled in the unimaginable luxury of linen sheets, my head swimming in the bravura light performance.

For the soldiers of the Western Front, there were no *son et lumières*, but shows of all kinds were ubiquitous behind the lines. Music halls had been integral to pre-war working-class life, and the soldiers yearned for the sentimentality of familiar acts, popular songs, and actors in drag, unconcerned by the quality. Walter Cook of the Royal Army Medical Corps recalled one performance coming together. 'Captain Tindall had an idea. He said, "These troops want cheering up, you know – we will form a concert party." Well, I helped with the sewing, a little gang of us. We scrounged sheets and things; anything we could find... We found enough to dress them all... The troops, once they got something they really liked, they brought the house down.'[7] The types of acts in the concerts varied, but singing usually featured. There might be comedy, sketches, jokes, dancing and poetry recitals.

In the 25th Royal Fusiliers, the quartermaster had been persuaded to appear onstage as a woman, his audience 'indulging in delightful fantasies that brought them substantial memories of the girls they had left behind in London, Manchester, Glasgow'.[8] How the soldiers must have yearned for female company. 'Keep constantly on your guard against any excesses,' War Secretary Lord Kitchener warned new soldiers in words that anticipated the unworldliness of the headmasterly advice I disregarded as a school leaver. Wine, women and song we were told to avoid. 'In this new experience,' Kitchener continued, 'you may find temptations both in wine and women. You must entirely resist both.'[9]

Some hope. 'We were not monks,' protested Lieutenant Dixon, 'but fighting soldiers with an abundance of physical energy... And if bought love is no substitute for the real thing, it at any rate seemed better than nothing.'[10] Home leave to wives and girlfriends occurred only once a year, or less, for ordinary soldiers (officers might expect leave every three or four months, though often not taken up). So with little opportunity for sexual intimacy at home, and no chance for relationships with girlfriends in France or Belgium, resorting to 'bought love' was commonplace behind the front lines. 'Drink flowed freely,' recalled Corporal George Ashurst, 'and as the music and singing went on, the boys danced with mademoiselles in the flimsiest of dresses, or flirted with them at the tables, using the most vulgar expressions. All the evening, Tommies could be seen either going to or coming from the girls' room upstairs...'[11] Being surrounded by death only increased their libido. 'That last fling by the young conscript... was due to an instinctive urge. For the very young soldier, it was probably his first fling, as it might have been his last.'[12]

For a few brief moments, the soldiers found some peace. But at what price? The prospect of the excitement trumped their caution. 'There were well over 150 men waiting for opening time... Right on the dot of 6 p.m. a red lamp over the doorway of the brothel was switched on. A roar went up from the troops, accompanied by a forward lunge towards the entrance,' recorded seventeen-year-old George Coppard in his diary.[13] Nearly 420,000 British and Commonwealth troops were admitted to hospital because of venereal disease in the war: 5 per cent of those who enlisted, and over five times higher than the number admitted for trench foot and frostbite. British military law punished only concealment, not contraction, of venereal disease. The army tried to provide a mix of alternative recreation and moral exhortation to discourage soldiers, though never, for fear of a backlash at home, provided prophylactics. It preferred to dock the pay of those who contracted it: with prostitutes costing some 2–3 francs a session, and the weekly pay of a private the equivalent of 10 francs, hitting soldiers in their pocket was seen as the best way of mitigating pain in their privates. Parliament was far less tolerant of the *maisons tolérées* (brothels), and, with cases of venereal disease soaring in 1918, legislated against them, to howls of protest from the army and the French.[14]

Breakfast is served in the palatial dining room overlooking Place Stanislas. We imagine we are guests in a palace. But sadness is in the air too. Sarah flies back today from Basle. As we approach our car in a multistorey car park, we see the petrol cap is ominously open: some of our fuel siphoned off. It is the first unpleasantness on the trip – people have hitherto been unfailingly kind. We have a long journey east to get back to Ménil, where Sarah drops me off one last time by the river. It'll be a completely different experience on my own without her, and I don't know how I'll cope.

A long hug, a moment of uncertainty with so much unsaid, and she is gone. She is flying down for Susie's wedding, but it seems a long way off. I look at the time. It's 11 a.m. and I have a car collecting me at five from my destination, 31 kilometres away. My route takes me mostly south of the front line and north of the Meurthe along roads. I'm feeling pretty low physically and mentally this morning but tuck my chin in and step forward. I lose myself in dictating an article for the *Independent* about the lessons of the First World War on what's happening in Afghanistan. No clear objective nor exit plan ranks high in it, nor learning from history – my constant theme. I suggest that partition could have been a workable option, with a Taliban-controlled and a democratic state side by side. It is the kind of compromise that

Gillespie the lawyer might have favoured. No one takes it up. Probably a stupid idea.

I arrive back in Lunéville, this time by foot, determined to give the town a fair hearing. I walk in past where the military airfield had stood: from it flew the war's first 'fighter plane' which deployed a synchronized machine gun on its nose spitting out bullets through the rotating propeller. For a few weeks at the start of the war, the German army had occupied the city. Inhabitants were forbidden to leave their houses during the daytime except to buy food or provide water for livestock, and not at all at night. Proclamations were put up across the city declaring 'anyone trying to leave the neighbourhood by night or day, on any pretext whatsoever, will be shot.'[15] Well that puts Covid restrictions in context. I pass people in open doors staring out at the grey streets under a grey sky as I make for the Versailles-style gardens of the chateau. While I eat a baguette for lunch, I muse how the confidence and opulence of the gardens sits uneasily with the straitened town of today.

Marie-Marguerite Wibrotte was a primary schoolteacher in Lunéville who became concerned that the bodies of those killed in action in August and September 1914 might be denied a proper burial, and face a nameless oblivion. So she persuaded volunteers to go out with her to the battlefields to help dig them a temporary grave. Later, she bought the Mouton Noir farm just to the west of the town. She and her team of helpers transported the dead to it, constructing a chapel and a meeting room in an old inn for relatives of the deceased to visit. Her endeavours were to become the foundation of a French National Necropolis, the military cemetery of Friscati, for 3,751 soldiers, many of whom died in military hospitals during the Battle of the Grand Couronné.[16]

As I wander around the gravestones and photograph the French tricolour in the gathering wind, I reflect on the power of determined women during the war to achieve extraordinary things. I think of my grandmother Eileen defying officialdom to save her husband, of the imbalance of life without women. I start worrying that Sarah hasn't called me to say she's arrived at the airport. My mind always imagines the worst: I fret she was very tired, that her satnav is faulty, driving on the right. Has something happened to her? It makes for an anxious afternoon. Eileen constantly fretted. So my mother did too. The circle is complete.

It is here I have my most profound intimation of what the Via Sacra could be, on the Allée Marie Marguerite Wibrotte, created in 2004 in this schoolteacher's honour. I am walking along the side of the hill, with a low hedge to my right and, to my left, trees with a series of crosses along the path's border, marking the deaths of four fallen soldiers from both sides of the war. Can there be any better illustration of Gillespie's 'tree-shaded path' past the graves of 'the silent witnesses from both sides'? Borders of present and past, life and death, dreams and reality blend and dissolve. For a few precious paces, Douglas Gillespie is walking silently by my side.

Then it's down to earth as I trudge on through village after village, on and on, till I reach the town of Dombasle-sur-Meurthe where my taxi awaits me. I have just managed to achieve the 30 kilometres in six hours, but it drains me, and when I get back to the hotel, I'm exhausted. A steak and a litre of local beer for dinner in the Place Stanislas fail to lift me, and I'm up all night drinking water, fretting about my progress. The unwanted habit of anxiety has passed down through the generations, from Eileen, to my mother, to me. Was it all started here, by this war?

* * *

Sky News wants to interview me at 8.45 a.m. about the recall of Parliament today to debate Afghanistan, an event occurring only thirty-four times since 1945. After a terrifying race in driver Carl's BMW taxi, who insists on playing Sade loudly the whole journey because last night I had told him I liked 'Smooth Operator' on his playlist, we arrive back at Dombasle. I position myself in front of the war memorial dedicated to '*Enfants de Dombasle morts pour la France*'. A father is reading to his three children from a history book called *1914 1918*. Kay Burley, the presenter, has no option at the end of the interview but to ask about the walk – more publicity.

The morning is heavenly, walking along the Canal de la Marne au Rhin (connecting the River Marne to the Rhine at Strasbourg) before I switch to the banks of the Meurthe. As the Nancy suburbs loom into sight, I leave the river behind and walk in through a district unpromisingly named Jarville. Poverty and depression are everywhere, and for the first time, I feel concerned for my safety, as quick-eyed youths loiter on street corners with mobile phones and electric scooters. The atmosphere is menacing. As I pass a bus shelter, a man darts out to offer me a swig from his bottle of Jack Daniel's, surprised when I decline.

I know next to nothing of those who live on the margins of society. I was reminded of this on one of my preparation walks along the River Thames with John Casson. I had first met John when he was senior foreign policy adviser at No. 10, but after being ambassador to Egypt he left the diplomatic service to follow his faith and become head of the charity L'Arche, which provides homes and support for those with disabilities. As we walked along the banks of the river, this brilliant man now sporting purple hair prompted me to question why I lack the courage to make such a leap myself, for all my faltering attempts to do so at different stages in my career. If I do land another elevated and detached leadership job, isn't that just another distraction from confronting reality? Would I finish it exactly in the same place as I am now, but perhaps even more lost and apart from the truthful life I yearn for?

Pop-up tents are everywhere on the pavements with the stencilled lettering DÉPISTAGE COVID-19. Long queues snake back, pushing pedestrians into the road. I take a side street and arrive at the vast Nancy Southern Cemetery for French soldiers killed throughout the war. At the far end I find eleven Commonwealth War Graves Commission (CWGC) graves on gravel, two abreast, including six from the Great War. I message CWGC historian George Hay to ask why they are here. He thinks they must have died while a Royal Flying Corps airfield was being created in the latter stages of the war to fly bombing raids into Germany, had the war continued into 1919. They all served in the Indian Labour Corps and died in the winter of 1917–18, when, as a commentary notes, 'Indian companies working around Nancy suffered extensive sickness because of a long delay in getting adequate warm clothing and shelter.'[17] How cruelly they must have suffered, so far from home. As I pass by my hotel, I pop up to my room to put fresh bandages over my blisters, before pressing on for a further 6 kilometres along the banks of the Meurthe, ending the day at Champigneulles. I've managed another 30 kilometres today, but it's taking an ever more troubling toll on my feet, and the Compeed plasters are not stopping the blisters grow. A prolonged altercation between two lovers in the square below wakes me at 2 a.m. and I remain awake to dawn. My mind goes back to lying sleepless in a motel in Kansas City in 1978 when researching my doctorate. 'Feel very alone in an unfamiliar world,' I record in my diary.

Next morning, I call in at the *pharmacie* for a personal blister seminar. It is better than spending three hours waiting in a doctor's surgery, and I have a taxi to catch. Even before I see him driving round the corner, I hear Sade blasting from Carl's car. Then, out of a black sky, I have my best walking day of the trip so far. I tramp along the Meurthe for the final stretch before it blends at the town of Pompey into the River Moselle, which also arises in the Vosges; 545 kilometres later, it flows into the Rhine at Koblenz in Germany. After too short a distance walking along its sinewy north bank, I wrench myself away as it turns due north and I need to travel west. Kilometre after kilometre I trudge along farm tracks and forest paths, serenaded by butterflies and swifts, stopping after 32 kilometres at Bernécourt.

On my way back to Nancy, where I'm spending my last night, Adam telephones me with the news none of us wanted to hear. He has caught Covid. Typically calm and thoughtful, he knows at once the implications for Susie's wedding in a few days' time, cranking extra strain into what has been fraught wedding planning. I don't drink tonight, which means I can have a long yoga session before going to bed. Together with meditation, I have found it over many years a powerful way to centre and calm myself. But not on this occasion. For the first time in many years, as I lie awake in bed yearning to be lost in sleep, I have a panic attack.

* * *

Today will be my first day when I'm having to carry all my clobber in my rucksack and shoulder bag. Surplus clothing and items are jettisoned into the hotel room's billowing wastepaper bins. Washing powder doesn't make the cut: from now on, I'll be relying on whatever soap I find at each overnight stop. Much of what remains is medical for my increasingly blistered feet. Carl and I chat like old comrades as he drives me back to the action for the last time, and then I'm on the old front line. I walk through Seicheprey and Richecourt, to Montsec. Early on, my path stops abruptly as a farmer has planted a vast field of sunflowers in the way: 'The heads are enormous, the size of saucepans, and stare back at me with that passive-aggressive look of a student caught doing something wrong, defiantly saying "not me".' Back on the track after an enormous detour, I notice trench remains in the woods. I message my friend, military historian Philip Stevens, who later that day sends me an image of a trench map from the Library of Congress, showing them as American 'jump-off' (i.e. front-line assault) trenches from 1918.

I'm boyishly excited to be walking along the front. From 19 September to 11 October 1914, the Germans fought the French for control of this very land. Joffre's forces were prised out of the town of Saint-Mihiel, creating a vast German salient jutting into the French lines, a southerly equivalent of the Ypres salient. Victory gave the Germans a valuable observation post over the vast, dry Woëvre Plain, and cut essential rail and road communications to Verdun further to the west, which restricted the French ability to provision this vital stronghold.

German writer and philosopher Ernst Jünger saw his first military action here, at Éparges Ridge. He kept a diary, published in 1920 as *Storm of Steel*, in which he spares no gory detail. 'Through a stuttering swathe of machine-gun fire, we plunged back into our communication trench, and moved to a position on the edge of the wood previously held by the French,' he wrote. 'A sweetish smell and a bundle hanging in the wire caught my attention. In the rising mist I leapt out of the trench and found a shrunken French corpse. Flesh like mouldering fish gleamed greenishly through splits in the shredded uniform. Turning round, I took a step back in horror. Next to me a figure was crouched against a tree… Empty eye-sockets and a few strands of hair on the blueish-black skull indicated that the man was not among the living.'[18] Jünger was wounded shortly after, the first of seven. After fighting in many of the war's major battles, his final injury was in August 1918. He lived for another eighty years, becoming an honoured figure, though lingering suspicions about his writing glorifying war, and his condemnation of democracy in the 1920s, never fully went away.

Gillespie had travelled to the US before the war, which can only have shaped his internationalist outlook. I'm thinking of his trip as I encounter for the first time American soldiers in action. The Germans held the Saint-Mihiel salient for four years, until a US force on 15 September 1918 wrested it back. General John Pershing, commanding the American Expeditionary Force (AEF), had insisted that his troops fight as an independent army, not under French or British command. As French tanks provided cover, and British, French and Italian aircraft provided support, thus was launched the predominantly American offensive. 'D-Day' entered the historical lexicon at this point, ascribed to the day planned for the attack, with the assault time known as 'H-Hour'.[19] It was to prove the biggest deployment of American armed forces in battle since the Civil War fifty years before. What happened here also helped shape the Second World War twenty years later, for helping plan the operation was George C. Marshall, later President Roosevelt's and Truman's army chief, while George S. Patton, later commander of American forces during the Second World War, led a unit of American tanks.

Raymond Austin of the 6th US Field Artillery wrote to his parents about how, on the morning of the attack, US front lines advanced just in front of Seicheprey: 'The Boche put up some resistance, but it didn't last long, and we got a lot of prisoners... I don't believe there is a man in France who does not feel there is no doubt about the final outcome, although it may be far off...'[20] The battle lasted just three days, with 16,000 German prisoners taken, and put the entire salient back in Allied hands.[21] The American success proved their worth to the British and French. Pershing wanted to press home the advantage, but held back from attacking the historic fortified town of Metz, 25 kilometres to the north. It proved to be the last major battle fought in Lorraine during the First World War; though, had the armistice not come on 11 November, a massive Franco-American attack was to have been unleashed towards Germany just three days later.

I walk up to the American memorial at Montsec on the path curling towards the summit. With my baggage and the heat, it takes me half an hour. I see the American cemetery nearby which contains the graves of 4,153 American dead. American generals determined that, even if their politicians were turning their backs on Europe in the interwar years, the memory of the soldiers' sacrifices should not be forgotten, and they fought tenaciously for their memorials. The mighty Montsec monument, completed in 1937, is strongly reminiscent of the Jefferson Memorial in Washington DC, unsurprisingly as the latter was constructed from 1939–43, both consisting of a classical circular colonnade, approached by a broad stairway. At the centre of the covered circle at Montsec is a bronze relief map of the salient, showing where the military operation had taken place in September 1918. The Germans were back in control of the area for much of the Second World War, but left the monument untouched, damage to it only occurring from shrapnel from American guns in 1944.

I am left wondering why the United States is far more attached to the memory of the Second World War than to the First. Some 5 million Americans were drafted by 1918, though far fewer went into battle; had the fighting continued into 1919, as Pershing envisaged, many more would've seen action. American economic muscle had been powering the Allied war effort since 1914: Britain spent around half its war budget in the United States. Fear of the almost limitless American population and its economic capacity made the Germans desperate to win the war before the 'Yanks' arrived in significant numbers, hence their massive offensive launched in March 1918. It almost succeeded.

Some 116,000 Americans died during the First World War, double the number killed in the Vietnam War. A mere 52,000 of them were killed in combat in 1917–18, with 63,000 dying of disease, mostly from the Spanish flu epidemic. In total, some 320,000 US personnel became casualties (sick or wounded).[22] Before their victory at Saint-Mihiel, the American troops had fought in July at the Battle of Château-Thierry as part of the Second Battle of the Marne. From October they fought in the massive Meuse–Argonne Offensive, where they were successful in breaking through the German defensive position, the Hindenburg Line (built in the winter of 1916–17 behind their front). American forces played a pivotal role in the Allied victory, in contrast to their humiliation in Vietnam. The AEF's contribution is the chance for national recognition and pride, surely?

Well no. The Meuse–Argonne Offensive proved the deadliest campaign in American history, with the number of graves in its military cemetery at Romagne (14,246) far eclipsing those in the much-visited

Omaha Beach cemetery in Normandy (9,386 graves).[23] When I stopped here on my exploratory walk in the summer of 2016, we were surprised to be told by guides there that no American president has visited Romagne, despite it being the biggest American cemetery in Europe. So why so little interest in America in this war?

The First World War was the first American war not to bequeath a prominent commander as president. The War of Independence gave George Washington a national profile that helped him become the new country's first head of state. Later, the Mexican-American War (Franklin Pierce), the Civil War (Ulysses S. Grant), the Spanish-American War (Theodore Roosevelt) and the Second World War (Dwight D. Eisenhower) all helped propel a military leader into the White House. But Pershing never even ran for president, another marker of the way the war is regarded in the United States.

Distancing from the war within Congress and beyond had begun even while the guns were still raging. Memories of the Civil War were still vivid: this, not the 1917–18 war, was to Americans their own 'Great War'. It had lasted four years, divided the country, and killed over 650,000 people.[24] The First World War, in contrast, was a faraway war, with American forces only fighting in the final months as subordinate forces to Old World powers. After the armistice, Congress had rejected President Wilson's vision of a continuing American involvement in world affairs, spurning his idea for a League of Nations, and opting to return to isolationism. In 1937, a Gallup poll suggested 70 per cent of Americans thought involvement in the war had been a mistake.[25] American involvement from 1941 in the Second World War quickly eclipsed memory of the earlier war. Over 400,000 Americans were killed as part of the 'greatest generation' from 1941–5, and Hollywood, still in relative infancy in 1918, helped implant visions of American heroism and military prowess in popular culture with wave after wave of films from 1945 continuing to the present day.

So we should not be surprised that only in 2021 was a memorial to the First World War unveiled on the National Mall in Washington DC, long after similar memorials for the Second World War, the Korean War and Vietnam War. Unlike in Britain (after 1915), American families too could repatriate bodies. Those bodies that did return across the Atlantic were often buried in individual family plots or local cemeteries, militating against a unified national memory. One can find many explanations for the First World War being America's 'forgotten war'. But I hope, defiantly, as I walk on, that the Via Sacra will help awaken the United States to a hundred years of shame in overlooking what happened in these fields and hills.

The day has caught up on me. It is already late afternoon, and I'm looking for my lodging for the night. I have booked the hotel at Heudicourt-sous-les-Côtes, the only bed available nearby. I experience quite a thrill arriving on foot, pack on back, as I had long envisaged. There is a new bounce to my stride as I walk into the Lac de Madine. I'm shown up to my room on the first floor with a balcony overlooking a red-tiled roof out on to stone cottages. I sit down on the bed, take off my heavy boots and do my foot stretches and rotations for the first time today. Then a long yoga session on a bathroom towel, a shower, and I start to feel human again. Refreshed, I collapse on the duvet, catch up on messages and record my diary, before going to dinner on the patio outside, with a choice of yellow, purple and orange chairs. No one could accuse the restaurant of being stingy with food. Enormous plates of smoked salmon, shoulder of lamb, and an overflowing fruit salad, all interspersed with *amuse-bouches*, are placed in front of me.

As I drink a half bottle of Chablis *premier cru*, I read Patrick Leigh Fermor's *A Time of Gifts* propped up on the water jug. How I wish I was meeting people along the way as he did ninety years ago. Covid and my lack of his bountiful connections continue to rule that out. What bliss, though, to have a tired body, a balmy evening, wholesome food, perfect wine and a book. Very heaven.

The price of the Chablis is a restless night, and a very early wake-up. I abandon hopes of going back to sleep and read the overnight news and papers on my phone: dominated by the retreat from Afghanistan. I cannot understand why the Pentagon did not foresee what would happen and achieve a more orderly withdrawal. This is still too early in the morning for the Saturday *Today* programme to begin broadcasting, so I turn to Classic FM, and listen to Shostakovich's second piano concerto, second movement. In no time I am in floods of tears and have to lay down my book as I can no longer see the words. It's a mystery to me why some music moves people to the core while leaving others cold. Why should this affect me rather than his more famous 'Leningrad' Symphony, composed in 1942 at the height of the Second World War?

My hopes for an early start are frustrated by breakfast not being served till 8 a.m., and when I come down on cue, a long line has already formed. So I do not leave till 8.45, and spend the first hour walking by the side of a long and busy main road in the rain. At its end, a supermarket, where I buy 4 litres of water, sufficient for the day ahead as I'm not expecting to pass any community where I can restock. The plain is dominated by a plateau, with the village of Vigneulles-lès-Hattonchâtel immediately above me. Google Maps points me to a farm track up, which then becomes a path, before turning into a battleground through bramble. At the top, a delightful hamlet, with a memorial to the children who lost their lives in the war. The heavily damaged village was rebuilt by an American benefactor, Ruth Isabelle Skinner (or Miss Belle Skinner as she was known locally), in the 1920s.

Nearby, the remains of the Benedictine monastery of Château de Saint Benoît totally command the surrounding countryside. Founded in the twelfth century, it was damaged in 1791 amidst the turmoil of the French Revolution. The Germans commandeered it in 1914, and until July 1916, when it transferred to Flanders, it was the General Command HQ of the III Bavarian Army Corps, with visitors including Kaiser Wilhelm II and Bavarian King Ludwig III. Contemporary photographs show a hive of military activity, with staff, guards, officers of every stripe and a hospital.[26] It remained an important German military centre until 13 September 1918, when it fell to the 161st US Infantry Regiment. They found the Germans departed and the chateau abandoned. Douglas MacArthur, prominent US commander in the Pacific during the Second World War, used it as the headquarters for his infantry brigade. He later wrote about standing in the cupola and being able to view German forces retreating in the far distance. The chateau was destroyed by German shelling on 24 September 1918 and is now just an empty, ruined facade, another scar of the Western Front.[27]

I am now on the high plateau, and walk westwards for nearly 25 kilometres through the forest, with trenches and shell holes clearly visible to my left and right. For five hours, blissfully, I am out of radio contact, with no messages coming into my phone, nor newspapers and weeklies. For years since I was a student, I have religiously read daily newspapers, weekly political journals, and kept up with the news on radio. For what? I must have spent a year of my life doing so, the ever-changing news mostly ephemeral, and the comment too often rehashed and lacking originality or insight. Yet still, like an alcoholic, I remain attached to it. Attached too to my phone, obsessively checking it every few minutes in range. The walk is slowly prising me away from this addiction. Funny thing, I'm loving it when I can just ignore it. A few days ago, when I thought I had left it behind, I experienced not panic, but a deep peace.

By pure chance – I wish I could say otherwise – I stumble across the spot where Alain-Fournier, champion of France's belle époque destroyed by the First World War, inhaled his last breath. Born in 1886, Fournier established himself in the pre-war years as a societal and literary giant. He tutored the young T. S. Eliot, wrote gossipy and literary columns for *Paris-Journal*, and conducted expansive affairs, one of them with his boss's wife, daughter-in-law of former French President Casimir-Perier. His great and only masterpiece, the novel

Le Grand Meaulnes, was published in 1913. I first came across it in the diaries of diplomat and politician Harold Nicolson when I was a student. He thought it the most impressive novel published in France in his lifetime. I became enchanted by the tale of adolescence, romance, and the fraught journey to adulthood. In the forest clearing, a stone memorial to Fournier portrays a copy of *Le Grand Meaulnes* and an officer's cap. A short distance away, a glass memorial preserves the site and markers of the mass grave where Fournier was later found. In a state of high excitement, I send a message and photograph to Nicolson's granddaughter, author Juliet, a friend since university.

When war came, Fournier was recalled to the army. 'I don't know exactly where God is in this war,' he said, 'because none of us can solve the riddle of existence, but I know that I'll be shot down only when He wants, how He wants, and where He wants.' Where He wanted was exactly in front of me in the forest. On 22 September 1914, Fournier's company had crossed the forest road on which I was walking, where he charged towards the German positions, and, waving gun in hand, disappeared from life.

The circumstances of his death and location of his body remained a mystery until the 1970s, when two admirers managed to pin down a mass grave dug here by the Germans. After prolonged petitioning, they secured permission from the French Veterans Secretary to excavate it. By examining surviving buttons and nails used in boot soles from his regiment, experts identified the skeletons as belonging to it. Fragments of a lieutenant's coat were then found, with records showing our man to be the only lieutenant reported missing from that day. The skeleton matched his height, and biological analysis showed the bones belonged to a soldier aged about thirty. He had complained of tooth decay in a letter to his family shortly before he disappeared. Close analysis of the skeleton's jaw revealed tooth disease exactly where he had written about it. Case proved, he was reburied with full military honours, along with his comrades, at the nearby French National Cemetery at Saint-Remy-la-Calonne.[28]

We pass later by this final resting place in my taxi, nestling on the side of the hill leading up to the forest plateau. My head still full of my discovery, I was brought down to earth when the car met me at a Kentucky Fried Chicken outlet, no less, on a busy road north of Verdun. With no phone reception in the forest, I had been unable to let my driver know I was running late. When we met up, Alain-Fournier didn't seem a promising line of excuse. He leaves me in no doubt that he is displeased at my hour-late arrival. I can understand that, and apologize profusely in faltering French. Back at my hotel, I find it the social centre of the entire Woëvre district, with expectations running high of a singer brought in to entertain dinner guests that Saturday evening. As it starts to pour outside, I have to come in and sit near her. When she sings 'Wonderful Life', the 1986 song by Black, with so many memories, emotion again is pricked. For the second time in twenty-four hours, tears surge to my stinging eyes. I go to bed dog-tired, having spoken to Sarah, and disappear into the world of sleep.

So tired, that I hear not the heavy rain that goes on all night. I fail to remember that I had spread out my sole set of clothes when it seemed the storm had passed over on the warm red tiles outside my bedroom window. They are sopping in the morning. Thus do I bid a wet farewell to Lotharingia.

6

Verdun

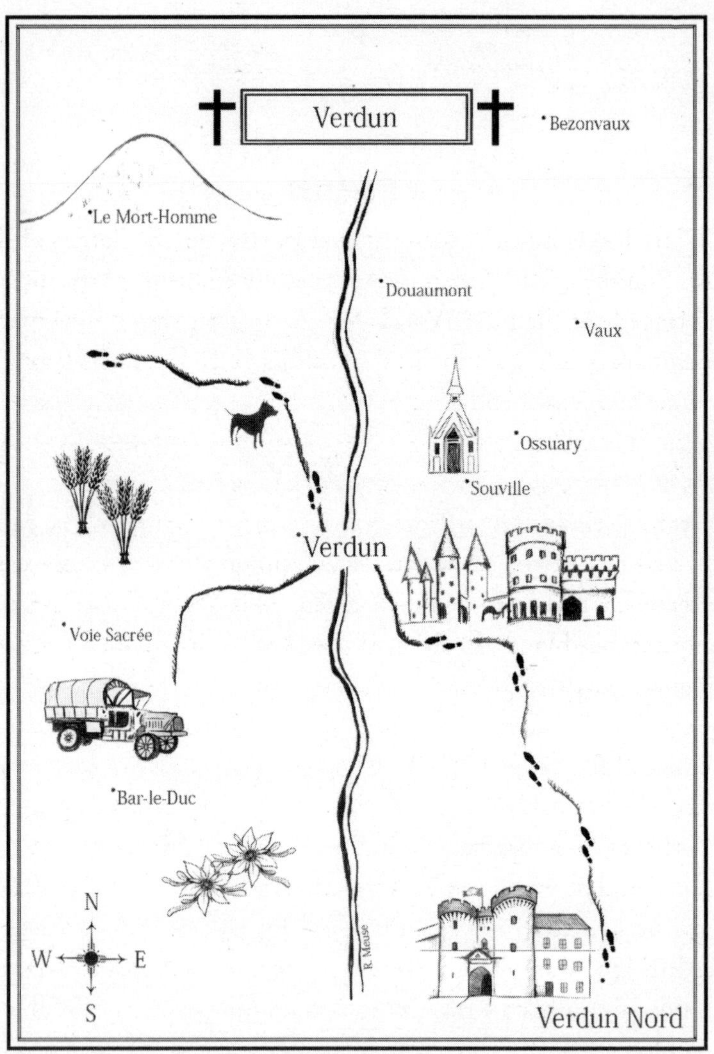
Verdun
Bezonvaux
Le Mort-Homme
Douaumont
Vaux
Ossuary
Souville
Verdun
Voie Sacrée
Bar-le-Duc
N
W
E
S
R. Meuse
Verdun Nord

THE BRITISH ARE COMFORTABLE portraying the Battles of the Somme and Passchendaele as the very emblems of the futility and tragedy of the First World War. A stronger case can be made, though, for Verdun, on the north-west tip of Lorraine. At least the Somme and Passchendaele had territorial objectives, starting with a major breakthrough in the German lines, however unrealistic that ambition was. But the Germans initiated the Battle of Verdun with no strategic ambition for fresh territory. Sitting pretty on the gains they had made two years earlier in the summer of 1914, they were perfectly content to settle for that. No, their aim was not land and conquest, but blood. To drain French blood dry, terminating any remaining Gallic appetite to continue in the war, so Germany could concentrate its whole effort against the Russians on the Eastern Front, as Schlieffen had always intended, and then to strangle Britain by its submarine blockade.

It fell to Helmuth von Moltke to enact Schlieffen's plan. When it failed and he was dumped, his successor, Erich von Falkenhayn, knew he had to avoid a similar fate. He did not mask that his Verdun aim was nothing less than to bleed France 'to death'. Supposedly, in his 'Christmas memorandum' to Kaiser Wilhelm II in December 1915, he claimed he had selected Verdun because it was the one location where 'the French Command would be compelled to throw in every man they have' a place which, for patriotic reasons, the French would never abandon.[1] When after

302 days, and a quarter of a million dead, the guns finally fell silent, the front had not moved at all. But nor had the French determination to continue in the war.[2]

I love Verdun, one of the most evocative and affecting towns in French history. On this Sunday morning, Day 14, I set off towards it in my damp clothes from my unpropitious finishing point of last night. My driver is in much better humour when he collects me from the hotel. He is Turkish, called Moran, and, like so many expats, longs to go to the US. I listen as he tells me with rising emotion about his itinerant family, and his hopes for a better life for his children. Just as he speeds away, with the greasy Kentucky Fried Chicken smells in my nostrils, the clouds open. I realize that my trousers that have served me so well are not waterproof, and water is trickling down my legs into my boots. For the first time, I unpack my bright red waterproof top, and place my passport and other documents in the zip pocket. My blue hat, which returned to active service following the loss in the line of duty of its brown replacement, also fails to prove water resistant. Worse, my trusty phone, my secret weapon to date, also decides it's had enough of the incessant rain, and shuts down. So the sylvan route I had plotted to take through the woods and fields into beautiful Verdun falls at the first hurdle. With no map, I have no option but to stick by the grizzly A4. Visibility is poor, and even in my red top, the traffic often picks me out late, which means last-minute swerves and regular spraying with sitting water. When I can, I sidestep into the verge, but that is now a furious stream of gushing liquid. I console myself with spotting a knee-high memorial, proclaiming this route the 'Voie de la Liberté 1944'. The only liberation I'm after right now is from the rain.

The 10-kilometre journey humping my full kit seems to take forever, but when I at last reach the outskirts of the city, the skies clear, and the sun makes my clothes steam. I walk in on the Rue de Sauveur past the canal and admire its overhanging houses. I'd like to live here, I muse; I often think I'd like to live in striking places I visit rather than where

I now live – not that now I live in any one place. Perhaps I should move here? As I near the centre, I walk past a cross-legged man with a well-sculpted face, gazing down at the hat in front of him, asking for money. I think at first he is crying, or praying, but then I see he is deeply immersed in a television programme on his iPhone. He doesn't notice me as I steal by. I find my hotel easily, Les Jardins du Mess. Built in 1893 for officers in the French Army, it retains a splendour and grace despite its conversion to its present use early this century. It commands pride of place on the banks of the River Meuse: my third river of the walk, and, at 925 kilometres, one of the longest (and not to be confused with the Meurthe). Arising at Pouilly-en-Bassigny south of Nancy, it flows due north, forming for a time the western border of the Holy Roman Empire, before surging through Belgium, up into Holland past Maastricht (the river is known as the Maas in Dutch), and out into the North Sea in the Rhine–Meuse–Scheldt delta.

The river is critical to understanding of Verdun. It explains why it was first settled, and why the Romans chose to create a fortified city, named after the Latin word *verodunum*, 'strong fort'. For the next two millennia, its importance in European history went way beyond its comparatively small size. Here it was that in 843, the three grandsons of Charlemagne, crowned first Holy Roman Emperor in 800, divided his empire. An ecclesiastical centre for a thousand years, it became in 1552, along with nearby Metz and Toul, one of three major bishoprics annexed by France. In 1670, Louis XIV's celebrated military engineer Vauban visited, drawing up extensive plans for the fortification of the city, which took decades to be fully realized. In 1870, in the Franco-Prussian War, it became one of the last French forts to surrender, cementing its iconic status in the French patriotic mind. Plans to make it impregnable envisaged over a dozen polygonal forts up to 8 kilometres from the city to its north and east facing Germany, and an inner ring of six forts, to ensure Verdun would never again be taken. Even though the plans were only partially completed by 1914, several forts, including Vaux and Douaumont, had been erected, rendering it the strongest defensive position in the whole of France.

As I wait for the receptionist in my hotel, dripping on their new carpet, I read about a strange prequel to Covid hospital pressures currently filling the news. Winifred Kenyon, aged twenty-four, was one of a small number of British nurses sent to Verdun in a Voluntary Aid Detachment (VAD) in mid-1916. 'The work here is terrible,' she wrote in her diary. 'We have had a lot of deaths. It is simply awful, for the number of wounded is impossible to cope with, and they lie unattended for days.'[3] Images of queues of coughing Covid patients waiting to be seen is never far from my mind. The receptionist, eyeing me suspiciously, tells me my room is not yet ready. So I slip guiltily into the large downstairs wheelchair bathroom to dry my wet clothes, wash, and apply deodorant.

I am off to meet another Brit who found himself in Verdun: Jonathan Williams, who contacted me after seeing my daily Twitter photos, and said he would be eager to help out with his car. Lacking the time to walk around the extensive battlefields, I grab the opportunity. I am very excited: this is my first Leigh Fermor-style encounter with a local person. A Mancunian, Jonathan left England eleven years ago to settle here with his French girlfriend and to work in a nearby transport depot. His two passions are birdwatching and cricket, but it transpires he is a notable local historian as well, and as we drive up into the hills north of the city to see the remains, he teaches me much about why Verdun was such a deadly battle.

In early 1916, the city and its surrounding forts jutted out in a salient into the German line. The attack was due to begin on 12 February, then 16 February, but heavy snow delayed it again. Massive artillery bombardment, Falkenhayn believed, would be the key to undoing the French. He began as he meant to continue: at 7.15 a.m. on 21 February, over 800 guns lit up the dawn with a ten-hour barrage on French lines just 30 kilometres wide, delivering 1 million shells. The noise could be heard 160 kilometres away. I ask Jonathan to repeat that figure, because it seems hardly believable: 1 million shells, 30,000 raining down on every kilometre.[4]

Just four days later, on 25 February, the unimaginable happened. Early that day, a unit of the 24th Brandenburg Regiment noticed that only part of Fort Douaumont was still firing, so the soldiers approached it stealthily, crept inside through a shell hole, and with the aid of other German forces, rapidly and bloodlessly subdued the French garrison. By evening, Fort Douaumont, the strongest in France's invincible ring of forts, was in German hands.

A bitter argument raged after 1918 among German veterans. Who deserved principal credit for the triumph?[5] Heroes were in demand in a Germany reeling from its defeat in the war. One contender was Lieutenant von Brandis, who long after became French president Charles de Gaulle's personal guest in 1966 on the fiftieth anniversary of the battle, even though he was probably one of the last German attackers to enter the fort that day. De Gaulle felt the history personally: he himself had been bayonetted in the thigh, gassed and taken prisoner near the fort on 2 March 1916.

On the day Douaumont fell, General Philippe Pétain was appointed to take over command of Verdun, despite having pneumonia, in part because of his reputation for not wasting French lives. In his memoirs, he recalled his anguish as he watched three-quarters of the French army march to the front from Bar-le-Duc, the assembly point on the 72-kilometre supply route into Verdun, a route of almost mystical significance to the French, the Voie Sacrée.[6] Following the German advances of 1914 at Saint-Mihiel, through which I recently walked, all railway lines and roads that might supply the salient were lost except this one. From 21 February, horses were forbidden on it to free up space for what became a stream of 3,500 trucks, mostly Renault and Berliet, and 800 ambulances, many of them Ford Model T. By the side of the road, a narrow-gauge railway was constructed to carry up more supplies, including food, and to bring back the wounded. During the first month of the battle, it carried nearly 50,000 tonnes of ammunition and 263,000 men.[7] The route is sacred still to the French. In 2006, on the ninetieth anniversary, it was renamed 'RD1916'. The French government, understandably, has not wanted us to use Gillespie's name 'Via Sacra' because of its similarity to Voie Sacrée, and hence refers to the path we are establishing as the 'Western Front Way'.

Pétain's appointment stiffened French resolve, but did not reduce the pace of the slaughter, with his own 33rd Regiment being one of those to suffer most heavily. Multiple assaults were launched to retake Douaumont: in May 1916, French forces reached the roof of the fortress, but were unable to penetrate inside. An estimated 100,000 French soldiers were lost trying to recapture it.[8] Their willing sacrifice was evidence enough that Falkenhayn's diabolical gamble was well grounded.

In March, Falkenhayn decided to change tack and broaden out the battle to the west bank of the Meuse, from where French artillery had been creating havoc with German infantry. In March and April, desperate hand-to-hand fighting raged around Le Mort-Homme and 'Hill 304'. By the end of May, the Germans had succeeded in taking both peaks of Mort-Homme, the relentless bombardment reducing one summit by 10 metres in height.

Pétain knew that Fort Vaux must at all costs avoid the fate of Douaumont. Charles Delvert was one of his men fighting in front of it who learnt what all costs entailed: 'The shelling continues night and day. It's deafening. I'm punchdrunk. The formidable artillery duel never lets up for a second. The slopes of Vaux have been disappearing beneath shells… With the whistle of projectiles criss-crossing over our heads, it's like being by the sea, ears ringing as heavy waves pound the shore… We really are in hell. The night is black as ink; the ravine, a gigantic chasm, the surrounding hills, fantastic masses of dark shadow.' Delvert survived the war to become a history teacher, before dying of wounds in 1940.[9] Did he deploy this vivid language to convey to his students in those interwar years the reality of war? Or was he, I wonder, like so many veterans who taught in schools in Britain after 1918, as after 1945, unable to speak about the horrors seen?

Commandant Sylvain Eugène Raynal, organizing the resistance inside Fort Vaux, marshalled his forces as best he could to resist the German attacks. It was a losing struggle. At the start of June, German soldiers managed to breach the fort, and found the French barricaded inside ready to fight room by room to the end. Using flamethrowers and explosives to break down walls and doors, the Germans pushed the defenders back and back. By 4 June, the French had only one cup each of dirty water a day to drink, some resorting to sipping their own urine. Dehydration was in the end responsible for the surrender on 7 June of the remaining 600 men and one dog. Their first act on leaving the smouldering remains was to head straight for shell holes to lap up rainwater. The Germans were so impressed by their courage defending the fort that German commander Crown Prince Wilhelm (Kaiser Wilhelm II's son) presented Raynal with a sword, before dispatching him into captivity.[10]

With Douaumont and Vaux now secured, the Germans edged closer to the city, and by 23 June were only 4 kilometres from the Verdun citadel. But on 11 July, Falkenhayn pivoted. With German strength under severe pressure on the Somme, just eleven days old, and the Eastern Front, he suspended further attacks at Verdun. His forces were exhausted, engineer Christian Krull for one: 'At night, we tried to get an hour's sleep in flooded dugouts, while we were covered in thick, wet mud. We could not sleep because of all the vermin, the cold and the dampness, so we dashed over to the cannon and relieved the dead-tired gunners, just to get warm.'[11] Myths of German military invincibility and prowess nevertheless gained currency, fuelling the rise of National Socialism in the 1920s, with a series of authors celebrating Verdun as the birthplace of a new type of heroic, militaristic German.[12]

The reality is that from July, the French began to seize back the initiative, recapturing Douaumont in October and Vaux in

November. By December 1916 when the fighting ceased, the line was where it had been in February 1916. The French had bled, though, severely: their intention to join the British attack on the Somme as equal partners in July 1916 had been blunted, and the morale of its soldiers badly dented. In this sense at least, Falkenhayn had not totally failed. Neither chief of army was to survive in post. Falkenhayn was replaced by Paul von Hindenburg in August, and the enigmatic Joffre, blamed for poor preparation, by the dashing Robert Nivelle in December.

Never before in history, nor since, had bombardment been so intense. 'The pleasant landscape of fields and forests was reduced to a vision of hell, a lunar landscape of horror, filth, fear and confusion,' wrote one author.[13] The whole ecology of the Verdun salient, including the water systems, had collapsed. The ground was so full of toxic chemicals, undetonated artillery, decaying bodies and war debris that the French government decreed that several villages, mostly in the Meuse *département*, could not be rebuilt safely, and debarred dwellers returning home. Thus were established a number of ghost towns named '*villages détruits*' to preserve their memory. Altogether, France had 11,000 schools, town halls and churches and over 350,000 homes destroyed in the war. On top of this, over 2,500,000 hectares of farmland were devastated, an area larger than the size of Wales, as was the transport system: 1,800 kilometres of canals, 5,000 kilometres of railways and 62,000 kilometres of roads all required rebuilding.[14] Nowhere was the destruction more concentrated than at Verdun.

Jonathan takes me to my first *village détruit*, Bezonvaux, in a valley surrounded by wood-covered hills. It reminds me of two other abandoned villages I have known: Oradour-sur-Glane, near our home in France, and Tyneham in south Dorset. Laurence Olivier's voice opens the epic 26-part television series *The World at War* recounting the wanton Nazi murder in 1944 of the entire population at Oradour, while Tyneham was requisitioned in 1943 for a firing range, and never repopulated.

Both ghost villages still attract visitors in their tens of thousands. Not, though, Bezonvaux.

Before August 1914, a noticeboard informs us, Bezonvaux had been a small rural community, with, 'according to the Meuse telephone directory of 1913', 149 inhabitants. As the front line edged closer after August 1914, most left. Then the soldiers came. A memorial honours one young Frenchman, André Maginot, who used the village as a base for launching raids and ambushes on German forces nearby.[15] After the war, he returned to politics, and became increasingly troubled by what he considered insufficient protection offered to France by the Treaty of Versailles against a resurgent Germany. Impressed by the defensive forts he remembered around Verdun, but also their paucity, he advocated a series of permanent fortifications along the northern border of France. In 1926, money was voted to begin the building of what eventually became the 'Maginot Line', completed in 1938. Just in time for the invading Germans two years later to sidestep it.

Bezonvaux was captured by German forces on 25 February 1916, which they used as a logistics and supply centre, with a hospital installed in the chateau. After the French took it back later in 1916, the Germans repeatedly shelled the village, leaving it, by 1918, a ruin. We walk along the 'Remembrance Path', which follows the route of the abandoned Upper Street, passing by where the church and the *mairie* (mayor's office) had once stood, and finishing up in front of the chateau. All that is left of the village are fragments of wall, remains of windows and doors, and piles of rubble and tile. The inhabitants were proud of their vegetables, we learn, grown in the kitchen gardens homes had at their rear. As we look, I hear a distinctive bird sound. 'What was that?' I ask Jonathan. In no time, he identifies a nuthatch. He spends large chunks of his spare time travelling to distant parts to observe birds: I learn much listening to him talk. I am reminded that my grandfather Wilfred, invalided by the war, became a keen ornithologist. I hear his voice too in Jonathan's.

We return to Verdun via a stop-off at the 'Trench of Bayonets'. On 12 June 1916, a company of French infantry was killed and buried by shellfire in a ravine between Douaumont and Thiaumont. Protruding from the ground at regular intervals was seen a number of bayonets, carried by the soldiers buried by the earth below. In December 1919, American banker George F. Rand visited the site, and, moved by what he saw, wrote that, while the men buried are mute, 'their appeal to the world is eloquent'. It distressed him that the weather was corroding the bayonet metal, and trophy hunters were taking remains as souvenirs. So he petitioned President Clemenceau to act, and made a personal gift himself of 500,000 francs to preserve the site. Just the following morning en route to London, Rand's plane crashed and he was killed. The plan nevertheless went ahead, the decision taken to move the monument to flat land 30 metres from where the bodies were buried. A concrete covering was built over the repositioned trench, and white crosses erected to represent where they had stood. Jay Winter, the American historian of the war, approves of the simple recreation: 'The Trench of the Bayonets,' he writes, 'is a war memorial of a special kind: a tomb frozen in time and preserved not by, but from art.'[16]

A final stop – I am anxious to be back on the road – is at the Douaumont cemetery and ossuary. In my farewell trip for parents as head at Brighton College in 2005, one of the party, a French mother, suddenly leapt up on the low perimeter wall of the cemetery, and, with the tricolour behind her, burst into a French folk song dear to her heart. We all stopped dead, transfixed. Her limpid voice floating in the May evening air will always stay with me. Some 16,000 French soldiers are buried in the cemetery below which she sang. The 'Lion of Verdun', as Marshal Pétain became known, is not one of them. A plot had been earmarked for his body, but his collaboration with the Nazis and leadership of the Vichy Regime in the Second World War destroyed his reputation and lost him this revered final resting place. After 1945, he was tried, convicted of treason and sentenced to death, a sentence commuted because of his old age. He was imprisoned and then buried in 1951 on the Île d'Yeu, south-west of Nantes. In 1973, a group of fanatics stole his disinterred coffin, and pressured President Pompidou to rebury him in the cemetery. A formidable police presence was deployed night and day to stop it happening.[17] Eventually, the coffin was recovered and reburied on the Île d'Yeu. Pétain had been unable to rest in peace; perhaps he still doesn't.

On rising ground above the cemetery stands the ossuary, containing the remains of 130,000 French and German soldiers, gathered up from the battlefields in the early post-war years. Built between 1920 and 1932, the bald design is intended to resemble a sword thrust into the ground. The tower was paid for from American donations, further evidence of the strength of US interest at the time. Inside the ossuary, forty-six stone coffins, each representing remains found in different parts of the battlefield, allowed mourners to have some form of personalized connection to their loved ones.

Verdun, like all the war's battles, left behind vast numbers of dead who could not be identified, because of mutilation or nametags lost. I'm puzzled, though, by why the French built ossuaries rather than opting for individual graves for unknown soldiers, as the British chose. But the French had form on bone collections. In the late 1700s, with mounting pressure on cemetery plots in Paris, bodies began to be dug up to be reburied below the streets in catacombs or charnel houses. Human decay, as seen, ensures bones take up much less physical space than a whole body in a bulky coffin. The Parisian necropolis is the largest ossuary in the world, with the bones of some 6 million in spaces connected by 300 kilometres of tunnels. Difficult to imagine this below the streets of London: somehow, it doesn't seem quite British. But it leaves me pondering the difference between the nations, not least in something so significant as the treatment of death.

In December 1915, French legislation called for the creation of national cemeteries across the front to bring together the bodies of soldiers who had 'died for France' with perpetual graves to be maintained at the expense of the state. True to the egalitarian ideals of the French Revolution, the headstones are austere, each virtually identical. For soldiers of Christian faith, as most were, a concrete Latin cross stands at the head of the body. Solid headstones replaced crosses for non-Christians, with Muslim soldiers having headstones angled slightly to face east – the direction of Mecca. In 1922, the French government bowed to pressure, and allowed families to relocate bodies to plots in their home towns: some 30 per cent of those with a confirmed identification were reburied.[18] In Britain, the government early on flatly ruled out repatriation. If British families wanted to see their loved one's grave, they would have to travel to the Continent. Could this explain something of the powerful British pull to the trenches, in contrast to a certain diffidence from the French?

I need to start walking again. Back in Verdun, Jonathan joins me for the first 2 kilometres, past the start of the Voie Sacrée, now a busy main road. We talk about the third Test match against India at Leeds which we've been following closely, then dive into a patisserie to share an apple tart before bidding fond farewells. What a great guy, I think, hoping I will see him again. I do, quicker than either of us expected. I walk on the straight road north-westward out of town, and pick out a farm track that takes me up into the hills. Coming over a ridge near Le Mort-Homme, I spot a gorgeous-looking stone farmhouse in the valley, straight out of North Yorkshire or the Lake District. I stop as I pass the farmyard to take a photograph.

'Jonathan, I've just been bitten by a farm dog. I might need a tetanus booster,' I texted him at 3.13 p.m., less than an hour into the journey. 'Do you have any idea how I can do so quickly without holding back my rhythm on the walk?' I didn't see it coming. A couple of collies were barking in the farmyard, but I've had dogs barking at me many times each day. The smaller one advanced towards me, and I couldn't work out if it was grinning or snarling. It proved to be the latter. As I shooed it away, it suddenly charged at me, a greyish foam around its gums, biting my shin hard through my trousers and leg re-educator. I made menacing sounds at it as it considered coming back for a second go, before retreating to the yard, job done. The farmer heard the kerfuffle, grabbed both dogs by the collars, put them back on the chain, and cast a knowing look of disdain in my direction. Incensed, I started towards the farmhouse, but stopped in my tracks, less out of fear of another attack, though the thought was certainly in my mind, but because I hadn't a clue what I could to say to him, let alone in broken French. So I retreated to a safe distance, pulled up my trouser leg, and rubbed the wound with antiseptic wipes. It stung. Four large teeth marks are very evident, punctured skin, blood and bruises.

Bloody irritating but it's not going to stop me, is my thought. Cross that as a dog-lover I didn't read the signals better, I'm damned if I'm going to lose time because of it, so onwards I go. There'll be no more *hommes morts* at Le Mort-Homme!

I do speak to Sarah, though, who says I should get it looked at immediately, and then to Lou, closest friend of Joanna and me, and for many years also honorary medic to the Seldon family. She too says emphatically that I have to get it checked, hence my text to Jonathan. Blast it, I think, and press on. For two hours, I am up and down in rolling hills through farmland, stopping finally at Esnes-en-Argonne. After a *tarte aux mirabelles* which I pocketed in Verdun, and some chocolate biscuits which have melted liberally in all directions, life starts looking up. Jonathan responds to my message while I'm coming back in a taxi, happy to help. After a long shower at the hotel and some yoghurt, I'm feeling ready for anything. Heavy lobbying continues from the UK and makes me think that I should again take up Jonathan's offer, rather more than he had bargained for.

We find *service des urgences* at Hôpital de Verdun guarded worryingly by armed security. A terrifying receptionist views me with deep suspicion, but after the ordeal of her interrogation, everything improves. An hour and a half later, we are on our way out, a tetanus test proving negative, antibiotic prescription in hand, and arrangements made to return tomorrow morning for consultation with a specialist about *la rage* (rabies). I am impressed by the French hospital care, the lack of ego (receptionist aside) from staff, and just high intelligence, observation and empathy from everyone we encountered. Without Jonathan's immaculate French, I would've been there half the night. Or shown the door.

Back in the hotel, I turn the lights off and look down over the lights of the city playing on the river, the boats swaying in the breeze, and the cafés bustling on 'London Quay'. London adopted Verdun in 1920 and gave money to create in the bombed-out city this elegant waterfront. The official inscription records the gift as coming from 'the heart and centre of the British Empire' to 'the heart and centre of the French fight'. For a long while I am lost in the magical scene. But then I remember the day. I'm more unsettled by the reaction of others than by the bite itself. Rabies I know is real: it killed my mother's first husband in India, Lieutenant Colonel Rex Perrott, on 4 November 1945, buried in Delhi War Cemetery, his name later added to the war memorial in the graveyard at the church in Matfield, Kent. I commit myself to trusting the advice of the rabies specialist when I see them in the morning.

I do not do justice to the loveliest bed in France, tossing and turning all night. I'm up at six starting to plan the route ahead. I know the next few days will be through the most isolated terrain of the entire walk. Jonathan is waiting for me at 9 a.m. by the citadel to drive me to the hospital for my consultation. A nurse spends half an hour collecting information before handing me over to the doctor: tall, distinguished-looking, with elegant hands. He explains that there have been no new cases of rabies in France from dogs since 2001, but is still cautious. He takes me through what the rabies vaccine would mean – two deep injections now, and then two more spaced out. I am not keen: the injections sound as though they would knock out my walking timetable, already stretched almost beyond the limit.

The specialist doesn't tell me the consequences of not taking the vaccine if I have contracted it. Sometimes, it's better not to consult Google, and only some weeks later does it tell me that 60,000 people die annually from rabies, a horrible death, 99 per cent of them from bites from domestic dogs. Would it have affected me if I had known this at the time? It would have worried me, for sure, but I would have pressed on all the same. The specialist was concerned enough to insist I tell him the location of dog and owner; I manage to locate the farm on my phone tracker which I show him, and he fills in documentation which I must take to the gendarmerie to test if the dog has rabies, and for them to discipline the farmer for not chaining a dog who bites passers-by. He asked me if I want to sue. Absolutely not, I say. I have no animosity towards the farmer, nor the dog. In that at least, I am honouring the path of peace.

The gendarmerie trip proves uneventful, then I'm on to the *pharmacie* to collect my prescription for Amoxicillin, bandages and antiseptic. The

Monument aux enfants de Verdun morts pour la France.

very least I can do to thank Jonathan at the end of my day walking is to take him and his partner Aurelia to La Clapier, the nicest restaurant I can find open in the city on a Monday evening. She is French but we speak in English, about the walk, the rise of the right in France, and their hopes for the future. We talk about Jonathan taking a degree perhaps in ornithology, and Aurelia in languages – she can speak English, German and Italian fluently. I think of all the highly eligible people who circumstances prevented going to university. After dinner, we stroll along the London Quay to part by the *Monument aux enfants de Verdun morts pour la France*. Brightly illuminated in the three colours of the French flag, it is composed of five figures of soldiers in stone, representing the different corps of the French Army.

Inaugurated in 1928, it upholds the famous motto of Verdun in 1916: 'They shall not pass'.

They didn't. But at what cost?

7

Champagne–Argonne

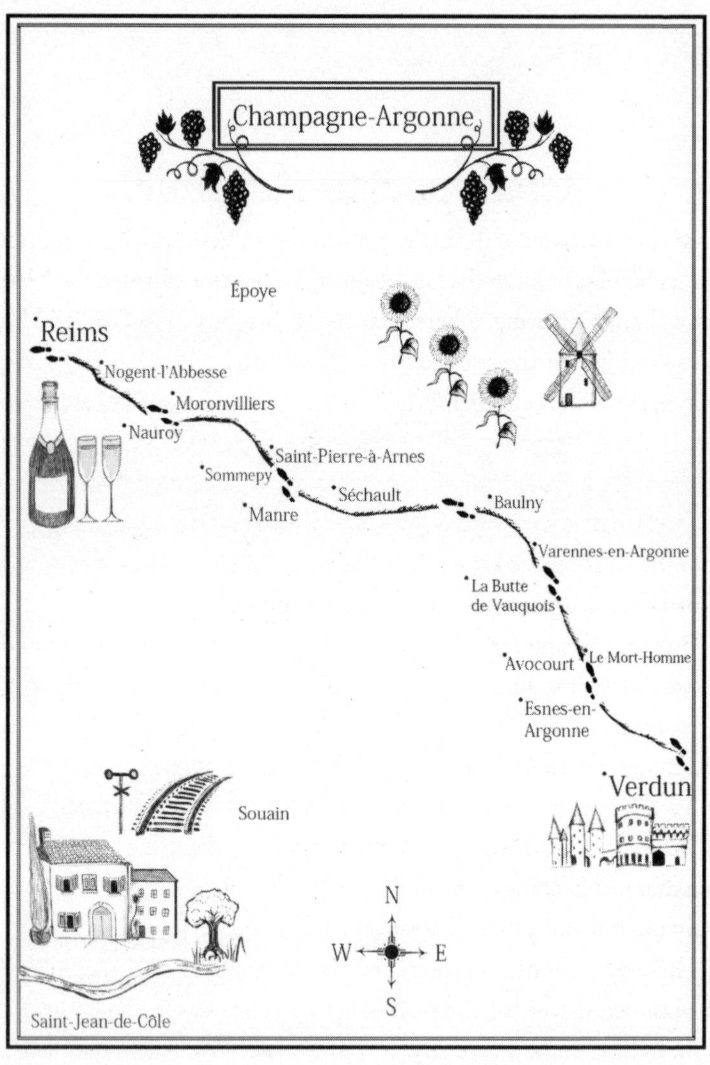
Champagne-Argonne
Époye
Reims
Nogent-l'Abbesse
Moronvilliers
Nauroy
Saint-Pierre-à-Arnes
Sommepy
Séchault
Manre
Baulny
Varennes-en-Argonne
La Butte
de Vauquois
Avocourt
Le Mort-Homme
Esnes-en-
Argonne
Verdun
Souain
N
W
E
S
Saint-Jean-de-Côle

I AM LOOKING OUT of my bedroom window in Verdun. The sun, already at its highest point in the late-August sky, has transformed the Meuse into a Signac painting, a kaleidoscope of bright red, yellow and blue flecks skating over the surface of the river, reflecting its dappled colours back on the hotel ceiling. It is after midday, though; and, hospital visit over, I want to be far away from *accidents et urgences*, from gendarmerie, and from Le Mort-Homme.

Day 15: the next few days will take me through wild Champagne–Argonne to Reims, to the railway to speed me to Susie's wedding on Saturday, and, amazingly, to my halfway point.

But completing the walk is not completing the journey. Gnawing away at me is my failure so far to provide satisfying answers to my questions: is peace more than the absence of war, how to find it in our lives, and what am I to make of my faltering life once the walk is over? I must have imagined the answers would materialize as the steps were marked off (400,000 to date and counting, thank you). The reality has been that just keeping going day after day has taken almost every ounce of my mental and physical strength.

I rake over all this as I look down on the car park, waiting for Alain Nicolas, taxi driver for the next few days. I am itching to be walking again. Itching somewhere else too. The antibiotics have unsettled my guts. Walkers' nightmare! I have become blasé about relieving myself in bushes. But not the Full Monty. My only remedy is not to eat. On this walk, always I am finding trade-offs. No food, no need for nonexistent toilets on the trail. But no food, and my energy will fall away. I am imagining runs in the trenches. Now that was something else.

Dysentery was common amongst the soldiers, caused by infected water, giving sufferers stomach cramps and diarrhoea. They had to rush to use the regular latrines dug over a metre deep as far as was safe from trenches (one of their trade-offs was privacy and smell versus danger). Latrines were considered full when there was less than 0.3 metres left at the top, whereupon they were covered. The men were often thirsty, and in the early years of the war, insufficient clean water was provided. So they sometimes resorted to drinking water from shell holes, which could be contaminated by human and animal detritus.[1] Their rations, though filling, were usually unheated in the front line, and eating receptacles often carried diarrhoea-inducing germs. Newspapers were a common form of toilet paper. For the thousandth time, I realize how lucky I am.

I will be stomach-cramping my way over the next five days through battlegrounds unknown to me, ones in which the British contribution was almost wholly absent. Major encounters took place here early and late in the war, while in 1916 and 1917, when the main action was to the east and west, this was a quiet sector. The First Champagne Offensive was in December 1914, when Joffre unleashed a series of corps-sized attacks on German lines. Some ground was taken, but in January 1915, Falkenhayn ordered a German counter-attack. Joffre's response was to launch a larger offensive, focused around Perthes-lès-Hurlus, 40 kilometres due east of Reims. He managed to advance some 3 kilometres before fighting petered out in March.[2] Over the summer of 1915, the French and British High Commands planned a coordinated offensive, with the British attacking on 25 September in Artois at Loos (where Gillespie fell), and the Second Champagne Offensive launched the same day between Reims and Verdun. In the first week of the offensive, French artillery fired over 3 million shells, churning up their own soil without a second's regret.

Second Champagne followed a now familiar pattern. Early French success saw German front lines taken before momentum was lost, units became disorganized, trenches clogged with wounded, communications cut, and men bogged down in the shell-ravaged landscape. The Germans then moved swiftly into action over virgin ground, reinforcing the areas under pressure with fresh troops. All territory lost was steadily retaken. When Second Champagne ended in November, the sides were back where they started. But with 190,000 French and 150,000 German casualties.[3] It was as futile as the disastrous Battle of Loos. What consolation could there be for those who loved them?

Falkenhayn was observing the back and forth of Second Champagne forensically. His conclusion? Full-frontal offensives to achieve a strategic breakthrough in the enemy's line would never succeed on the Western Front with contemporary technology. And what was the final objective of fresh offensives? The enemy's capital? It was never going to happen. He was asking the right questions, even if his answer was brutal: the Verdun strategy, of not aiming for any breakthrough, but to destroy the enemy's strength and morale.[4]

After the long lull, fighting returned in earnest to this sector three years later. The Champagne–Marne Battle, launched on 15 July 1918, was Germany's last desperate spasm on the Western Front, the final flowering of the Spring Offensive from 21 March. Launched to either side of Reims, its modest objective was capturing the city. By August it was evident it had failed. In September, Supreme Allied Commander Ferdinand Foch ordered US forces to advance into the Meuse–Argonne Forest. Despite heavy fighting and the mounting influenza pandemic, by the end of October, the US army had the Germans in full retreat. The fighting finished up north of where I will be walking over the next few days, towards the German border.

'This walk is proving harder than I estimated,' an understatement I recorded as I set out at midday from Esnes-en-Argonne. 'But I'm not going to let it defeat me.' Off I go due west along a long straight road, blissfully car-free, with the Hill 304[5] Memorial just to my north a reminder that I am still on the old Verdun battlefield. It commemorates the French soldiers who fell here, west of the Meuse. A short distance out of the village, I arrive at the vast Nécropole Nationale d'Esnes-en-Argonne, with 3,661 individual French graves, and a further 3,000 bodies in ossuaries, many from 1914–15. No one is visiting the graves of men now long forgotten. As I saunter slowly past the crosses, I am drawn in by the stillness of the departed. The numbers of these silent witnesses dwarf many times over the 136 living in the village today.

The silence stays with me as I walk along the lane past haystacks made up of bales piled on top of each other, as I remember from childhood farm holidays in south Devon. I'm now passing orchards with apple trees on either side, the fruit bright and red, their cidery scent filling my nostrils, another harbinger of approaching autumn. Dropping down into Avocourt, I find a village asleep, with *boulangerie* boarded up in the middle of the main square. I'm startled out of my thoughts by the loud neigh of a horse tied up by the side of a house. A display board, frayed at the edges, shows off pre-1914 photographs of the village, stationary horses and traps, smiling faces of men outside L'Hôtel-Café Antoine, and children in smocks by the fountain, all straight out of the pages of *Le Grand Meaulnes*. An aerial photograph taken after 1918 shows Avocourt '*totalement ruiné par les obus Allemands*' (totally destroyed by German shells). The village had been battered repeatedly from the war's earliest days, when French and German trenches to the north were just 10 metres apart. 'We insulted them and threw stones. Then one fine day, everything was blown up by a treacherous mine that had been embedded underneath us,' eyewitness testimony recorded on another noticeboard. I learn that on 26 February 1915, the Germans used flamethrowers here for the first time, killing fourteen soldiers from the 3rd French Infantry Regiment. Was being burnt to death worse than instantaneous expiry from shrapnel or bullet, if one died anyway? It must've been, surely. Did some receive a thrill from seeing flesh burning from the flames they were disgorging? Yes, I fear must be the answer. Assuredly, then, empathy is the first building block of realizing peace.

Leaving Avocourt by the Ancienne Rue de Varennes, I pass another French cemetery with more than 1,800 dead, many from 1916, killed on Hill 360 at the western extreme of the Battle of Verdun. Retaining their own cemetery rather than having the bodies transferred to the national necropolis at Esnes was one of many fights by the villagers post-1918. They hoped an important graveyard might bring vitality back to their once-thriving community which, according to the 1911 census, boasted 1,014 souls. Life from death. The post-war Reconstruction Commission estimated it would cost 13.5 million francs to rebuild the village, with work on public buildings starting in 1923, the church consecrated in 1926 and school opened in 1927. But not even the award of the 1914–1918 Croix de Guerre for its sacrifices restored the community to its pre-war glory. On the centenary in 2018, only 123 lived in the village. The Great War killed communities, not just people. *Villages détruits* took many forms. Human structures centuries in the building were destroyed forever in just a few hours of bombardment.

The war changed nature as well. A 6-kilometre brisk walk through winding lanes takes me to La Butte de Vauquois, which had 18 metres shaved off its top by explosions from underground mines. I'm not sorry to be saved that extra climb, I reflect wryly, as, low on energy, I puff up the hill. The road takes me to a village which I realize was built entirely post-war, before I choose a rough track up through woods to the summit. Once atop, and looking for kilometres in every direction, I understand why this supreme vantage point was one of the most fought-over pieces of land on the entire Western Front.

The villagers on top of their idyllic hill might have thought they would be spared when war broke out in August 1914. But Crown Prince Wilhelm's decision to bypass Verdun and plunge deep into Argonne made them vulnerable. So they rapidly departed for safety, though the mayor and his seven-year-old grandson were killed by shelling when sheltering in a nearby village. The French took the top of the hill on 15 September and immediately fortified the abandoned community. Nine days later, in a pattern by then familiar, the Germans took it off them, and pumped iron and concrete into fortifications around the perimeter, installing artillery capable of firing on the railway line to Verdun from Paris. Recapturing the summit now became a major French priority. Their assaults in October, November and December failed, with huge casualties. In February 1915, they managed to capture the hilltop four times only to lose it shortly after. In March, however, they managed to keep hold of the southern part of the summit, digging trenches just a few metres away from the Germans on the northern half of the hill. With No Man's Land that narrow, and shelling thus too dangerous, both sides resorted to trench mortars and, increasingly, to underground mines, facilitated by the favourable nature of the rock for digging. An extraordinary total of 519 mines were detonated in the war (320 French, 199 German). The village church, the school, and all the shops and houses, were totally obliterated. Not even low-level walls, cellars or foundations were left. It was as if a volcano had blasted them into oblivion.[6]

Both sides dug down deep into the hill, carving out a dense labyrinth with kilometres of tunnels, leading to barracks, dormitories, command posts and even hospitals. On 14 May 1916 at 4.10 p.m., the Germans detonated the most powerful single mine of Vauquois's war, with 60 tonnes of Westfalit (a high explosive developed in the nineteenth century for coal mines) killing over a hundred French soldiers.[7] In 1917, the French planned to blow the Germans off what remained of the hill with three giant mines dug 45 metres below the surface, loaded with a 145-tonne charge. But by this time, the war had moved on. The rapid development of new observation methods, aircraft and balloons, and stalemate at Verdun, meant that Vauquois lost much of its strategic importance. The French thus abandoned the plan for what would've been the most sensational pyrotechnic display of the war. Late in the day came elements of civility when both sides developed a code where mines would only be detonated at set times of the day. All very gentlemanly. The final French mine exploded in March 1918, and the last German one a month later. In September, during the Meuse–Argonne Offensive, the Americans stormed the hill. They were puzzled to find no trace of the village indicated on their maps. All that remained were row after row of deep mine craters.[8]

Now, 103 years later, I share something of the Americans' incredulity at the summit I am on, albeit covered over by grass and with carefully preserved display trenches. No one lives here any more. With the support of the city of Orléans on the Loire, from where so many had fought and died on the hill, the new village was built on the hillside through which I had walked on my ascent. The density of unexploded shells and mines after 1918 meant the French government had prevented the inhabitants rebuilding their village where it once stood. Explosives can become more unstable over the years – not just mines and shells, but mortar bombs, hand grenades and ammunition. Gas shells can leak poisonous chemicals. The figure of 1.5 billion has been given – no one can possibly know – for the number of shells fired in the war, of which perhaps 10 million, again a wild guess, remain in the soil, either duds that failed to detonate or munition dumps not used at the time. The Département du Déminage (mine clearance) destroys some 400 tonnes of old ordnance every year, from both world wars, with over 600 of its personnel killed since 1946 carrying out its work.[9] Some soldiers after 1918 were unable to get the sound of shells out of their heads; but, for others, the threat from the shells continued to be all too real.

I spend an hour at the monument (inaugurated in 1926; designed by a veteran) and walking around the battlefield, and spot just one group of three people. Suddenly aware of the time, I turn and hurry back down the hill, too quickly, miss my turning, and have to walk an extra 3 kilometres. I'm annoyed with myself because of the further pressure it puts on my schedule. The clouds are thickening, and it looks as if a storm is coming. After an hour, I'm in the small town of Varennes-en-Argonne, another on the front line destroyed in the war, and I take refuge from the muggy air inside its modernist church, collapsing into a pew. Waves of exhaustion envelop me, not helped, I realize later, by my strict lack of food. In the dark claustrophobic interior, I concede with considerable reluctance that what I want my body to do is out of step with what it will let me do. I must call it a day. I try phoning Alain to tell him that I've missed my target for the end of the walk, and could he meet me instead in the nearby hamlet of Baulny? But his English is no better than my French, and for a few moments, I fear he will give up on me. I imagine I might be holed up in this breathless church all night. But I track down Sarah who is calm and sensible, suggesting I phone the hotel and ask them to contact Alain to explain the new meeting point. Soon enough, all is settled.

Two fellow visitors would've given a king's ransom in an earlier day for such a quick exit from Varennes. On 21 June 1791, Louis XVI and Marie Antoinette were travelling through the town in an attempt to escape Revolutionary Paris, en route to friendly forces just 50 kilometres away at Montmédy on the Belgian border. Progress had been impeded by Louis's insistence on using a luxurious royal carriage requiring regular changes of horses, rather than a lighter coach. The stately progress allowed Citizen Drouet, the postmaster of Sainte-Menehould, to recognize the king, anticipate his route, jump on a horse, and gallop down a shortcut to Varennes, where he alerted the National Guard, who arrested Louis. News that the king had planned to escape France and join up with enemy forces helped shatter the experiment in constitutional monarchy, always fragile, and sparked violent insurrection in Paris in August 1792. The abolition of the monarchy, proclamation of the Republic in September, and the guillotining of Louis in January 1793 all followed. How different French, and world, history might have been but for events that June night in Varennes. The memorial clock tower, built in 1793 on the very spot of the arrest, burnt by the Germans and rebuilt after 1918, barely seems to do it justice. It all puts my mini Varennes drama into perspective.

The clock tower is eclipsed in scale and grandeur by the nearby Pennsylvania Memorial, erected in memory of the volunteers from America's seminal state who liberated the town at the end of the war. Built in neoclassical style, it consists of a series of columns, bearing at the centre a quotation from President Woodrow Wilson: 'The right is more precious than peace'. Below the monument, bunkers and concrete shelters are carefully preserved for no one to visit.

I contemplate Wilson's words – can indeed there be peace without right prevailing? What is the worth of 'peace' now in Hong Kong when the democracy protestors are subdued or imprisoned? Wilson must be right, as he was about the need for the US to support the League of Nations, I think, as I take my final steps of the day along leafy lanes above the valley of the River Aire, finishing at remote Baulny. I'm mightily relieved to see Alain's car parked up by a farm gate. He too is pleased to have located the meeting point, helped by his wife sitting beside him, with chihuahua Kiki commanding the back seat. '*Vous avez l'air très fatigué*,' she says sternly over her padded shoulder as I feel myself slipping down the rear seat dozing off. '*Vous devez dormir*' are the last words I hear. A long time later, I awake to see the rainy suburbs in Verdun. As surreptitiously as I can, I wipe the deep leather seat free of sweat before leaving the car. Hunger is my overwhelming sensation as I collect my thoughts on the wet pavement. I search out dried toast in a nearby supermarket which I consume hungrily for supper in my hotel bedroom, hoping it won't cause problems. The full force of Covid comes back to me when I have a conversation with oldest daughter, Jessica, working flat out in the Health Department. The position since I began walking is not improving in Britain. We talk too about Adam: it is more touch than go that he will be able to make Susie's wedding in six days' time.

I fall asleep on my bed with unsettling dreams about my leaving the university and what to do next punctuating my slumber. Who am I when not defined by my job? I still don't know the answer. At 8.30 a.m., Alain (we're on first-name terms now) is waiting for me with Kiki in the hotel car park. It takes well over an hour to drive back to Baulny. I have capped my walk today at 25 kilometres, rehydration tablets for diarrhoea (no, it wasn't a good night) my only sustenance as I push on due west through this quite extraordinarily empty part of France. The rain has blown over and the weather is perfect for walking: sunny with a light, cooling breeze. I follow farm tracks and lanes through a succession of unspoilt rural villages: Apremont, Chatel-Chéhéry, Autry and Bouconville. If I had felt better, I would have made more of them, but I am utterly fixated on arriving at my destination, Séchault, which I do by late afternoon. Evidence of fighting as I approach it has long since disappeared into the soil of the open fields, with their wheat crop newly harvested. But when walking through woods, I spot the zigzag lines of trenches, concrete bunkers, and rounded depressions amongst the trees indicating exploded shells.

American soldier Alvin York fought in trenches here. His religious beliefs made him initially apply to be a conscientious objector, but his application was rejected. After much soul searching, he decided that it was his calling to follow orders as an ordinary infantryman, which he executed with extraordinary vigour. When told to take out a German machine-gun emplacement holding up his regiment's advance in October 1918, he attacked the position alone, killing several Germans, which prompted their comrades to surrender. Making his way back to the American lines, he captured still more enemy soldiers. York found himself the reluctant recipient of a shower of honours, including every major American medal and France's Legion of Honour. 'I am trying to forget the war. I occupied one space in a 50-mile front. I saw so little it hardly seems worth discussing,' he protested. But the honours continued to flow. US presidents wanted to be photographed with him, as did celebrities, his story capturing the imagination of film-makers and novelists, including F. Scott Fitzgerald. Yet he was happiest living quietly on the farm given to him by the state of Tennessee, where he established a Bible school for the education of rural youth, continuing to protest until his death in 1964 that he was no hero.[10]

The aftermath of my dog bite necessitates one final long slog back to Verdun. The prospect of rabies remains far from my mind. What concerns me is my continuing upset gut, and the blisters on my feet, growing in size and number. I am not certain I could have done anything about the former, but I rue my inadequate preventative work on blisters before I left. I sit on my bed and, unable to concentrate on Leigh Fermor or W. G. Sebald's *The Rings of Saturn* about his walk through Suffolk, read up about soldiers' feet in a pathetic attempt to derive some consolation from *Schadenfreude*. From the start of the war, I learn, British soldiers were issued with two pairs of regulation boots; officers, who purchased their own uniforms, were required to buy polished brown long boots. Harrods was a popular outlet, from where hand-sewn boots with straps made of brown oil calf could be purchased for £5 (some £350 today). From 1915, the 'B' boot series began to be issued to the infantry to save leather, with woven cotton laces, a plain-leather counter, and leather toecap removed. 'Puttees' (derived from the Hindi word *patti*, i.e. bandage), a long strip of cloth introduced with khaki uniform in 1902, were wound tightly round the soldiers' legs from ankles to knees to provide support and protection from water, a poor man's knee-length boot substitute.

Boots and puttees, unchanged for the eight days the men were in the front and support lines, were far from perfect. British troops, excepting a minority within kilt-wearing Scottish regiments, wore tight boots and puttees that constricted blood circulation in the lower legs. Says historian George Morton-Jack, 'Combined with prolonged exposure to water on the trench floor, their boots and puttees could cause feet to swell, turn blue and develop blisters and sores.'[11] Henry

Williamson, the writer and friend of my grandfather Wilfred, recalled how 'when the frost came... our boots froze while we were sleeping – it was painful'.[12] Frozen feet combined with poor blood flow to produce varicose veins and 'trench foot'. Officially recognized from 1916, it was initially regarded by many top brass with dry feet and brightly polished boots as a disease of malingerers seeking a quick passage home, despite it resulting in growing numbers of amputations. Damage to fighting strength and to morale notwithstanding, the same unforgiving style of boot continued substantially unaltered, some 70 million pairs for Allied armies during the war, 50 million of them proudly made in Northamptonshire's factories.[13] The preservation of one such, Waulkerz Boots factory in Northampton town centre, was by coincidence being debated as I walked.

British soldiers envied the *poilus* (French infantry). 'We came across some French soldiers,' recalled Private Charles Colthup. 'They had thick felt boots and a kind of rubber outside. I thought to myself, "I wouldn't mind a pair of them."'[14] The Germans too were believed to have superior footwear: hobnailed boots used by the Prussian army since the 1870s, known to the British as the 'jackboot', as tough as they were durable. Technically known as the *Marschstiefel* (marching boot), they were a motif in Erich Maria Remarque's classic war novel *All Quiet on the Western Front*. When his comrades come to see their friend Kemmerich who is dying in hospital, they fall out over who should inherit his boots. They are then passed on from comrade to comrade after they in turn meet their end; the military footwear being far more tough and durable than its temporary human owners.[15]

The Poor Bloody Infantry (PBI) – as they styled themselves – certainly felt bottom of the heap when it came to footwear. Indian soldiers were envied for their oversized boots which allowed for blood circulation and two pairs of socks for warmth.[16] Envy turned to anger when the Tommies caught sight of the new-style American boot from January 1918 with its enhanced water resistance and a thicker sole (nicknamed 'little tanks').[17] British soldiers were particularly vulnerable as so much of their fighting took place in waterlogged Flanders, notably on the Ypres salient. One army response to boot envy drew on the emerging field of nudge psychology. Soldiers were paired with each other and held responsible for the feet of a fellow comrade. Each day, they were charged with looking at each other's feet for telltale signs of trench foot: itching turning to numbness, skin turning red or blue, or swelling and the smell of decay. Whale oil became widely available to rub into the feet.[18] Too little, too late, those affected must have felt.

No telltale signs of red or blue at least are evident on my feet as I now, companionless, examine them on my bed. I pick up my Mountain Warehouse Extreme Quest Men's Isogrip Boots with a new respect. Made from leather, they have heavily padded heels and ankle protection, yet weigh no more than my everyday black shoes. But even with these paragons of modern footwear science, and the liberal application of the modern equivalent of whale oil, the blisters are still growing, and hurt as soon as I put my boots back on. 'Stop bloody complaining,' the voices from the PBI are yelling at me. Bloody right.

I start Day 16 back at Séchault, at the German cemetery, beautifully tended and with generously spaced graves under plane trees. *AUF DIESEM FRIEDHOF RUHEN 6,454 DEUTSCHE SOLDATEN 1914–1918* (in this cemetery lie 6,454 German soldiers) declares a sign at the entrance gate. I'm surprised to find three-quarters of the graves are indicated unknown, suggesting the impact of decay in the long period between death and the cemetery's opening. My photograph has a protracted shadow stretching along an avenue between the German graves. 'I wonder if it is the spirit of Gillespie,' I write, indicative of my state of mind that sun-bright morning.

The village boasts a prominent memorial too to the 369th American Infantry Regiment, described as the 'Harlem Hellfighters'. A noticeboard tells how this regiment of black American soldiers arrived in France ready for combat in April 1918. Their military commanders, though, decided that the French army would integrate them more successfully, 'so they were re-organized as a French unit'. The men spent the first three months in the line defending the area around Avocourt, before taking part in the final Meuse–Argonne Offensive from September 1918. They took many objectives including Hill 188, captured large numbers of German prisoners and forty-seven machine guns, while shooting down three German planes. Of the 5,000 Harlem Hellfighters who fought, 1,400 became casualties.[19] In stark contrast to the American Army, the monument records the words of a French officer after the war: 'The French people could not understand the idea of social distinction on account of colour. They said the coloured men were soldiers... and they could not see why they were discriminated against. They received the men in their churches and homes.' The French government indeed awarded the entire regiment the Croix de Guerre with Palm. Corporal Stowers was one of many to perform acts of outstanding bravery, pressing ahead ferociously with an attack despite being severely wounded. Stowers never made it home, but several of his heroic comrades did. No American president, though, posed for a photograph with them, and none of their states gave them farms. Segregation remained in the US army throughout the Second World War, only being officially ended by executive order in 1948; even after then, vestiges of discrimination remained in the Korean, Vietnam and Afghan Wars.

Woodrow Wilson's words come back to mind. His vision of 'the right is more precious than peace' did not extend to black soldiers. Sadly, because he was a progressive in so many other ways, Wilson, the first president from the South since before the Civil War, and the child of slavery apologists, saw segregation grow in the military when he was at the White House. By today's, and even contemporary standards, he was a racist. So too was Churchill. But must we condemn them so vehemently? We are all, far more than we are comfortable admitting, figures shaped by the thinking of our time. I recoil from the strident denigration that characterizes our polarized and judgmental age. We could condemn a little less and understand a little more.

I walk along the busy main road to Manre, past the once-thriving Moulin de Manre and boarded-up Ancien Café des Sangliers, where I pick up farm tracks and lanes which I remain on for the rest of the day. Poppies are blooming by the side of the chalk track, together with all manner of wild plants: foxgloves, cornflowers, hawkbit and field scabious. The intense quiet, the butterflies and the profusion of flowers growing in the chalky soil make it difficult to imagine how it looked to war correspondent E. Alexander Powell, visiting this very region in September 1915. 'Over an area as long as from Charing Cross to Hampstead Heath, and as wide as from Bank to Marble Arch, the earth is pitted with the craters caused by bursting shells, as the face of a man who has had the small pox,' he wrote.

An American living in and working from London, Powell's neutral status gave him access behind German lines until America entered the war in 1917. 'I kicked a hobnailed German boot out of my path, and from it fell a rotting foot,' he records. The stench of the Champagne–Argonne battlefields was his abiding memory: 'It looked and smelt as though all the garbage cans in Europe and America have been emptied upon it.' Peering into a deserted dugout one day, he was driven back by the overpowering stink, till a soldier 'more hardened to the business than I' went in ahead with a candle, finding the shell-blackened bodies of three Germans. A postcard from a Bavarian village, clasped in the fingers of one, had its message mostly blotted out by crimson, but bringing it up into the light, he could read the opening words: 'My dearest Heinrich, you went away from us just a year ago today. I miss you terribly, as do the children, and we all pray hourly for your safe return...'[20] I choke up when I read words like these, imagining the long empty evenings, the dismay and grief, the desolate years ahead for that

Poppies by the side of my track through the Champagne battlefield.

fatherless family. Are my tears triggered in part by my own experience of the death of Joanna, and thoughts of the children without their deeply loved mother? Of course they are.

I pause to collect myself, allow the feelings to settle and soon after pass a sign announcing that I'm entering the Département de la Marne, arriving shortly after at the Sommepy American Monument on Blanc Mont Ridge. Opened in 1937 on the twentieth anniversary year of America joining the war, its most striking feature is an observation tower of golden-yellow limestone giving a commanding view over the battlefields. Together with preserved gun emplacements, dugouts and trenches, I'm struck by how this American memorial is aimed as much at instruction and history as at remembrance of the dead, as are British and French memorials. The site is open to visitors daily. The pity is, there are no visitors. No one to remember. No one to instruct.

The site looks down over the ossuary of Navarin, 8 kilometres due south, containing the remains of 10,000 French and American soldiers killed on the battlefields. The pyramid-styled monument is topped by a statue of three soldiers, one the pilot Quentin Roosevelt, youngest son of Teddy Roosevelt, president of the United States from 1901–9, the only child of an American president to die in combat. That's another stark contrast with the British experience, as we shall see with the sad tally of prime ministerial family loss on the Somme.

Just to the south of the ossuary lies Souain, where four French corporals were shot for cowardice on 17 March 1915, an example to their comrades. Later considered the war's most outrageous abuse of military power, it inspired Humphrey Cobb's anti-war novel, *Paths of Glory*, in 1935, and Stanley Kubrick's 1957 film, starring Kirk Douglas. After prolonged campaigning by their families, the four soldiers were exonerated in 1934. Their families received a symbolic single franc as compensation. The official verdict at least brought them some peace, far more than any money might have done.

Bemused at finding myself in the midst of all these epic monuments alone, and at the height of the tourist season, I sit down on a verge, which turns out to be a communication trench, and pull out my long-awaited lunch. I tuck cautiously into the bread and cheese, hoping for the best. I've been carrying all my clobber today as I'm at last moving on tonight from Verdun to a fresh location, and the relief of laying it down is intense. I think of the unexpected bliss that the soldiers could experience in simple things, as when warming themselves under the sun, sipping a mug of hot tea, eating a rasher of bacon or inhaling a cigarette. So relaxed am I that I don't feel myself being bitten multiple times by ants, which have penetrated my clothes and food-rich rucksack.

Sod it, I think, as I shake them off, apply anti-bite ointment, and pack up to leave. I have just 15 kilometres left to walk today. Optimism surges. I sense that I might have broken the back of this 100-kilometre section through No Man's Land of Champagne–Argonne. I allow myself to imagine I can even smell the champagne vineyards surrounding Reims, which I must reach by Friday, two days away. But I have been stung before by euphoria: one day at a time is the way to crack this.

One red line I decided before setting out was not to let work intrude into the walk, but an exception comes this afternoon, my final meeting after ten years as a governor and board member of the Royal Shakespeare Company and I want to convey my gratitude. Directing plays brought me the greatest joy at university, and deep down I would have much preferred to serve on the artistic side of the RSC. I know I lacked the talent, though, and still loved my association with it. Leaving it is a curtain falling, another mini death. The board meeting eats up 9 full kilometres as I stride, my phone on mute, on farm tracks along a plateau with views over low-sloping hills in every direction.

In no time, I arrive at my rendezvous at Saint-Pierre-à-Arnes where a jovial taxi driver whisks me to a gîte at the nearby village of Époye. It was the only open accommodation I could find, and it has wrenched me further north of the front line than I wanted. But it is at least the kind of stopover I envisaged I would be staying in every night, but for Covid: my bedroom is in a converted barn, it is in an unspoilt village, and dinner made from wholesome local produce arrives course after course on the patio in front of my room. The owners are eager to chat, and I am thrilled to have their company. I had not anticipated the loneliness of the walk. They laboured hard to create their appealing bedrooms out of their outbuildings, but business since has been poor, and now another season is all but over. Generous glasses of sweet local white wine are poured as they enquire about the walk and about Sarah. The lady of the house, who had spoken to her earlier about my arrival, is curious to know why I am with 'a French lady'. When I tell Sarah, I can feel a pulse of linguistic triumph surge through the telephone. I have no recollection of going to bed before I tip over into a drowsy sleep.

Relieved of my heavy baggage, which is going forward by taxi, I plan a 32-kilometre walk the next day, a Thursday, weaving in and out of the front lines, to finish within striking distance of Reims. With the weather grey and overcast, cold and very gusty, I take only two 500-millilitre water bottles. I will need less liquid, I reason, without the sun beating down. I set out in high spirits along farm tracks before 9 a.m. A bi-turbo tractor sails past me, the farmer waving gaily even as his behemoth blows my blue hat clean off into his cabbages. Cabbages and maize have been the staple crops all the way since the Vosges. I follow the wending La Suippe river valley through a succession of villages, each quieter than the last, entering and leaving Bétheniville on a track like so many, thousands of years old. I pass an abandoned railway line, a remnant of the 120-kilometre narrow-gauge local line partly destroyed in the war, and closed to passengers finally in 1936, which speaks of a world lost that puts me in mind of *Le Grand Meaulnes* again, with its evocation of a pre-1914 rural France so visible to me still every single day. Its lyricism and poetry uplifts me far more than the walking books I had expected. I have decided to part company with *A Time of Gifts* and *The Rings of Saturn* till back home. Like Alain-Fournier's heroes, I am on a journey looking for something I do not know I can find. 'I am looking for something still more mysterious. I'm looking for the passage that they write about in books… suddenly, as you part the branches in the dense undergrowth… you see something like a long, dark avenue leading to a tiny circle of light,' says François, the book's narrator. I too am looking for a lost estate, a long avenue leading me to a circle of light, to a place of deep peace. Is its existence a fiction, or am I too looking in the wrong place? Perhaps the answers will come when I am closer to the English Channel and can find more time to reflect.

Teeth, not peace, is what preoccupies my mind in the short term at least as I walk on. Randomly, it is fixated on Fournier's dental records, which allowed the authorities to identify his body. Shortly before leaving for France, I cracked a tooth down to the root and my dentist nicked it out, gone forever, an enamelled portion of me forging on ahead, an advance guard into the next world. That must be why teeth are looming large today. I hadn't realized until I saw Peter Jackson's colourized film of the First World War, *They Shall Not Grow Old*, quite how poor the condition of soldiers' teeth was, and how unselfconscious they were about it. Even young soldiers grin straight at the camera bearing remarkably few gnashers.

Until the 1860s, the British army required soldiers to have strong teeth for biting musket cartridges, but the emergence of copper cartridges removed the requirement. Little notice was taken despite the Boer War highlighting the often deplorable quality of soldiers' teeth.[21] Intensive lobbying for action came from the profession, with the *Dental Journal* quoting one soldier in November 1914 saying, 'There is nothing which takes it out of a man in the trenches more than toothache.'[22] Happily for the British soldier if not for its commander, Douglas Haig developed severe toothache in October 1914, but was unable to find a British dentist to treat him. Twelve were promptly dispatched to France with temporary commissions in the Royal Army Medical Corps, the total number rising to 850 by November 1918.[23] But with understanding of oral hygiene still basic, and regular toothbrushing in the line often impractical, the problems mounted, as did the requirement for speed with patients, who suffered terrible pain without anaesthetics. Royal Flying Corps officer Maurice Baring experienced first-hand how rudimentary wartime dentistry was: 'No matter how much you struggle and scream and kick... Holding my head in a vice, he dug the drill deeper and deeper into the tender tooth till the hole is finished.'[24] By the war's end, the government still didn't consider dental care a primary need. Even today, dentistry remains the Cinderella of the medical professions.

Mulling over teeth, human and dog, my tongue repeatedly seeks out the root of my lost canine. I continue along chalky upland tracks for the next few hours past large arable fields, with remains of cement fortifications a regular feature among the crops. Later in the day, deep rutting in the paths' baked mud caused by modern military vehicles puts me on high alert to the risk of turning or twisting my ankles.

Observation posts and double rows of wire fencing suggest the French military don't want people here. It's not First World War debris but nuclear war that is the source of the high security. Controversial simulated nuclear tests or 'cold firings' took place here, and a no-fly zone was in force to protect sensitive work inside on atomic energy. What have we learnt since 1918? The permanent route of the Western Front Way should pass by here. Armageddon has many forms.

I skirt round the side of dense woods which conceal the remains of the village of Moronvilliers. Armageddon came for the villagers early one morning with French commander Robert Nivelle's 'Battle of the Hills' in April and May 1917. It was conceived as a supportive attack as part of the Second Battle of the Aisne, but the village, slap bang in the middle of the main assault, never stood a chance. Moronvilliers was totally flattened by shellfire and declared a 'red zone': the government ruled out restoring it after the war and decided to rebuild it as an extension of the nearby village of Pontfaverger.

No fewer than fifteen *villages détruits* were designated in the Marne region alone. My track drops down on to another, called Nauroy, equally in the eye of the battle, as seen in the diagram below.

The roadside sign on the outskirts, white letters on a black background as opposed to the standard French black on white, tells me I am arriving

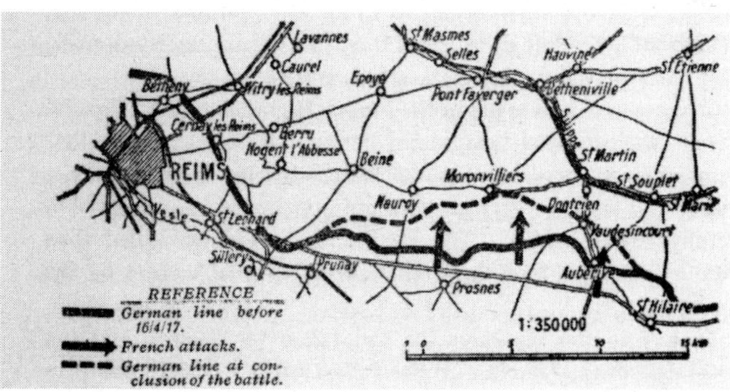

A contemporary map of the Nivelle Offensive.

at no ordinary place. Where the village once stood, now there are woods, with half-metre-high monuments dotted around the undergrowth. The first I see announces that Jean Isidore Guérin-Lemâitre, aged seventy, a *cultivateur*, lived here. A map and aerial photograph shows how his house and street looked before Nivelle and his forces arrived. I leave the main road to wander on wood paths through the former village and to make out more of the all-but-obliterated buildings; here the church, there the square. In one clearing, a black metal statue of a *poilu*, which took 300 hours to fashion from 300 kilograms of shells found nearby, is dedicated to all the men, women and children '*morts pendant la guerre 14/18*'. It was unveiled only in May 2017, on the centenary of the battle, welcome evidence of continuing interest in the war.

The citizens of Nauroy were forced to merge with Beine, 5 kilometres to the west. I imagine how they must have felt as I slug along the straight road to 'Beine-Nauroy', an unprepossessing village which, to my disappointment, has no café open. My water-light strategy has not proved a success, and for a good two hours in the warming afternoon, I've been without liquid. I manage to locate one shop, a *boulangerie*, but that too is closed. There is nothing for it but to keep going, hopeful that my destination for the day, Nogent-l'Abbesse, a tourist town on the champagne trail, will have shops and bars. Another hour's walk later, this time uphill, I discover it has several. All resolutely shut. By now, I'm seriously thirsty and hungry, and, when I hear my taxi is running an hour late, my temper begins to fray. Not even the champagne shops and hotels are open, though the town's dogs are outside in force. A large and angry Alsatian with bared white teeth almost succeeds in scaling a 2-metre fence separating us. I am cross I have been caught out by not carrying – or being able to find – enough water. Such a basic, stupid error for a walker. I'm clearly on edge, and my multiple bites are itching. I've made it to Champagne, and already walked through a few vineyards, but I feel no elation. I sit down on a bench by the church and meditate to calm myself. I was in such a good place mentally and physically last night, and I have blown it.

The taxi driver, the first person I've spoken to all day, finds me there and proves very amiable. We chat in French and English as I ask him to take me on a detour to a chemist for antihistamine and more antiseptic ointment for the ant bites, which have formed rashes on my arms and torso. Back in my barn room, I spend a long time washing away the day from my clothes and body. I push myself to do yoga for half an hour, but worryingly, it's a slog. I have reached nearly halfway on the walk, but in place of relief there is anxiety.

During another restless night, I dream several times about Joanna. 'I'm still here,' she tells me, perched improbably on a barstool. She is so vivid, her knowing smile so real, I could touch her. I wake each time wondering if it is my imagination, or if her spirit is coming to visit me on the eve of our Susie's wedding. It provokes nothing like the waves of grief that have swept regularly over me since she died in her ward at the Royal Marsden. This experience is neither sad, nor is it unsettling. It is the opposite. She really was here, still, as she said.

I have booked a ticket the next day on the 12.02 from Reims. I am up early, anxious about missing the train. My primary objective this Friday is to make sure I don't. I set out again from Nogent, which looks much more welcoming in the bright morning air. Good news by text from Adam: he is clear of Covid and out of quarantine just in time for the wedding. I have 15 kilometres to walk this morning with my full kit, choosing a remote woodland track down towards the distant city. This plan first goes wrong when I'm being bitten deep in the woods by several mosquitoes undeterred by my insect repellent. Then I lose my way. Not for the first time on unused tracks, I realize I am covered with cobwebs. In a trice, I feel a large spider crawling steadily down my chest. Careless of the buzzing mosquitoes, I whip off my top, and shake it violently in all directions, still gypped by yesterday's biting ants. Torso bare to the world, waving limbs like a lunatic, I must make a sorry sight. A moment of panic follows when I realize I'm lost in a vast wood and fear I will miss the train. Being a no-show at Susie's wedding is a horrible thought. When I calm down, I hear distant cars; I beat a way through the undergrowth towards the sounds, and soon I'm out into open fields. Discarding romantic notions of my early-morning pastoral walk, I opt for busy roads, marching quickly along them in the direction of the cathedral. No more risks today. Thus does this bedraggled, cobwebbed ambler enter Reims, along La Rue de Cernay; past, appropriately, La Ferme des Anglais.

As I push myself along the city's pavements, thinking how odd it is to be in bustling crowds again, I at last let myself feel some achievement on reaching this glorious city, the most populous of my entire walk. Reims, with its deep connections to its country's monarchy, shares something with Gillespie's school in the once royal city of Winchester. Arriving with time to spare, I am drawn to the cathedral, and am overwhelmed. Built in the thirteenth century concurrently with the two other great French cathedrals bearing the name Notre-Dame – Paris and Chartres – it became the largest and, for a long period, France's most powerful. In 1429, in the presence of Joan of Arc, King Charles VII was crowned here, as were no fewer than thirty-two of his fellow monarchs.

The dominant French city between Germany and Paris, Reims was fated to be heavily involved in the war. German forces quickly stormed it, transforming the cathedral into a giant infirmary. Following the First Battle of the Marne in early September 1914, the Germans withdrew and took up position on the surrounding hills, from where they bombarded Reims without mercy. Their first onslaught came on 18 September, when five shells hit the cathedral. Worse came the following day, when lead from the still-burning roof poured down through the medieval structure causing ancient stained-glass windows to explode. Some 300 shells altogether smashed into the edifice. Such barbaric acts against the heights of cultural and spiritual genius were of course, I remind myself, perpetuated by both sides.

After the war, fierce debate took place across France on whether this revered cathedral should be left in its mutilated state: 'One must not erase traces of war, or its memory will be extinguished too soon,' argued architect Auguste Perret. The traditionalists, though, prevailed, with reconstruction commencing in late 1919, and donations pouring in from across the world, including $2.5 million ($35 million today) from American magnate John D. Rockefeller.[25] Restoration took twenty years, and only in July 1938 was the cathedral reopened to the public. The city and the cathedral were badly battered again in the Second World War. Symbolically, the German surrender on all fronts was signed in Reims on 7 May 1945.

With 80 per cent of the buildings in the city destroyed by artillery, its remaining inhabitants took refuge in the 120 kilometres of champagne cellars lying beneath it. The war had not been kind to the wine. The 1914 vintage, supposedly one of the twentieth century's finest, was harvested only after an Allied offensive forced the Germans to abandon Épernay a week before grape picking was due. With many Champagne vineyards on the front line between German and French armies, an estimated 40 per cent were destroyed in the war. Production somehow continued, and with no apparent slippage in standards. In 2015, auctioneers Sotheby's sold a cellar visit to Krug and tasting of its fine 1915 vintage for £90,000.[26]

I resist the temptation to buy a small bottle of a more modest vintage on the sleek TGV as I speed southwards from Reims. I've always relished long train journeys, but on this occasion I am apprehensive of my fellow passengers, some of whom are coughing. It's several days since I have been this physically close to strangers. My mind races: if I pick up the illness, I could spread it at the wedding. It would wreck the walk. I put on a second, then a third mask as I change trains in Paris from the Gare de l'Est to Montparnasse to continue my journey to Angoulême.

At the station, I pick up a taxi for the hour journey to our home at Saint-Jean-de-Côle. I arrive to a house full of people, noise and spirits high all round. Adam looks very relieved, and Jessica is just in from her flight down with husband Alex. The children and their partners mesh together like clockwork as always. Dinner for family and oldest friends is at a restaurant on a long table in the medieval square under the shadow of chateau and church, the months of Covid uncertainty making this gathering all the more intense and sweet. I don't say much: the switch from solitude to high-intensity contact is taking me time, and before the church bells chime midnight I slip off home to sleep on the settee in the river room overlooking the water.

Susie is our second child to wed. Jessica's marriage to Alex had taken place in the summer of 2015 at Wellington, just before we left the school. Joanna was alive, and spoke beautifully after dinner, as she had done at our own wedding. Her absence is the unexpressed factor for all of us. How will we be?

I awake to delicious smells from the kitchen of heating croissants and to the chink of champagne glasses. The house is a blur of bridesmaids' dresses, flower arrangements and excited laughter. Every detail has been planned by the next generation. I am passive. I take the hint and retreat to a quiet spot upstairs with coffee to catch up on my walking diary.

The wedding ceremony is to be held in the garden in early afternoon. As guests arrive, the bridal party assembles in the house. Susie takes my hand as we emerge on to the patio; we walk down the path by the side of the river, turn and pause before proceeding along the floral aisle between the guests. We both have a moment, caught out by the suddenness of intense emotion. Now, I am to hand her over to another man, my father's job done. Once we collect ourselves, we proceed to the floral chuppah (a nod to the canopy under which Jewish weddings take place) and I pass my beautiful girl over to Jonny, and to one of their friends who officiates. Task accomplished, I take my seat beside Jessica and Adam, and fall into doting and dotage, lulled by sounds from the fast-flowing river swollen by the recent storms. Drinks follow in the village by the river, before everyone proceeds to another village and chateau for the wedding feast. Landing the father's speech for her at the dinner that evening is my personal challenge. The choice of words, and the emotion behind them, I know will last a lifetime. 'You nailed it, Dad,' Susie whispers later on. It means more to me than words can describe.

What of Sarah? She arrived late on Friday by car from Limoges airport. She is quietly sensitive to Susie, helping her with practical advice, talking to restaurants and hotels for guests, and working her way with agility around the complex family dynamics. I have invited three sets of old friends, all of whom I've known for many years. Sarah, who is staying in the same accommodation as them in the village, is at once very at ease with them.

It is surely an error to imagine that a widower with children will not be deeply affected by how they and his new partner relate to each other. However much I might be falling for Sarah, I could never be happy if the children were not. So the weekend is a perfect storm for Sarah: her first wedding of one of my children, guests she barely knows, the dream home Joanna and I bought close to where we had our honeymoon, and the wedding ceremony in the garden in which her ashes are scattered. The programme quotes one of her final poems: 'Here I am among all this… and always will be.'

The nature of a crowded weekend wedding party affords us no time to talk all this through. Sarah has not seen me for nearly two weeks since she left me in Lorraine, and has no prospect of seeing me again for a further three till I finish. But the luminous joy of Susie and Jonny, Jessica's and Adam's happiness, and Sarah's loving warmth and graciousness throughout, are telling me something, clarifying for me the future in one area at least of my unsettled life. Here among all this I hear Joanna's words, blessing the wedding we've celebrated. I'd like to think she would be blessing a wedding perhaps to come.

Susie marrying Jonny by the river in the garden at Saint-Jean-de-Côle.

8

The Aisne and Marne

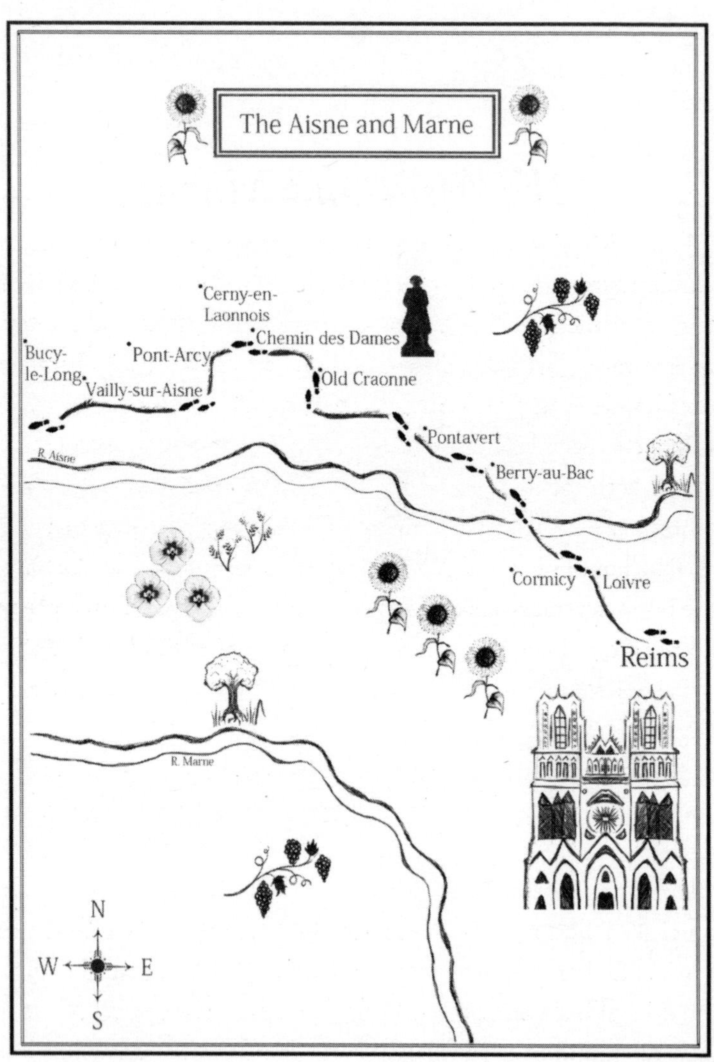
The Aisne and Marne
Cerny-en-
Laonnois
Chemin des Dames
Bucy-
le-Long
Pont-Arcy
Vailly-sur-Aisne
Old Craonne
Pontavert
R. Aisne
Berry-au-Bac
Cormicy
Loivre
Reims
R. Marne
N
W
E
S

EARLY MONDAY MORNING IN Saint-Jean-de-Côle. Song thrushes, blackbirds and reed warblers are filling the air with song. Mist still hangs over the river, the garden is covered in confetti, and the house has streamers, discarded lily buttonholes and half-empty champagne flutes on every surface. Upstairs they are out for the count after the prolonged festivities that went on all weekend late into the night. My heart is with the married couple and revellers, but my head is already turning back to the trail, while my body, unused to the leisure, is in full rebellion. Lou bandaged my feet again yesterday, but the blisters have burst, several layers of skin peeling off with the Compeed plasters, and the wound is raw. I worry about what she is thinking. With my having 500 kilometres still to walk, what prospect does she give me of completion? She is certainly not going to say anything, and I am glad she doesn't. I don some sneakers and pick my way gingerly along the cobblestones through the village in search of fresh bread for when the revellers arise.

I pause as I pass the war memorial in the square. It carries the names of eighteen who never made it back home to this tiny village: from François Dubarry, killed on 11 September 1914, to Jean Dussutour, who died of his wounds on 13 October 1919. The impact of the war on this community, as on villages across France, was utterly devastating. With over 1.35 million killed, and 4 million more wounded out of a total population of just 40 million, how could it be otherwise?[1]

One of the names on the memorial, André Rebière, was killed

in May 1916 at Avocourt, where I tarried last week. Another, Pierre Souriaud, died in April 1917 in the Second Battle of the Aisne at Berry-au-Bac, through which I will be passing early this week.[2] I might be 600 kilometres and a hundred years away here, but the names of the Western Front's war-scarred towns and villages, the valleys and woods through which I have been walking, would have been uttered in the most doleful tones by Saint-Jean-de-Côle's inhabitants in homes still standing today, perhaps even in our house with the blue shutters on the toll bridge. So many hopes dashed, so many marriages lasting no longer, so many weddings that would not now be taking place in the round twelfth-century church, into whose cool solace I retreat from the rising heat. I am returning later today to the front line, understanding anew how the cruel tentacles of the war wrapped themselves around every community across France.

* * *

By evening, I am back in Reims. It is already dark when I step off my last Covid-cleansed train of the day. Farewells with the children made me sad, with our heads so recently united in common cause all now scattered, and no time to talk amidst a lunch with friends at the Charbonnel in Brantôme. I reflect on the day as I gaze out of my third-floor window at the city lights playing on the water's surface. Water always lifts my spirits. Is that why I love France so much? Far more so than in Britain, life has revolved around canals and rivers. My Hôtel Campanile Cathédrale overlooks the canal linking the Aisne to the north and Marne to the south, the two rivers which sculpt this chapter. Reims lies on the modest River Vesle which flows into the Aisne, but such a renowned centre required far more robust and navigable water access. So a canal was dug in the seventeenth century, extended by Louis XIV's First Minister Jean-Baptiste Colbert, after whom the town harbour is named. The Canal de l'Aisne à la Marne along which

I will be walking tomorrow had the eventual aim of linking the mighty River Loire to the wetlands of north-west Europe. The ambition has been revived with the 100-kilometre planned canal from Compiègne to Cambrai, connecting the Seine to the Rhine basin. The digging of this vast modern-day trench has brought to light a slew of First World War bodies and mementoes. A reminder, if one is needed, that with every step, I walk over the bones and mulch of war.

All this week, I will be walking through one of the last sectors where the French bore the lion's share of the fighting. After the weekend, at last I'll reach the areas where British troops were in action. How ironic if I make it that far only for my feet to let me down. But I cannot fail. I do not know how I will manage it, but Gillespie's path of peace has to be created, and completing the walk will give it a big push. I do not care what toll it takes on me.

The Aisne and the Marne constitute the fourth and fifth rivers that define my walk. The former, arising in the Forest of Argonne and joining the Oise some 350 kilometres later, is my constant companion throughout this sector. The Marne is, like the Rhine, more of a shadowy presence during my pilgrimage. It arises near the Meuse's source in central France before snaking its 500-kilometre way into the Seine in Paris. Twice, at the start and near the end of the war, the soldiers' blood seeped into the Marne, but was not spilt in vain. Like a mighty spring, the river propelled the invaders back, preventing them reaching Paris and with it, changing world history.

How incredibly exciting to be walking through the very places where the initial prolonged encounters of the First World War occurred, all of which is virgin land and new history to me. I have been reading up on its main contours, trying to get it clear in my head.

Death and destruction were intense during the two Marne battles and the three great Battles of the Aisne. The First Battle of the Aisne (12–15 September 1914), which dictated the subsequent history of the war, followed swiftly after the Allied victory in the First Battle of the

Marne (5–12 September). The German forces retreated 60 kilometres and more to the high ground immediately beyond the Aisne, which flows here east–west. They destroyed the bridges as they retreated, slowing their pursuers, as did the River Aisne itself, 3 to 5 metres deep and 30 metres wide. Falkenhayn, succeeding Moltke on 14 September after the Marne failure, was having to adjust to the unexpected. The Schlieffen Plan envisaged victory after just six weeks, not digging in and defending themselves.

On the foggy night of 13 September, soldiers of the British Expeditionary Force (BEF) in hot pursuit crossed the Aisne at Bourg-et-Comin on pontoons. But when dawn came the exhausted troops found the wide arable fields on the other side afforded no protection from the Germans dug in on the higher ground above them on the Chemin des Dames. On 15 September, John French, the BEF's commander-in-chief, ordered his troops to entrench. This was a new experience for the British too. Without equipment or training in how to create trenches, they went off to nearby farms in search of spades and pickaxes, while others dug down into the soil with their bare hands. In these precarious conditions were established the first British trenches of the war, providing rudimentary protection from the vastly superior German artillery, trench mortars, and hand and rifle grenades. For two weeks, wave after wave of attacks were launched by the French and British on the Germans, but they proved unable to penetrate German lines or displace them from the Chemin des Dames. By the end of September 1914, the British and French recognized, as did the Germans, that achieving a breakthrough via a full-frontal assault was too difficult. So both sides tried to outflank and outwit the other.[3] Hence, the 'race to the sea' and the establishment of the Western Front.

But then, after this violent awakening, for the next three years this was an unusually quiet area, until the spring of 1917.

The Second Battle of the Aisne (16 April–mid-May 1917) is also known as the Nivelle Offensive after its strategist Robert Nivelle, 'hero' of Verdun, who succeeded Joffre in December 1916. Nivelle conceived the battle in April 1917 as a joint offensive, with the British attacking at Vimy Ridge and Arras on 9 April to draw off German forces, and the French then advancing a week later. Lloyd George was charmed by Nivelle, who spoke excellent English, and signed up British forces for the plan, much to the chagrin of British commander Douglas Haig.[4] Oh, the boons of being a good linguist.

His master strategy was based on saturation bombardment of the Germans, followed by a 'rolling barrage' (shells landing in parallel lines moving ever closer to the enemy trenches, behind which attacking troops progressively advanced), to allow infantry to make rapid gains. Not for him the merciless attrition of Falkenhayn at Verdun: no, Nivelle envisaged nothing less than a total victory on the Aisne and the ending of the war. Despite the Germans capturing his battleplan, he did not deviate, launching his attack on 16 April, a week after the British at Arras. His artillery pounded the Germans but his forces proved incapable of achieving the decisive result that he promised, and despite some tactical gains, the battle was called off on 25 April. French headquarters had been planning for some 10,000 casualties: the number proved over 130,000. The failure of his grand strategy led to Nivelle's sacking and his replacement by the more cautious Pétain. The Germans were not finally pushed off the Chemin des Dames till late October 1917.[5]

The Third Battle of the Aisne (27 May–6 June 1918) was launched by the Germans as part of their grand Spring Offensive, aiming to recapture the Chemin des Dames and threaten Paris before the Americans arrived across the Atlantic in full strength. Though it was predominantly a French battle, five British divisions were caught in the front line and suffered heavily. The German advance was finally halted on the Marne on 6 June.[6] The final German offensive in this sector, the Second Battle of the Marne (15 July–6 August 1918), was the attack on both sides of Reims. The French were fully prepared this time, even firing on

German positions forty minutes before their preliminary bombardment was timed to begin. The Germans nevertheless made some advances, crossing the Marne at one point, but when French and Americans counter-attacked, they began to crumble.[7]

I spend an hour in my Reims hotel room before breakfast, minding my Aisnes and my Marnes, trying to remember their complicated sequencing, while applying fresh gauze and bandages on the right side of my right foot. 'It's frankly looking a bit of a mess this morning,' I write; then, more hopefully: 'I have enough plasters and antiseptic ointment to last four days, and I'll spread out my remaining dog-bite antibiotics in case the wounds become infected.'

I'm relieved when I get outside into the morning air, and start walking north along the canal, with the throbbing city giving way to open countryside. Joggers, cyclists and walkers with dogs on the towpaths soon dwindle and I find myself on my own. After 8 kilometres, avoiding a wide bow in the canal, I take a track into the town of Courcy. The war memorial bears the names of some fifty of '*ses enfants*' killed in the war, together with eight civilians, caught up in the battle when the town was 'contested territory' between French and German front lines. Courcy was recaptured during the Second Battle of the Aisne on 16 April 1917 in a rare appearance on the Western Front of Russian forces, in the form of the First Brigade of the Russian Expeditionary Force (REF). As they fought, 2,000 kilometres to the east their country was falling apart.

The French had initially requested the capital St Petersburg send 300,000 men to help on the front; Russian generals, under pressure on the Eastern Front, said no, but Tsar Nicholas II overrode them and this one brigade was dispatched. Four days before they captured the town, the troops learnt of the February/March Revolution, which their officers had tried keeping from them. Following heavy casualties, and the failure of the Nivelle Offensive, some Russian troops rejected their officers' orders and elected soldier committees, suppressed by troops loyal to the new Kerensky government which had succeeded the abdicated Tsar. Turmoil at home, as Irish troops also experienced, was disconcerting for the Russian soldiers. Following the Communist October/November Revolution, all remaining troops on the front were recalled to Russia by the Bolsheviks. Lenin immediately signed the decree of peace to end Russian involvement in the First World War while the barbarous civil war began soon after. The REF had to wait till 2010 for a memorial to their sacrifices to be unveiled on the Marne, and until 2011 for one in Paris.

Sitting down by the town memorial and munching on chocolate biscuits, I recall the most invigorating school trip I ever ran, to Moscow and St Petersburg in the mid-1980s in the last days of Communism, the students brimming with curiosity and gratitude. When two returned at breakfast having spent the night wandering Moscow and calling in at all-night Orthodox Easter services, I was not angry but thrilled. As I rebandage my feet, my diary strikes a note of optimism: 'I'm establishing a daily routine. A pause after 5 kilometres for a drink, a biscuit for elevenses at 10 kilometres, some dried fruit and nuts at 15 kilometres; then, with the back of the day broken, lunch after 20 kilometres, and onward to my next place of rest. Meanwhile, constant sipping from the water bladder reinforced by rehydration tablets might do the trick.' Unlike First World War generals, I was trying to learn from my mistakes. Events, though, were to conspire to torpedo my neat plan.

Before leaving my perch on the memorial steps, I read an overlaid plaque listing the Second World War tally: two '*morts en déportation*'. So similar was the French experience of the First World War to the British, it's easy to underestimate how utterly divergent it was in the Second. I start walking along a track called 'Libération 8 May 1945', with white butterflies dancing around my head serenading my every step. A country road takes me to the small town of Loivre before I hook right, then dogleg left back on to the Aisne–Marne Canal. A *péniche* (motorized barge) glides silently past, one of some ten a day carrying grain harvested from the fields through which I have been passing. I come off at the village of Cormicy, whose *nécropole nationale* contains the graves of over 14,000 French soldiers, more than the number of burials in the largest British cemetery in the world, at Tyne Cot on Passchendaele Ridge. As I wander between the crosses, I encounter the grave of Pierre Chèvre who died on 4 November 1918, one week from the war's end, exactly 100 kilometres south of where Wilfred Owen died on the very same day on a very similar waterway joining two rivers, the Sambre–Oise Canal. Did Chèvre too have a brother to whom his apparition appeared in full military uniform, as Owen's brother claimed, and was the church bell tolling at 11 a.m. on 11 November too when his parents opened the awful telegram?

As the canal makes another long bow eastwards to follow the hill's contours, I opt for a more direct but very noisy main road for 4 kilometres into Berry-au-Bac. Here it is that Pierre Souriaud from Saint-Jean-de-Côle died, and where my joyous canal flows into the Aisne (more precisely, into Canal Latéral à l'Aisne, which runs alongside it). On the other side of town, cleverly positioned at a big trunk-road roundabout, I find the French memorial to the 'armoured cavalry' (the tank), first deployed on the opening day of Second Aisne, 16 April 1917. Some 130 of the contraptions were ordered into action here at the very eastern tip of the Chemin des Dames. While many were knocked out by German artillery before they even crossed their own front line, a few made it to the third German line, attacked, and managed to return. On that unsuccessful baptism day, more than seventy tanks were destroyed, thirty-six broke down, and 180 crew were killed, missing or wounded, many burnt alive inside their armoured cavalry.[8]

Opened in 1922, this first memorial erected on the Chemin des Dames commemorates 900 French soldiers killed in tanks, the majority in the summer and autumn of 1918. By then, tanks with radios, swivelling turrets and improved mechanics ensured that the weapon was far more resilient than proved on that first day. By the end of the war, the French army had 2,700 light tanks, performing a key role in the final offensive.[9] I stroll over to a further memorial added after 1945, commemorating tank crews killed in the Second World War. It is an inspired decision to plant a tank museum where the engines of war actually saw action: not an option, for obvious reasons, for the Tank Museum – 'the world's finest collection' – at Dorset's Bovington.

After my fill of the mechanized cavalry exhibits, I depart due west for a 5-kilometre slog into Pontavert, dropping my reading glasses on the way which is frustrating. On the outskirts of the village I visit a civilian cemetery, which has one solitary CWGC grave in it (to add to the two at Cormicy). Dog-tired, I arrive at the Relais de Fleurette Hotel, in vernacular farmhouse style built around a central courtyard. I surrender myself to end-of-day tasks in my bedroom before coming down to loud 1950s music. Perry Como's crooning turns the restaurant into an American diner. The first course is salad with goat's cheese, followed by the same salad with a jacket potato and flecks of dry beef, rounded off by chocolate mousse. An amazing effort considering the impact of Covid. I say to the hotel manager when he looks at me anxiously, '*Absolument délicieux.*' I go upstairs to my room worried. My will is as strong as ever, but my feet are aching from the walk, and show no sign of benefiting from the rest over the weekend. How foolish I was to imagine they might. If only I had been able to set out from Reims with my body as fresh as when I started just three weeks ago on the Swiss border, I would be blazing ahead now. But the damage has been done and I'll have to live with it. On top of that, my lower back is twingeing from lugging a full rucksack since morning. I am trapped. A whole week out might allow recovery. But with time so tight due to the oft-postponed start, what else can I do? I feel I am heading for a fall.

The result is a restless night, full of anxieties about my ability to complete. I wake out of a demi-sleep at 6.30 a.m. for an early breakfast. Not the best, understandably. I crave healthy cereal, fruit, seeds and nuts. But I smile and say my '*superbe*' after bread and orange juice.

Upstairs, I wipe cream on to my feet, and apply the surgical tape that Lou left me to secure my gauzes and ankle bandage, repairing my spare glasses with the same tape. Slightly alarming how many things go wrong when I get tired.

It is Day 21, 1 September. The weather is already turning, with a cold chill in the air. I leave after 8 a.m. cross that I've squandered an early start, feeling despondent for the first 3 kilometres, with heavy traffic along what I expected to be a quiet road out of Pontavert. But then my spirit brightens, as does the sunlight, and I find a tranquil track to complete my journey to new Craonne, built after 1918. The bell atop the art deco church tolls nine as I walk into the village. Where once the air reverberated with screeching shells, all is silence but for birds, dogs and an occasional cock crow. Swallows, deciding they've had enough, are gathering on the telephone wires ready to migrate south in search of warmth. Nothing, it seems, wants to live here. I leave the village by the D18 in the wrong direction, adding 2 kilometres to what will be a long day. But for a giant hare on the road staring me down, and giving me a moment to check my route, I would have walked on for ages before realizing my error.

Here I am ambling along the Chemin des Dames, which follows the D18 for 30 kilometres due west on the ridge above the Aisne Valley. Its name is derived from the specially paved road taken by Louis XV's daughters, Adélaide and Victoire, when travelling between Paris and the Château de la Bôve just by Craonne, home of their close friend the Countess Françoise de Chalus (and former mistress of their father). To the Germans, it was the Damenweg, deeply etched on their memories. By whatever name, throughout 1915, 1917 and 1918, it was the centre of the war, repeatedly fired on, mashed up and reddened with blood.

I follow a track to old Craonne further up the hill, another *village détruit* and as moving as any I've seen so far. An inspired arboretum over 7 hectares with fifty-seven varieties of tree types has been cultivated on the site of the old village. I walk along the Rue Saint-Rémi, the former high street, which tracks past the once-fashionable Voyeux Café-deli in a half-timbered dwelling. The 320 homes housed over 600 villagers, I learn, many taking to their cellars on 13 September 1914 during First Aisne. Those not killed in the bombardment were allowed by the Germans to cross to the Allied lines. The heaviest damage was done by French artillery in Second Aisne, when remaining buildings were smashed to pieces. After the war, only forty inhabitants returned to the smouldering remains, and in 1921, the local council agreed to move the village to the present site in the valley. But the authorities never persuaded more than 160 to live there. Most either settled down elsewhere or had died.

Craonne's war has been immortalized by the song 'Chanson de Craonne'. It gained fame amongst the exhausted French *poilus* in the months leading up to the Nivelle Offensive (*Goodbye to life, goodbye to love / goodbye to all the women, / it's all over now, we've had it for good / with this awful war. / It's in Craonne upon the plateau / that we are leaving our skins, / cause we've all been sentenced to die, / we're the ones they're sacrificing*). Sung to the popular 1911 tune 'Bonsoir m'amour', it was one of many songs from the war, and though it was officially prohibited both at the time and afterwards, it has become the most popular in France today. The song came to epitomize the French army's anger at the failed Nivelle Offensive, when resentment swelled amongst the ranks, with up to half refusing to go into battle and demanding better conditions. Pétain brought the mutiny back under control by July 1917, with over 600 death sentences meted out (of which some thirty took place), and 5,000 rebels dispatched to prison or penal colony.[10] Restoration of order came at a price: longer periods of leave for the men, and the promise of no major offensives until the Americans arrived.[11]

The French army somehow managed to conceal news of the mutiny from the Germans. Even British troops picked up only patchy information at the time. I wonder why British troops didn't follow suit? How much worse did conditions have to become before the men rose up and

The remains of trenches near the Chemin des Dames.

screamed 'enough'? Historians are divided on whether their respect for their officers deterred them, or fear of the consequences, or whether their experience of the war, incredible though it may sound, was less harsh than the French. After all, some 50 per cent more French soldiers were killed than British defending their soil. I seek out George Hay back at CWGC HQ in Maidenhead, who tells me relatively better conditions were indeed significant. The British were in the front line for less time, had more appetising food, and more home leave than the *poilus*.

British troops did, however, mutiny albeit on a small scale at Étaples, the principal base and transit camp for the BEF in France. Relations between Tommies and army instructors could be brittle here, with the resentment sparking protest in September 1917 when some 1,000 soldiers marched on the town and refused to obey orders to return. One was shot dead by military police, further inflaming the men. A full-scale riot threatened, until unrest was quelled by armed soldiers, with 300 protestors arrested. Some fifty were court-martialled, and many were given hard labour or field punishment. One lance corporal in the Northumberland Fusiliers, Jesse Robert Short, was sentenced to death for attempting mutiny, encouraging comrades to lay down their arms and to attack an officer. Executed by firing squad on 4 October 1917, he was buried in Boulogne Eastern Cemetery.[12] I have always had time for protesting students, ever since the rebellion I helped lead as a sixth former at Tonbridge School in the early 1970s against the Vietnam War and the school cadet force. The former folded soon after; the latter continues till this day. A small victory.

Before I leave Craonne, my attention is caught by the most easterly 'Jardins de la Paix' built to commemorate the war's centenary. A striking Arab and Muslim design, based on the legendary gardens of the Maghreb, it is a tribute to the 9,000 Moroccan soldiers who died in the faraway war on French soil. I walk up to another recent addition, a substantial wooden observation tower on the summit of the plateau looking down over the entire Chemin des Dames and Aisne Valley below. All is quiet, apart from a frolicking young French couple.

A reminder of all that lies beneath the ground came with the discovery in 2020 of the Germans' Winterberg tunnel, whose entrances were targeted by the French. A direct hit from an ex-naval gun struck one end, causing multiple explosions of ammunition within, entombing large numbers of German soldiers. Over the following six days as the oxygen ran out, the men inside suffocated, took their lives, or asked comrades to kill them. Just three survived long enough to be brought out by rescuers to tell the story. Untold numbers of dead men and unexploded ordnance remain buried along the entire Chemin des Dames Ridge.[13]

It's nearly midday, and I've only travelled 5 kilometres. I return to the D18 and walk past a series of monuments along this most historic of roads, noticing the shell holes and trench lines in the woods. This is France's Achilles heel: to the west it has the Atlantic; to the south, the Pyrenees and the Mediterranean; to the east, the Alps. But to its north, no natural defence, unless we count the Chemin des Dames, just 100 kilometres from the capital, protecting it from invasion – but only as long as the French army was powerful enough to hold the ground. It was here on 7 March 1814 at the Battle of Craonne that Napoleon confronted the forces of the Coalition, succeeding in driving the Russians off the plateau, winning him a tactical victory but at a heavy cost. His presence is still here. Dominating the landscape is a statue of the Little Corporal erected in 1974, legs a-strut surveying the battlefield, while a memorial chapel built for the centenary of the battle in 1914, and inaugurated just weeks before war broke out, was obliterated by shellfire. A joint memorial statue of an 1814 and 1914 soldier holding up the French colours was erected after the war, at Hurtebise Farm. Despite the triumphalism, neither battle a century apart can be considered a real victory. Further along the Chemin des Dames, I pass by where the romantic California Restaurant, popular with its clientele for its commanding views, once stood. All that remains today is a viewing platform with a semicircular orientation table pointing to '*Offensive Française*'.

My plan is to reach the medieval city of Laon tonight. Like another shorty, however, who planned to reach Laon immediately after the Battle of Craonne, my hopes are dashed. Within an hour of abandoning the Chemin des Dames to take a shortcut due north towards the city straight through the forest, I am beaten, if not as dramatically as at the Battle of Laon on 9–10 March 1814. All is going well for the first kilometre or two in the forest, but then at a crossroads, my path clean disappears. The map, which I check several times on my phone, is unambiguous – my route is straight ahead. I peer into the undergrowth, and dimly make out a steep incline down the other side of the plateau, with no bottom in sight. I spend ten minutes debating what to do. Throwing caution to the winds, shortening the straps of my rucksack and clinging tightly to my shoulder bag, I plunge forward through the narrow gap. Suddenly, I lose my footing, and slide down and down on my back through brambles and tree roots. At the bottom, I take stock, checking no bones are broken. My shoulder bag has burst open, distributing the contents to either side of my track downwards, and my glasses have gone too. With some difficulty I manage to find them near the end of my slide, with recently applied tape flapping freely. I stick them back together, but I am still in trouble with no phone signal to show me where to go. My clothes are covered in moss and insects, and the mosquitoes are amassing. As I'm bitten on my upper arm, I whip out the insect repellent only to discover it is empty. 'This is the worst moment of the trip so far,' I record. I shrug and advance in what I hope is a northerly direction. But the path, if it ever existed, has vanished.

With Laon still 20 kilometres away, I realize reaching it on foot tonight will not be possible. My best hope is to return to the Chemin des Dames. But how? Lacking the strength to clamber back up the slope with full kit, I seek out a path running parallel along the valley. After half an hour of groping, I come to a clearing. My phone is now picking up a signal, and I find a track that eventually brings me slowly back up to the Chemin, two hours after leaving it. I'm now desperate for something to eat. I forge onwards to Cerny-en-Laonnois barely noticing that I'm passing the Senegalese Riflemen's Memorial and the path to the *village détruit* of Ailles, one of six on the Aisne. Only later do I learn that a vast number of 192,000 soldiers from French West Africa, including those from Senegal and Mali, fought in the war.[14] Heavily involved in Second Aisne in April 1917, some of their battalions lost three-quarters of their men. An installation, consisting of thin Giacometti-style statues, opened in 2007, is magnificent with the riflemen highlighted against the valley below. I want to know how much freedom these men had over whether they fought, and what precise cause they believed they were supporting. I lack the time to find out, especially when I learn too that my planned destination, the village of Cerny-en-Laonnois, was another wiped off the face of the earth by constant shellfire and rebuilt on another site in the 1920s. On land earmarked for it, the French and Germans agreed in May 1917 to a truce of whose compassion Gillespie would have heartily approved. It allowed for the safe collection of dead bodies from the battlefield, many of whom were to be later buried in adjacent German and French cemeteries on the main road. This is the first time on the walk I see Gillespie's silent witnesses lying en masse side by side. Adding to the poignancy, the grave of Albert Truton, sentenced to death in June 1917 for his part in the *poilu* mutiny. As I wander around the site, I see a solitary stone British memorial column, one of the most easterly on the front, commemorating the sacrifice of the BEF in First Aisne in September 1914.

It is mid-afternoon and, by the time I arrive at the Brasserie Le Poilu at the new village's crossroads, lunch is long over. I consume several packets of crisps, the most on offer, and several bottles of tonic water while I try to find a taxi to meet me. Ten calls and much mutual incomprehension later, I am at my wits' end. Sarah's new school term is beginning and I'm trying to avoid asking her for help. But I'm so stumped I call her apologetically and ask her to charm one of the most promising leads into submission. Eventually, a driver agrees to meet me at Bourg-et-Comin to take me to Laon, if I can be there in an hour. I readily assent before realizing that it is 6 kilometres south. So I yank on my bags and equipment hurriedly to set off at full pelt, watching closely my Gaia app which tells me I'm managing a record 6.7 kilometres an hour, which in the heat, and with full kit, is a bit of a schlep, but quite fun. As the traffic whistles past, I amuse myself by comparing the sound of motorbikes to whizzbangs, cars to small shells and lorries to heavy artillery flying overhead.

I make it to the *mairie* at Bourg-et-Comin with a minute to spare. I converse with my taxi driver in broken French as he speeds me to Laon, agreeing to pick me up in the morning. I've booked in to l'Hôtel Les Chevaliers, a niche establishment not open till late afternoon. So I take advantage to explore this exquisite hill town with its twelfth- and thirteenth-century cathedral and preserved buildings. A similar town in Britain, Lincoln perhaps, would be full of life; here I observe no tourists, with the bite of Covid evident in those begging and in the desolate faces that pass me.

The hotel soon opens, and up in my attic room, with paint peeling off the ceiling and walls, I start worrying about bedbugs. The manager,

British and French war graves at Vailly-sur-Aisne.

the brother of the owner, is very friendly and reassures me that the bed is new and clean. I sit on it to catch up on diaries and messages and start my second blog for *The Times*. Today, I write, has been the best and worst day of the trip so far. To cheer me up, I go for dinner at the Restaurant Le Parvis in the cathedral square, with polished wooden tables and swirling white cutlery. Having had no lunch but for the crisps, I order salmon and egg brioche, followed by *pièce de boeuf bien cuit et légumes*, and then a fruit salad made specially for me for dessert. One of my greatest joys in life is eating out with friends in restaurants in France or Italy, but there are consolations to being on your own with a good book (I am reading Gillespie's letters), propped up on an ice bucket cooling a half bottle of Chablis, which followed a generous glass of Moët. I justify it by saying I drank no champagne amongst the vineyards, and need cheering up. It works, and I skip back to the hotel looking up at the picturesque floral canopy covering the streets.

The world looks very different wide awake at 2 a.m. staring up at my distressed ceiling. I reach for the remains of the Chablis, which knocks me out for a few hours. I awake tired but free of bedbug bites at 7 a.m., wash holding the broken shower head in my hand, and rush downstairs for a quick breakfast of fresh baguette, butter and marmalade, with heavenly coffee to revive me. The car is waiting outside and I'm back at Bourg-et-Comin to walk with the sun rising above the stone houses at 8.45. On the way, I ask the driver to stop just south of Cerny at the Vendresse British Cemetery, which I had hurried past on my yomp yesterday. This most easterly British cemetery confirms that I am moving homewards. Designed by Edwin Lutyens, it contains the bodies of 727 British soldiers, many killed in September 1914 during First Aisne. Encountering it provides a telling contrast to their French and German counterparts I have been passing by. Whereas the French by choice, and the Germans by necessity, favoured large burial grounds, the British opted for smaller and more numerous cemeteries close to where the men fell. British cemeteries like German ones are carefully landscaped, while the French are sparse. Like American cemeteries, they have white gravestones in contrast to the dark stone and granite used by the Germans.

In the very left of Vendresse's front row I spot the grave of 24-year-old J. E. L. Clarke, awarded a posthumous MC. On the day he died, 14 September 1914, Captain C. J. Paterson was fighting nearby, who wrote in his diary: 'We crossed the river [Aisne] with shells dropping around us. The Germans have destroyed most of the bridges… [but] we cross and line a ridge to the north of Bourg-et-Comin.' Two days later he wrote: 'I have never spent a more ghastly and heart-tearing 48 hours than the last… We have been fighting hard ever since 8 a.m. on the 14th and have suffered much… Swarms of the Germans on the ridge, rather massed. Our guns opened on them at 1800 yards… not much success, and Germans are too numerous. Several men killed…'[15]

I feel the men's presence keenly as I wander the streets of Bourg-et-Comin before setting off west on the busy Rue de Soissons. I've placed Sarah's bright orange covering over my dark rucksack, and her two luminous yellow rings on my arms alert the traffic whistling tightly past my right flank. After 3 kilometres, I turn left by the abandoned railway station into the hamlet of Pont-Arcy, which takes me across a Bailey-style bridge over the Aisne. I continue walking west through farmland along the south side of the river and its lateral canal, on and off the towpath. For three hours, I walk through crisp air, urging myself on. I wave to a fisherman on the other bank, too immersed in his world to notice. I'm lifted by a long conversation with Western Front Way's Rory who tells me he will be out for a few days when I am on the Somme next week. It makes me realize afresh how much I'm missing company. By lunchtime, I have reached the village of Vailly-sur-Aisne, and sink down in the heat at a Second World War American memorial commemorating liberation hero Robert Whalen. The sun is high in the sky and I can find no shade. I take off my boots and socks, and rebandage my feet, which are growing steadily redder.

After a snack and protracted cool drink of water, I'm back on my feet, walking through the town to the British and French cemeteries on its other side. Unusually they adjoin each other, and in some places, French and British graves are placed next to each other, as seen on p. 161. The French were mostly killed in April 1917 in Second Aisne whereas most of the British seem to have been killed in First Aisne in September 1914. Sergeant Thomas Painting, one of their comrades in the battle, later wrote: 'We got over the river and on to the high ground over a mile in front of the Aisne... Private Wilson of the Highland Light Infantry and one of our men attacked a machine gun. Our man got killed but Private Wilson killed the machine gunner, captured the position and got the Victoria Cross. Our man got a wooden cross. That's the difference, you see. One killed, one a VC.'[16] Wilson's heroism, cheating death several times that day, was more worthy than implied here, as recognized in his VC citation. But he couldn't cheat tuberculosis, dying from it aged thirty-nine at Craigleith Hospital in Edinburgh in 1926.[17]

Arthur Martin, a surgeon serving in First Aisne, reflected the shock of many at their first experience of modern industrial war: 'I walked a few yards down the road... Here was a scene of ghastly horror. On the road lay mangled and bleeding horses, dead men lying in all sorts of convulsed attitudes, upturned wagons... Add to this the agonised groans of our wounded men, the shrill scream of dying horses... One man, a burly Sergeant Major, had a big hole in his head, another a huge hole in his neck, a lacerated wound in the chest, and one boot and foot blown completely away. All had widely open staring eyes. The expression seemed to be one of overwhelming surprise and horror.'[18]

I'm a long way from Soissons, and I walk without a break to complete 36 kilometres during the day. I described it in my diary as the hardest slog so far, but I can remember little of it now except the afternoon heat shimmering on the road in front of me. I leave behind me the three Aisne battles, but not the Aisne, whose valley I follow through the aptly named Bucy-le-Long which seems to never end. At last I am in the outskirts of Soissons, walking towards it along the 3-kilometre Roman road past signs for electronic stores and sex shops, evidence I am approaching modern civilization. My hotel, the Best Western on Boulevard Jeanne d'Arc, is on the other side of town, which I scarcely notice as I dig deep into my energy reserves to get me there.

It is 6 p.m. when, panting, I reach hotel reception. Up in my room, I spend twenty minutes staring blankly out of the window, back muscles aching, before I find the strength to begin my daily routine of showering, clothes washing, bandaging and stretching. By the time I've finished it is past 8 p.m. I had wanted to explore the town but have strength only to walk to the lift which takes me down to supper on the patio looking out over the Abbaye Saint-Jean-des-Vignes. All that is left is its western facade with two tall spires, the rest a victim of the French

Revolution. I worry that all I will have left at the end of this walk is a facade with nothing behind it.

I am so tired I manage to fall asleep swiftly but wake every hour. I'm locked into a bind: wine at dinner helps me go to sleep, but wakes me after two or three hours. Yoga relaxes me during the night, but puts my back under pressure. In the morning when I start walking about my room, pain shoots up from the blisters, which now cover the ball of my right foot and toes and are spreading to my left sole, while the open wound on my right ankle is not healing. I'm in no state to walk the planned 40 kilometres to Compiègne today where the armistice was signed. I absolutely hate changing targets, but accept that I must do so if I am to avoid more serious problems, and opt for just a half day to walk past battlefields along the Aisne to the west of the city. So I cancel my reservation in Compiègne, relieved to discover I can remain in my Soissons room for another night, and now have a morning unexpectedly free. With no spare shoes, I buy some flip-flops to explore the town, which avoid rubbing the wounds on my ankles but afford no cushioning for my bruised soles on the hard pavements, pain stabbing my every step.

All this is forgotten in the enchantment of this stunning place, a powerbase long before the Romans arrived, and the location of their final defeat in 486 at the hands of Clovis the Frank, a rather fascinating figure celebrated as the founder of France. Soissons duly became a key centre of the Frankish Kingdom. It was seldom out of the news: Henry V was supposedly seeking vengeance at the Battle of Agincourt in 1415 for the massacre of English archers garrisoned in the city. The Anglo-Spanish War of 1727 was ended by the Congress of Soissons in 1729, Napoleon used it as a crucial military base, and it sustained a five-week siege in October 1870 during the Franco-Prussian War, only to be overrun.

Then came the First World War. The French retook the city after First Aisne but, as at Reims, it was within comfortable range of German artillery, which battered it remorselessly. The cathedral, together with

Soissons in 1919.

much of the town, was left in ruins. The tide of the war was turned here from 18–22 July 1918 in the pivotal Battle of Soissons (part of the Second Battle of the Marne). Primarily a French effort but with American and British (notably Scottish) support, it aimed to reverse the gains made in the German Spring Offensive of March 1918 when Soissons fell and the Allies were pushed back to the Marne. But superior Allied numbers and equipment, with the largest American deployment in the war to date, eventually prevailed. By cutting critical German road and rail supply lines, it forced them to retreat from their salient on the Marne and to give up final hopes of reaching Paris. On 2 August, Soissons was retaken, and the front line was restored from Soissons to Reims. For the remaining three months of the war, Germany was on the run.[19]

The British sustained 7,000 casualties during Second Marne, the Americans 40,000 and the French 80,000, with German losses around 110,000.[20] I stop by the city's prominent CWGC memorial to the BEF, with sculpture by official war artist Eric Kennington. Its fading engraving tells me it commemorates the 3,987 British and Commonwealth soldiers who died on the Aisne and Marne between May and July 1918 with no known grave. I flip-flop down to the River Aisne and walk along the sunlit quays before returning to the hotel via the twelfth-century cathedral. Inside, I study the sepia photographs by the door of the bombed building and town, then sit for a long time quietly in the nave. The purpose of the walk floods to the forefront of my mind. I'm distressed at how far I still am from achieving peace, even in my prayers.

I set out at 1 p.m. for my truncated 20-kilometre walk. It's almost a relief to put my boots back on because they at least fit my feet, and the padding eases the pain. I'm fed up sinking so many Nurofen because they upset the stomach, but I have no other pain plan left in the locker. What a blessing, though, to be free of equipment. As I walk west through silent suburbs, a well-heeled beggar approaches me. I'm torn between giving him euros but showing him where my money is, or feigning incomprehension.

My trail follows the south bank of the Aisne, crossing over the river at Pommiers, then along the Route du 11 November 1918 through Osly-Courtil to my destination at Fontenoy. I am walking exactly where the fleeing BEF crossed the Aisne in August 1914, retreating south after their defeats in the Battles of Mons and Le Cateau before rallying and stopping the German advance in the First Battle of the Marne. Sadly, I can find no evidence of their crossing on my route. But at Fontenoy, I gain more sense of the French counter-attack in August 1918 after Soissons was retaken, when the Germans were pushed back on a 10-kilometre front for two days.[21]

Tomorrow morning, I will bid farewell to the Aisne, and head north to Noyon and into mid-Picardy. Surely, I tell myself, my burden will lighten once I start to walk through oft-visited and familiar haunts. How wrong I was.

9

Picardy

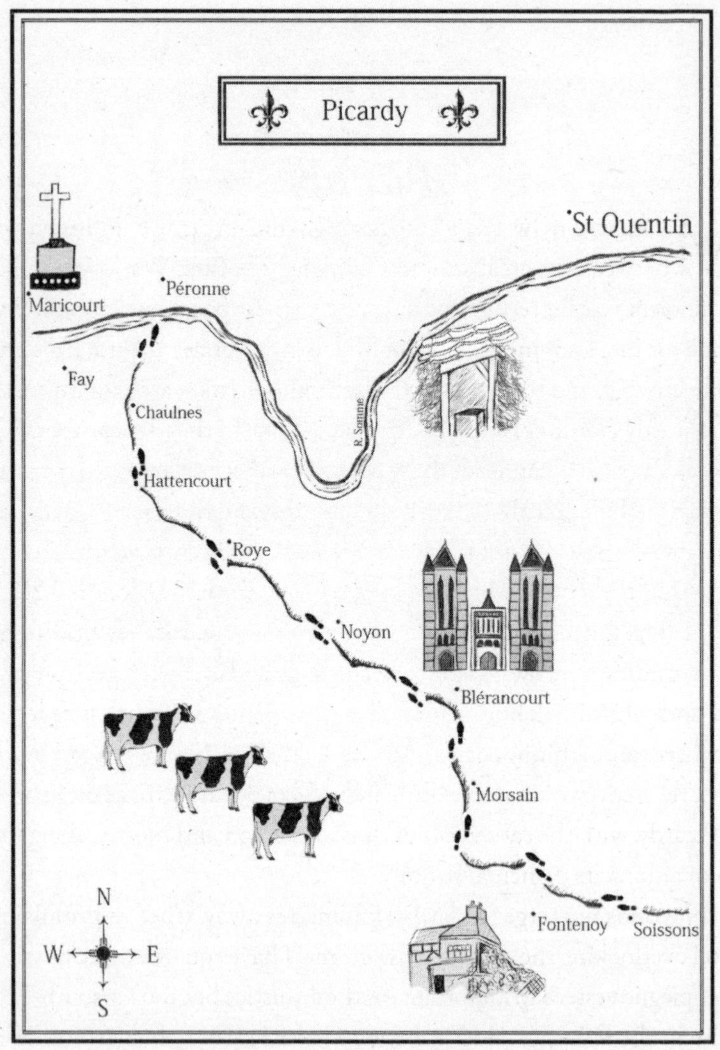
Picardy
St Quentin
Péronne
Maricourt
Fay
Chaulnes
R. Somme
Hattencourt
Roye
Noyon
Blérancourt
Morsain
Fontenoy
Soissons
N
W
E
S

MY ROUTE NOW TAKES me through mid-Picardy, a liminal space between the great set-piece battles of the First World War. Like an indolent volcano, eruptions did occur in these parts, but sporadically; while for me, I am inescapably fighting battles of my own to keep my body moving, and to focus my restless mind on its search for answers.

Picardy (*Picardie*) stretches from Soissons in the east to Abbeville and the English Channel in the west. Its boundaries fluctuated over the centuries, though it always sat between Paris and the Pas de Calais. Its very name is steeped in blood, derived from old French '*pic*' (pike), the AK-47 of the day, with battles never far away, from the Hundred Years War to the Battle of the Somme. It wasn't all gore. Picardy developed its own culture, its own distinctive language and architecture, from the red-and-white brick homes in its villages to giant Gothic masterpieces, nowhere more striking than at Amiens Cathedral, France's largest if not most revered. Gothic architecture indeed can be said to have originated in Picardy, with the cathedrals of Soissons, Laon and Noyon along my route among its principal triumphs.

Noyon is my target today, 30 kilometres away, where a promising hotel overlooking the cathedral awaits me. I have squared away missing Compiègne yesterday, important for the armistice but too far south-east to be in the fighting, and I'm in good spirits after a shaky start. Men talking loudly at 5 a.m. on the street outside the Best Western wake me early. I call down to reception and ask my taxi to arrive earlier, but am told '*pas possible, désolé*'. So I prop myself up in bed and reach for the collected letters of Douglas Gillespie. 'We have a new game this morning, "hunt the general", but I do not enjoy it much for I had only three hours lying down, and have been up since 4,' he wrote from the trenches on this very day, 3 September, 106 years before.[1] Ha! Douglas had even less sleep than me: this is exactly what I need to hear. I read on: 'For an hour I stood in a puddle waiting for him at the corner of my trench. I was cold and my feet were wet, and it was raining, and I'd had no breakfast.' What am I worrying about, I ask myself, as I rebandage my dry feet and prepare to go down to a hearty breakfast in a warm dining room with no risk at all of trench mortars landing on its roof?

A slick BMW 3 Series is idling on the hotel forecourt to whisk me back to Fontenoy. The forecast is for hot weather from eleven, so I am keen, as I will be carrying my full kit today, to cover as much ground as I can early on. I set off, tired but in good spirits, hoping that my chosen route will not let me down with zero leeway or humour for error. I'm desperate to arrive at Noyon by three, or soon after, so I can get on top of my diary and messages.

As I leave the Aisne behind me, I walk due north through woodland paths and along farm tracks, past fields of maize and cabbage. Liberal quantities of insect repellent applied to the skin as well as clothes are doing the trick, with mosquitoes on the whole giving me a wide berth. I'm walking on or near the front line, but see little evidence bar a solitary concrete dugout. After 10 kilometres, I reach the village of Morsain built in honey-coloured stone. I imagine I am walking in a crowd-free Cotswold jewel till I pass a shop flaunting a prominent *BOULANGERIE* sign. Closed, naturally. Time at least for dried fruit, nuts and several Choco Leibniz biscuits, my pick-me-up after some internal disagreements with too many *pains au chocolat*. The heat is now up, and I drink deeply from my hydration-tablet-reinforced water bladder. Right, I'm ready to go, up goes the rucksack and I'm soon walking past plentiful poppies on the verges of my path. After another 10 kilometres, and without passing person or car, I arrive at Blérancourt, hometown of

Louis Antoine Léon de Saint-Just, close friend of Robespierre, overseer of some of the French Revolution's repellent guillotinings, and known as its 'Archangel of Terror'. At least, he was until his own date with the guillotine, moments after Robespierre, during the 'Thermidor coup' of July 1794, at the end of the revolution's 'Reign of Terror'. His unassuming home is now a museum to the events of 1789–99. How could a man raised in this idyllic village have developed so much hatred?

I sit down in the porch of the sixteenth-century church and tuck into Brie and rolls from the hotel. Shaded from the sun, I pick out Leigh Fermor from my rucksack, determined to finish it. To my annoyance, people are still greeting and welcoming him into their homes. I find myself yearning again for the conversations that punctuated his walk. When I meet local people, they are friendly but transactional – and in truth I barely meet them. I reflect too that he was just eighteen years old, fifty years younger than I am. My equipment will surely be lighter and stronger than his, but not my body: 'Every step this morning hurts my heels, like pins sticking up into them. I just hope I'm not doing myself long-term damage if I do last the next 14 days,' I write.

The exquisite church protecting me from the piercing heat was severely damaged by shellfire in the war, a comfort of sorts that I'm on the front line. The town's suffering stirred the feisty Anne Morgan, youngest of the four children of US banker John Pierpont Morgan who had died in 1913, to fund a civilian relief organization. Help came from brother Jack, who headed J. P. Morgan bank, which, even before the United States came into the war, was heavily financing the Allies. After it joined in 1917, Anne raised money for ambulances and medical supplies, founding the Committee for Devastated France, one of the significant charities that sprouted in the US during the war. Pétain personally arranged for its HQ to be established in the nearby Château de Blérancourt, then behind the front. Anne travelled here first in 1917 soon after the town had been recaptured by the French, encouraging 350 American volunteers to reconstruct it and reseed the land with her. A commanding figure, she required her volunteers to speak French, to hold driver's licences and pay their own expenses: 'we do not want to have sightseers', she informed the *New York Times*. In 1924, Pétain made her an officer of the French Legion of Honour in a ceremony at Blérancourt, later elevated to commander, the first American woman to receive the distinction.[2]

In 1919, Anne bought the chateau in which the National Museum of French-American Friendship and Cooperation was founded in 1924. Dedicated to French–American relations since the sixteenth century, it includes many exhibits from the war. 'The Museum welcomes you today in a unique setting… Surrounded by the gardens of the New World,' declares a notice at the entrance. When I walk around this afternoon, I see no Americans nor French to engage in friendship and

Anne Morgan.

cooperation. 'Perhaps the Western Front Way will bring the Americans back, and revive the area, as did Anne Morgan,' I write.

I am in nostalgic mood as I depart for the final stretch to Noyon. How can anyone understand the need for peace without an appreciation of history? I wonder. So many Americans and French all the way up to their presidents know little about the past. I feel this as a personal responsibility, reflecting on my faltering attempts over the last ten years to make British prime ministers and No. 10 more aware of recent events. Bringing in lunchtime speakers, historians, writers and former aides to speak to staff in the Pillared Room was one device. The last, in December 2019, was Peter Frankopan, author of *The Silk Roads*: his closing point emphatically made was that the greatest threat to the West was not China but a global pandemic. Two months later, Covid struck. No. 10 is a strange place: many are eager to work there, if successful most find the experience exhilarating if frustrating, and then they spend the rest of their careers rueing they are no longer there.

I know deep inside that peace will only be found following a path of acceptance for what I have, not regretting what has gone. That's real learning, I think as I pass a magical field with five white horses. But a few minutes later, when my track disappears altogether in a field of tall maize, frustration returns. I pause, take a drink of water, and let the negative thoughts subside.

My map is absolutely clear: the path runs straight ahead but the farmer has planted his maize shamelessly on top of it. I walk to one side of the crop then the other, seeking a way around, but realize I must backtrack. As I do so I beat myself up, wondering if the dead end is a metaphor for my faltered career. Gloomy imaginings circulate as I retrace my steps. Finding a track that will take me to the main road in the distance shakes me out of it, but I've already clocked up 34 kilometres for the day and am hoping it isn't too much further.

As I approach Noyon, I cross over the River Oise for the only time on the walk. Robert Louis Stevenson paddled on the water under this very bridge on his famous canoe journey in 1876 through Belgium and France, stopping briefly at Noyon where 'I believe people live very reputably in a quiet way.'[3] Very quiet indeed they are still. This part of central and northern Picardy has suffered from industrial decline and depopulation since Stevenson's trip, so I shouldn't have been surprised when I find dilapidated houses, a boarded-up tourist hotel, a railway station with an abundance of platforms but no passengers, and streets with no shoppers.

Limbs aching, I stumble across the threshold of the Hôtel Le Cèdre opposite the cathedral. With such an appealing name as my destination, my spirits have been rising for several kilometres at the prospect of a roast with apple sauce and an apple Charlotte dessert rounded off by a glass of Calvados (Sarah later tells me *cèdre* means cedar). I am famished, but the receptionist explains they have no restaurant, and draws a blank calling around to find me a table for dinner. Tired as I feel, I dump my bags behind his desk, and scour the town without much hope of locating open shops. I find a small supermarket where I buy a tub of pasta, some yoghurt and fruit. The security guard's eyes never leave me as I travel up and down the aisles.

Lugging rucksack and shoulder bag upstairs to my hotel bedroom, I have a sharp stab of pain in my lower back. Blast, blast, blast. I haven't put it out for a couple of years, and I thought strengthening exercises had cured it. I manoeuvre my load the rest of the way but can't stay still with so much to do. I wash my clothes and leave them in the bath to soak while I busy myself in my room. A sound of running water becomes louder but I assume it is outside. Then, horrors, I see my bathwater begin to spread across the bedroom floor, the plughole having been blocked by my clothes. I use up all the towels I can find drying the floor, a challenge with piercing pain. Pasta and yoghurt have seldom tasted less appetizing. I lower myself into bed and leave the large ceiling fan on all night, mercifully loud to drown out the sound of the cathedral bells tolling every half hour. 'Feeling very, very low,' I write, before turning out my light.

I wake after the best night's sleep in a long time, helped by an enormous glass of wine, chased by 400 milligrams of Nurofen and half a magic pill which I brought along with me 'just in case' (I know, I know). After the rest I feel that I can manage the back pain, aided by texts from Lou and physio Rupert on how to minimize the ache. A wholesome breakfast awaits me in a first-floor room, and my spirits are raised further by a stroll to the cathedral and its close. This is a stunningly beautiful town: why is it not buzzing with visitors? I ask again. The cathedral, built between 1145 and 1235, is erected on the site of its burnt-down predecessor where Charlemagne (no less) had been crowned joint 'King of the Franks' in 768. Its replacement retains its Romanesque remnants but is mainly Gothic, one of the earliest examples in France. I gaze at the west porch, added in the fourteenth century, and the two incomplete towers before going inside and sitting quietly in a pew for twenty minutes, wondering how such an extensive building can possibly be maintained with a congregation so small. Soon, I am lost in thoughts and prayer.

Noyon en Ruines, a stunning war relief, sums up the pain this poor town has had to suffer. Few places on the Western Front changed sides more frequently. For two days at the end of August 1914, the British based their headquarters here till the town fell to the Germans on 1 September. The French regained it in March 1917, and the Germans took it back at the beginning of the Spring Offensive in March 1918. Only at the end of August 1918 did the French finally repossess it. By the end of the war, and after prolonged bombardments, the town was in ruins. It sustained a second pulverizing during the Second World War when the Germans occupied it again; a plaque near the cathedral remembers the rear-guard action from 5–9 June 1940 by a doomed French tank unit trying to slow down the German advance, '*forçant l'admiration de l'ennemi*'.

Prudence dictates that I head straight to Roye today along the Roman road, jettisoning my planned loop to the west exploring what

I can find of the Battle of the Ailette. Foch ordered this attack on 17 August 1918 a week after the Allied victory at Amiens, launched from French-held trenches to the south-west of Noyon. Boosted by tanks and aircraft cover, the French advanced on a 15-kilometre front, pushing the Germans back, and recapturing Noyon on 30 August.

I know today's walk will be tough, but I calculate I can manage 22 kilometres with my back if I take it slowly and carry my water bottles in my hands to relieve weight on it. By the time I set off at 11 a.m., the sun is already beating down, and within 2 kilometres, perspiration on my forehead is mixing with insect repellent to make my eyes sting. Idiotically, I keep looking back at the twin towers of Noyon's cathedral which stubbornly refuse to retreat further into the distance. Supporting the weight of my rucksack with one hand behind my back seems to help, alternating between left and right. It remains painful, but bearable. As bikes, cars and lorries (despite it being the weekend) whistle past, I walk inside the dotted white line at the side of the road, or on the verge itself where the grass is flat, wary of hidden dips that could lurch me sideways. Most oncoming vehicles give me a wide berth, lorries particularly. I provoke two angry horn blasts from young men with girlfriends sitting upright at their side. I think of the Roman soldiers walking this very route. Did they receive heckles from young bloods in carriages hurtling past them at speed the other way?

The kilometres slowly pass. I press forward through the noise, the heat and the gnawing pain. Rare evidence of the war includes a broken column by the side of the road signifying the life cut short of a 22-year-old French soldier killed in March 1918. As I approach Roye, I pass a British cemetery which contains 565 killed in 1918, and the graves of forty-three airmen killed during the Second World War. The Herbert Baker-designed graveyard is beautifully tended. I place two small stones, as is the custom, on a Jewish grave. Jewish soldiers fighting for Britain suffered from anti-Semitism, but less it would appear than those who fought for France, with the embedded anti-Semitism evident in the

Dreyfus Affair (1894–1906) still raw. The 100,000 or so Jews who fought for Germany in the war would appear to have suffered less. A recent Wiener Library exhibition in London testified to their sacrifice and the importance of their contribution: hard to conceive how untold numbers were murdered on the orders of the German state in the Holocaust shortly after.

Roye, half the size of Noyon, had a similar story. It was captured by the Germans on 30 August 1914, then the French took it back in March 1917, only for the Germans to retake it in the Spring Offensive of March 1918. They evacuated the town on 26 August. For a day, till the Allies arrived, it was a ghost town, and a ghost town it seems today – I feel like Wyatt Earp walking into a silent Tombstone film set in *Gunfight at the O.K. Corral.* The residents hide behind twitching curtains. I'm on my guard, waiting for them to emerge brandishing guns.

I locate the Airbnb accommodation – the only bedroom I could find in town – in a Corbusier-style block of flats close to the artillery-flattened city centre. Olivier, my host, is at the door to greet me, very affable, a financier who travels 40 kilometres every day into Amiens, a city he says is thriving. Thank goodness, I say, with a little too much feeling. Once alone, I spread myself out on the floor, legs raised on a chair as Rupert has advised, then hitch myself up improbably on to the settee for a Sky interview about Michael Fawcett, Prince Charles's former aide accused of offering to help secure citizenship for a donor to royal charities. This one is easy: go! Tonight, I'm going out to dinner. Olivier says he will drive me in his classic 1960s Maserati-engine Citroën to the best in town. The food in the modern roadside bistro is indeed nourishing, and after my feast he is there outside to greet me. I'm pathetically happy to be talking at last to someone while the throaty roar of his powerful engine speeds us home. Sad though I am not to be staying at a historic hotel had one existed in the centre of town, I rejoice at the opportunity that Airbnb gives for human engagement.

I'm up before seven because it takes a good hour with my back to shower and apply gauzes and bandages. Every time I reach down towards my feet I have a stab of pain. Olivier points me in the direction of downtown Roye for breakfast, and we bid fond farewells. Only once there do I appreciate how widespread was the destruction, including the eighteenth-century town hall blown sky high by the retreating Germans in March 1917. I admire its 1932 replacement rather more than I do the concrete 1930 Église Saint-Pierre which replaced its twelfth-century predecessor. Unable to find a café open for breakfast, I buy fresh orange juice from a patisserie and a small baguette which I eat on a street corner by a large refuse bin, luggage on the ground beside me. A tramp comes up to me approvingly, gives me a knowing nod and strolls on. Well, it's company.

My target for midday is the town of Chaulnes, walking along the front between it and Roye which the French successfully fought for in late September 1914 in the First Battle of Picardy, as part of the 'race to the sea'. The heat is already up as I walk fully laden north-eastwards along the Avenue General de Gaulle, three times busier than my road yesterday. My blue top is still not dry from its overnight wash before it becomes soaked again, this time with sweat. The orange juice on an empty stomach is sitting unhappily. Am I much more conscious of these minor irritations because I'm not working? I ask myself. With the insistent demands of a full-on job, there was less time and reason to notice the stomach, back, neck and head aches that punctuate my days now. I try coming off the road westwards on a path but lose my way at the Bois de l'Abbaye. I return reluctantly, but half an hour later, head down another track that looks promising but brings me back round on to the same main road, 'now even hotter and noisier and angrier'. After a few minutes, I pass a sign which tells me that I'm just 4 kilometres from Roye which I left two hours ago. Bloody, bloody hell. As I stop in a lay-by to adjust my bags, a swarm of midges descends, tens of thousands, and I lack the speed to run them off.

I can't take much more of this main road, even if it means walking further to reach Péronne, my target for tonight. So I take the next track off west, determined to tough it out. It skirts me past the hamlet of Liancourt-Fosse and then ducks under the A2 motorway and the Paris–London TGV railway into the bucolic village of Hattencourt, a hundred years apart from the world whistling by on northern France's principal artery. I find my dream bench – shaded by a wooden barn, free of crawling insects, midges and sun – and I slowly recover. The transformation is aided by my swallowing 1,000 milligrams of paracetamol, 400 milligrams of ibuprofen and two bars of nutty biscuit. My back is holding up. I might just be over the worst of it. I can do this.

Famous last words. When will I learn to be suspicious of optimism? So often, darkness comes on the walk after such moments. I walk out of Hattencourt on a country lane past its military cemetery and on to the village of Hallu, another destroyed in the war. I stop at the war memorial, which includes a dedication to the thirty-five killed between 8 and 11 August 1918 from the 78th Battalion of Winnipeg Grenadiers, '*morts à Hallu pour libérer la France*'. As a dominion, Canada's foreign relations were London's responsibility, so it too went to war on 4 August 1914. Some 620,000 went on to enlist in the Canadian Expeditionary Force (CEF), with 424,000 serving overseas, fighting mostly at the Somme, Vimy and Ypres, of whom 61,000 were killed.[4] Winnipeg and its province of Manitoba suffered particularly severely, with its economy depressed for years afterwards. Whether connected or not, the province saw a spike in seances in the 1920s, designed to make contact with the departed. Arthur Conan Doyle, whose son Kingsley died in October 1918 in the influenza epidemic, was a keen practitioner and author on spiritualism: indeed, he praised the province for its seances on his visit in 1924.[5]

Back in the world of the living, I trudge on to Chaulnes, whose very name calls to my mind gloomy associations, like Chelmno, the Nazi extermination camp, or charnel house (place of death), appropriately, as

The ruins of Chaulnes in 1918. © National Library of Scotland

it became one. I have now reached the southern tip of the French sector of the Battle of the Somme which opened on 1 July 1916. Chaulnes was repeatedly bombed, as seen in the photograph above, taken by official British war photographer John Warwick Brooke.

It is past 2 p.m. when I buy lunch on the Avenue Aristide Briand, named after France's eleven-times prime minister. Searching for shade from the intense sun, I place my chicken sandwich on the ledge of the *notaire*, and stand in the shadow cast by a lamp post, trying to find a shaft of cool air to eat in. My map last night said very clearly that it would take just two hours from Chaulnes to my hotel outside Péronne. But it now says it is well over three. To do that and risk damage to my back would be folly. So I decide to call it a day. I phone every taxi company in a widening radius – to no avail. Another bad moment as I realize that, despite new blisters on my toe and heel, I have no option but to press on. I jettison every last superfluous item, including my shoulder bag, in an innocent street bin. The heaviest weight remaining by far is the hardback copy of Douglas Gillespie's diaries. No diary, no point left to the trip. Back in the rucksack it goes. Summoning every drop of strength left in me, I set off. I choose my route very carefully at the fork at the top of the town. But I'm back at the same spot half an hour later, realizing the direction I chose is going to deliver me plumb on the detested fast road. I worry that if I started again back on it, I would no longer have the lateral strength to avoid keeling over into the path of oncoming vehicles if I hit a ditch.

So a longer journey on the lanes it is. On and on the walk goes, and as it does, I feel, miraculously, a new release of energy. Two hours nineteen minutes, one hour fifty-two, one hour twenty-six, on I press through Berny-en-Santerre and Barleux. England is playing in the fourth Test against India. Listening to every ball played at the Oval, with 199 runs to go, I draw vicarious strength from our batsmen holding out against the odds. Just 158 runs now to victory. What joy! We're going to do this together. I'm at the crease with you, lads… But then, the collapse. I still have fifty-five minutes to go. I will have to bat on alone to victory.

Nine and a half hours and 35 kilometres after leaving Roye, I arrive at the Kyriad hotel on the outskirts of Péronne. Reaching this pivotal town on the Somme had always been a marker from the start. I reasoned that if I could make it here, I could go all the way. So why am I not feeling jubilation? On a few occasions in my life I have become seriously unsettled, and it's difficult to find the way back when I do. The death of Joanna in 2016 was one, and my stopover now reminds me uncomfortably of another, in a similarly bleak bedroom in a similar motel on a similar noisy road, the I-70 in Kansas City, when writing my doctorate in September 1978. I worried then too I would never finish, and in the soulless environment with no known points of reference 8,000 kilometres from home, I was utterly lost.

Keep moving, I tell myself now, stop ruminating. I take my boots off but recoil suddenly at the look of my feet. A long bath provides little relief, and I go down to the restaurant for the self-service microwave dinner, the only option available. The one other guest glances across the tables at me dismissively. Back in my room, even meditation fails to bring peace, so I turn to Gillespie's missive. 'Today I had a curious experience,' he writes, 'for I walked a few miles across country to see if I could find that château which Tom described in his last letter.' Douglas was searching desperately for a connection, for someone who remembered his beloved younger brother. Thrilled to locate the chateau's French owner who had looked after him, Douglas is unable to show her his final postcard written from it before her attention is claimed by French officers arriving by car for billeting. I think he too is still grieving desperately. He leaves the chateau despondent.[6] I turn out the bedside light.

I am excited at breakfast as I have long anticipated this day. It is something of a pilgrimage. After many years I can see where R. C. Sherriff set *Journey's End*, written to expunge his guilt at surviving the war, and to commemorate those who did not. Directing it in my first year teaching in 1984, at a time I was still unconvinced the profession was right for me, gave me profound joy, similar to directing plays at university. To immerse the cast in the war, I took them on my first trip to the trenches, albeit not this far east to the exact location. I can see Tim Davie, now director-general of the BBC, holding up part of a machine gun the students had found. I directed the play a further three times at schools, then spent five years badgering film producers to bring it to the big screen. Eventually money and director were found, and cast assembled: Paul Bettany (Osborne), Sam Claflin (Stanhope), Toby Jones (Mason), Stephen Graham (Trotter) and Asa Butterfield (Raleigh). The film went out on general release in February 2018. Hibbert, played by Tom Sturridge, drew heavily on Sherriff's own experience of nerves. The story about a group of soldiers, their officer holding himself together only with whisky, all doomed to die in the battle hurtling towards them, speaks to us all today. Its truths were aided by the author hearing every word uttered by the soldiers with whom he served. My one impact on the film was to urge the team to reimagine the script as Sherriff might have done for film, as he did for

R. C. Sherriff in 1918.

The Dam Busters (1955), taking the story beyond the battleground. But did it work? The sister/girlfriend in the final scenes? I'm not sure.

One speech has always stood out to me, when Stanhope tries to reassure the frightened Hibbert that death cannot be so frightening, given all they know killed in the war so far: 'It can't be very lonely there with all those fellows,' he says. Then he whispers as if to himself, 'Sometimes, I think it is lonelier here.'[7]

Lonelier here. Words that frighten me. And comfort me.

I do not think that death is the end. But I do wish I could discern more about what follows it.

Sherriff set the play in British trenches near the town of Saint-Quentin during the three days leading up to the German Spring Offensive (or 'Operation Michael') launched on 21 March 1918. Fortified by hundreds of thousands of soldiers released from the Eastern Front, the Germans enjoyed a rare moment of numerical superiority on the Western Front, which they sought to exploit. Preceded by a ferocious bombardment, and using innovative 'stormtrooper' infantry tactics, they gave short shrift to the British Fifth Army, making rapid gains along the 100-kilometre front. Ground that the British had taken weeks to achieve at the Battles of the Somme and Passchendaele was retaken in days, with the Germans surging forward through Bapaume, Péronne, Roye and Noyan. I want to know how close the Germans came to success. Could they have actually won the war? I consult Nick Lloyd, author of the seminal *The Western Front*. 'It is tempting to say that the Allies were never close to being defeated and the German offensive would run out of steam,' he tells me. 'But it did not feel that way in late March and early April 1918, with a real concern the Allied armies would break, run, and never stop.' But as reinforcements arrived, resistance solidified, and the 'dangerous moment', as he described it, passed. The Germans failed to take the British strongholds of Arras to the north of the front and the still more important town of Amiens. Eventually, their Herculean effort petered out 20 kilometres short of it at Villers-Bretonneux in April. The German strategic gamble to win the war had failed, just like in 1914.[8]

By 1918 the front line had moved 30 kilometres east of where my hotel is today, so I take a taxi. Some 177,000 British soldiers became casualties in the offensive; 1918 indeed saw the highest British casualties of any year.[9] Some of them lie in the Savy British Cemetery I visit outside Saint-Quentin, including Private W. E. Lowe of the Machine Gun Corps, killed on the opening day of the battle, 21 March 1918. I taught a W. E. Lowe. Kneeling by his grave to read the dedication, 'Mourned Deeply by Mother & Brother', I move two red roses gently aside that conceal his age: nineteen. Did his mother and brother travel to France to see his grave, I wonder: how did they manage without him? I reflect on this often. As a head, it fell to me to break the news of lost parents and children. The thinnest of margins separates tragedy from life. In the horror of death, the grief and pain can be without end: what is the matter with us that we do not savour more our loved ones while we have them with us? So many friendships, so many families, miss out on joy through pettiness. I am as guilty as the next person.

Like the Germans, I don't make it to Amiens today. But I was staying there five years ago showing American politician and financier Mike Bloomberg the battlefields on behalf of the government's 14–18 NOW culture committee. He was intrigued that the war turned at the Battle of Amiens in August 1918, when the Allies started what became known as the Hundred Days Offensive that ended in Germany's military collapse. He was surprised, I think, at the lack of US interest in the war. His rat-a-tat mind fired out questions throughout as he surveyed battlefields, cemeteries and museums. At the time, he was a contender for the American presidential election to be held in November 2020. Had he become president, I have no doubt attitudes to the war in the US would've changed. I remember talking about his age – it would have been seventy-eight had he been successful. 'Same age as Churchill when he came back the last time in 1951,' I said. He looked at me sceptically. Perhaps he knew Churchill was a stripling at seventy-six. Besides, when has age been a barrier for the White House?

Everywhere we went, he was ringed by armed security personnel, more than I have seen for any head of government or state. Out of our conversations came the idea for a trip to Auschwitz in June 2018, the first by such a senior American political figure. Again, the same forensic questioning and deep intellect. Joanna and I were married by Hugo Gryn who as a boy was an inmate here between 1944 and 1945. As we walked around the gas chambers partially destroyed by the retreating Germans, I saw Joanna perched daintily on the piece of concrete she had sat on some years earlier as she contemplated her partially destroyed body and composed 'A cancer patient visits Auschwitz'. Mid-poem, she writes: 'For each of us a railway line / Stretches ahead / And we must walk along it...'

The chance to explore the French Somme story is one too good to miss, so I push back my planned walking time and ask my taxi driver to show me what's there. Some context: the Somme had been chosen as the location for no better reason than it was where the French and British lines met on the river. It had been envisaged as an equal French and British offensive. Despite Verdun preventing that, some 40,000 French soldiers were still killed, with 200,000 casualties in the four-and-a-half-month battle, a tragically high figure, but paling in significance against the British toll of 125,000 dead and over 400,000 casualties.[10] The French captured more ground early on than the British, aided by a significant artillery advantage and the Germans deeming the French sector south of the River Somme of less strategic importance to defend.[11]

The French necropolis at Villers-Carbonnel just south-west of Péronne marks the furthest point the French reached in the Somme battle: they never managed to wrest Péronne back from the Germans. I visit the deserted village of Fay which French colonial forces captured on the opening day: 1 July 1916. Great care has been taken on the preservation of the trenches, with sepia photographs of soldiers peppered around to show how they looked. But the pictures are fading, the lettering rubbed off, and the trenches and destroyed village unvisited. The *village détruit* has become the *village oublié*.

During the car journeys that morning, I catch up with my diary. I leave the hotel at 11.45 feeling in high spirits. It has been a brilliant start to the day. Exactly as I had anticipated every day being. The rest of the day looks exhilarating too. I am due to meet Rory on the road to Albert: he has come out that morning to spend four days walking with me. This time, nothing was going to go wrong.

On the short walk into Péronne, a young man drinking a can of lager comes up behind me and breathes heavily in my face. Covid, which I have put to the back of my mind, flooded back yesterday when Adam told me he has long Covid, as has my colleague Diana, despite both having double AZ jabs like me. I still have no Plan B should I catch it – is that foolhardy or brave? Had I thought about the risks too long before I left, I never would've set out. No point in thinking about it now. Especially as there is no Plan B.

I walk to the centre of Péronne before turning west, past the inspired Historial de la Grande Guerre Museum in the chateau to which I have taken so many groups, and then up the hill out of the town en route to Albert, the beating heart of the British Somme. At 12.53 – I make a note of the time – a large white van drives slowly by and the passenger throws a sack of liquid out of his window. I don't see it flying through the air before it hits me four-square in the abdomen, splattering all over my body. I turn to see the van speeding away, a head leaning out of the window looking at me, but moving too quickly for me to take a photograph. I'm drenched. I think at first it's urine, but it doesn't seem to be. It smells sweaty and rank. I don't feel angry, or even upset; but I do feel a shame and humiliation at becoming a victim.

I realize I can't drink any more of the plentiful water I have been carrying because my face and lips are smeared with the unknown liquid that I would inevitably ingest, so I press on, regardless of the heat picking up. It is a full 24 kilometres into Albert. That'll be fine, I reckon, because Rory will join me on the road soon, and we will go straight to the hotel where I'll take a much-needed shower. Then a long, long drink of water.

Rory calls. He has caught a train from Lille Eurostar to Albert but is having problems finding a taxi at the rural station. There'll be one somewhere, I tell him. There always is. I walk on along the winding D938 I know so well between Péronne and Albert. I am damned if this episode is going to distract me. This is the hottest day of my walk so far. Half an hour later, Rory calls back. He has spoken to the tourist office, who happen to be fans of the Western Front Way, but they say there is no taxi available till late afternoon. By now I'm over halfway, and approaching Maricourt. I'm thirsty, I tell him, but I'll be fine. I'll be in Albert soon. Rory luckily realised that dehydration was taking its toll.

Sometime after that, the tourist office appears to have panicked at the prospect of a walker pegging out on their pitch, and they dispatch an ambulance to me. This is not what I wanted: left alone, Albert would've been quite manageable I still thought. As I am passing the Péronne Road CWGC Cemetery, I receive an infuriating message via the tourist office to say the ambulance is waiting outside the *mairie* at Maricourt.

This means reversing my direction; my heart sinks when I see the flashing blue lights on the parked vehicle. I tell the crew that I'm absolutely fine, all I need is antiseptic to clean my face, some water to drink, then being left alone, *merci*, to resume walking. But they won't let me go. They refuse point blank to give me surgical wipes or water despite my protests. Not even the intervention of Sarah, who I caught just before she gave a briefing to staff on relationship education, convinces them to change their mind. 'The Englishman is very determined,' she tells the ambulance crew on speakerphone. It sounded pretty convincing to me, but they insist that they are worried about my condition, I'm very severely dehydrated and they are taking me to Péronne for immediate treatment.

I am deposited by the crew at the hospital reception at about 4 p.m., where no one is willing to give me any water. Dehydration is the key to the exhaustion I'm no doubt experiencing, I keep telling myself. But my attempts to tell this to anybody I can find in a white coat adds to the impression that they have a delirious Englishman in their precinct. I manage to get hold of Sarah again, her training session over, who repeats to a junior doctor that Mr Seldon is '*un homme très têtu*' (stubborn) and he has no intention of staying in the hospital overnight, but needs water. No response, but a porter points me to a supply of bottles – I end up swigging three. A nurse called Jade seems empathetic. Am I hallucinating? I babble on that I'm not at ease in hospitals, how I never needed them till the dog bite two weeks ago, about my endless visits to the cancer wards with Joanna. She smiles at me sweetly, but I don't think she understands a single word I say.

Soon after, I'm given blood pressure tests, an intravenous insertion is crafted into my upper arm to prepare for unknown fluids, my blood is repeatedly taken, I have an electrocardiogram, and no one – no one – is telling me what is happening. My cubicle's curtains regularly twitch open and medics look at me, I know not why. I'm beginning to wonder if they know something I don't.

Bloody Picardy indeed. Will it mark the end of my walk?

10

The Somme

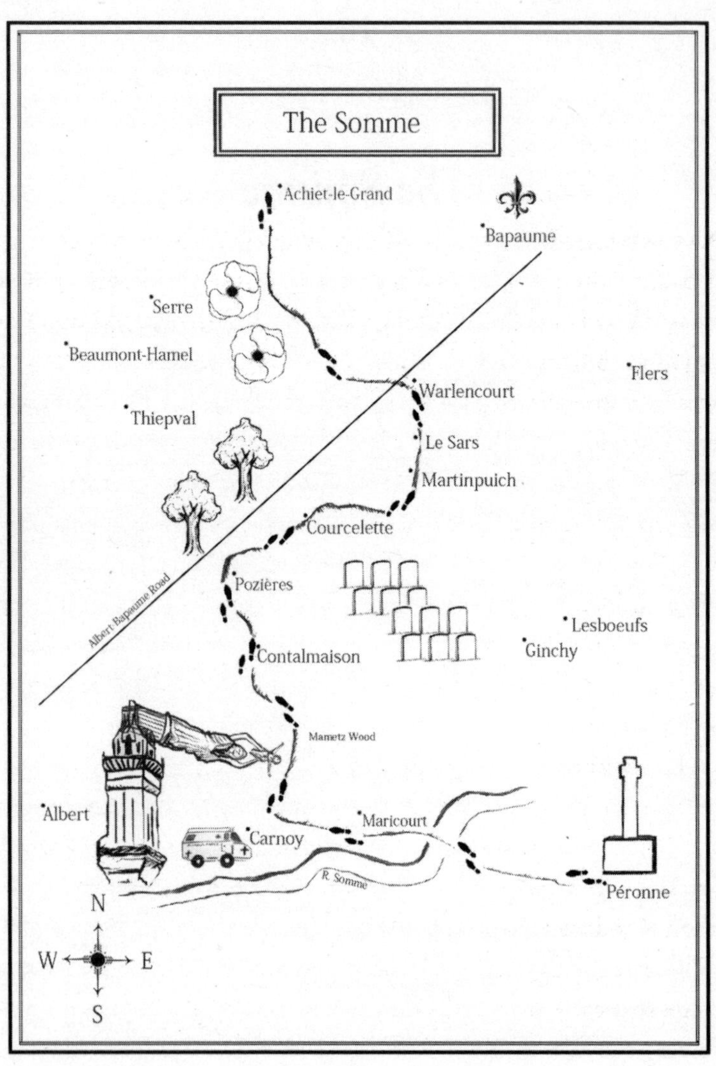
The Somme
Achiet-le-Grand
Bapaume
Serre
Beaumont-Hamel
Flers
Warlencourt
Thiepval
Le Sars
Martinpuich
Courcelette
Pozières
Albert-Bapaume Road
Lesboeufs
Ginchy
Contalmaison
Mametz Wood
Albert
Maricourt
Carnoy
R. Somme
Péronne
N
W
E
S

'PLEASE CAN I LEAVE?' I call out whenever I hear someone go past in the corridor or they peer in at me inside my cubicle. Silence. Why is no one listening? I worry I'll be drugged up in an anonymous bureaucracy, days lost while my timetable, hanging as it now is by a thread, will be shot. Images of the Cruella de Vil matron at the Tonbridge School sanatorium, forcing sleeping pills down my schoolboy throat, come suddenly to mind from years before. My eyes keep turning to the clock in my screened-off cubicle: 6 p.m., 7 p.m., 8 p.m. My heart is still racing despite the rehydration. The curtain suddenly swishes open... The humourless doctor is back! 'You are free to leave,' he intones in English, stony-faced. No reason given. I suspect it's less because the hospital is satisfied: more, they have had their fill of this protesting foreigner.

A hospital bed, though, may not be a wholly inappropriate place from which to embark on this chapter of my walk. The Somme's innocently sloping chalk hills and valleys, so like verdant Salisbury Plain on which the troops cheerfully trained, became to the British the epitome of the wanton bloodshed of the entire war.

The Battle of the Somme was conceived in confusion and executed with incompetence. After a year of stalemate on the Western Front following the 'race to the sea' in late 1914, the Allies decided at the Chantilly Conference in December 1915 that something 'decisive' was required. A series of mighty offensives on all fronts was their answer.

Disagreement ensued over the exact British contribution. Newly appointed BEF chief Douglas Haig argued for Flanders, which offered the strategic objective of recapturing the Belgian coast and ports. But Joffre preferred the Somme, where the French and British armies met. They compromised on a British diversionary offensive to take place in Flanders before the main joint attack on the Somme in mid-1916.

The joint plan was torpedoed, as we've seen, when the Germans attacked Verdun. As the French forces bled to death around Douaumont, Joffre demanded that the British attack in order to relieve the pressure. Plans for the diversionary offensive in Flanders were shelved too as it became clear that the heaviest burden of the Somme offensive would fall on the British alone. Haig's inexperienced 'New Army' began intensive preparations for the massive battle that would begin on 1 July 1916.

The seven-day preliminary bombardment along the Somme front failed to cut the German barbed wire, damage the deep bunkers where the defenders sheltered, or destroy their machine guns. How did the planners fail to anticipate any other outcome? When Haig's soldiers advanced at 7.30 a.m., the German soldiers emerged largely unscathed from deep underground dugouts and 'opened up a terrific fire'.[1] The result was carnage along large sections of the line with wave after wave of attackers shot to pieces. To this day, the bald tally of death never ceases to shock. The opening day on which such high hopes were pinned ended with 19,300 British dead and 60,000 casualties. The worst day in British military history.

Further major British assaults followed on 14 July and 15 September, the latter seeing the first use in the war of the tank, with limited effectiveness, as the French experienced. Fighting continued till 18 November by which time British casualties had risen to over 420,000, including some 60,000 from the Empire (25,000 each from Australia and Canada, 7,500 New Zealanders and 3,000 South Africans). Up to 600,000 Germans became casualties in the battle, and 200,000 French.[2]

And for what? Verdun had been relieved of German pressure, true. But the British never made it to their early objectives, including the German-held town of Bapaume, while the French never took back Péronne. There was no war-winning breakthrough or damage. The German army had, despite terrible losses, contained the attack.

When fighting returned in earnest on the Somme with the Spring Offensive in March 1918, the Germans swiftly recaptured all the pitifully few kilometres taken two years before. That August, the British grabbed it all back again at the start of the Hundred Days Offensive.

The Somme, my sixth river, arises near Saint-Quentin, and flows 250 kilometres into its wide estuary on the English Channel. From Péronne, the river slithers away west from the scene of the crime like a naughty schoolboy or politician protesting 'nothing to do with me'. Beyond lending its name, the River Somme played no part in the fighting, while the River Ancre which wends its way through the British sector of the battlefield, at times tinged red with blood, is known only unto God. In the halcyon pre-war days, its tranquil valley had been a beauty spot, the location Sebastian Faulks chose for a pre-1914 picnic in his novel *Birdsong*. Within months, it was transformed into 'The struggling Ancre [which] ran through my heart / I heard it grieve and pine / As if its rainy tortured blood / Had swirled into my own', as poet Edmund Blunden wrote.

A taxi is waiting outside the hospital to take me to Albert, to the Hôtel de la Paix, where Rory is waiting for me on the street. On my bed, he has laid several Boots bags full of medical goodies from Blighty. I am so happy to see him: more than anyone, he is making the Western Front Way happen. Ever patient, he reads while I shower slowly; then, arm over my shoulder, supports me as we progress to Le Hygge Brasserie in Albert's main square, overlooking the basilica. Smoked salmon and steak restore my iron, if not my spirit levels. Sitting at a table on the street, we chat away about the walk and my setbacks. Doing so feels a release, as it is to be back in beloved Albert. I have ached all walk for this moment, but it is not how I imagined it.

We gaze up at the illuminated golden statue of Mary with the infant Jesus on top of the basilica. It isn't the original statue. But neither is the church. Nor the restaurant. Nor the town. Nothing indeed is real here, if by real we mean original. A German shell struck the statue, crafted less than twenty years earlier, on 15 January 1915, leaving it hanging precariously in a horizontal position. There it remained, the Tommies upholding a legend that the day she fell, the war would finish. In the end, her fate was determined by British shells, knocking the statue down along with the rest of the basilica in April 1918 to deny the Germans a machine-gun post after they had captured the town in March. Untold numbers of shells rained down on Albert throughout the war, the soldiers and the few remaining citizens sheltering in its cellars. The decision was taken after 1918 to rebuild the entire town, including basilica and Madonna. Some politicians thought the church should be rebuilt with the statue leaning. But the inhabitants wanted to forget the bloody war. Poet and composer Ivor Gurney, who marched past the precariously hanging Madonna in November 1916, didn't have the option to forget. 'For myself it sometimes comes that death would be preferable,' he wrote to close friend Marion Scott.[3] In 1922, he was institutionalized in a mental asylum where he died in 1937, unable still to forget the war.

We stroll back past the illuminated fountains in the square, casting their shadows on the basilica. As soon as I'm alone, gnawing anxiety floods back. I wonder if the dehydration, ambulance and hospital visit have disorientated me. I turn out my lights at 10.30, but my heart is still racing furiously. Why did the medics seem so concerned? The dark, the unfamiliar room and the fatigue magnify my fears. Absurd thoughts swim through my mind. If I go to sleep I might never wake up. I don't want to die in this town of death, to abandon those who need me. Can it be so bad, where so many have gone before? Even alcohol,

Stanhope's resort in *Journey's End*, is no good at quelling the thoughts from the pit. On and off my lights flick for the next three hours until, terribly selfishly, I ring Sarah. She talks to me gently and says a prayer till I feel more settled. Around 2 a.m. I float away for a few hours to the sounds of bells and hospital orderlies.

With a start, I wake at seven. I spray insect repellent over the raw wounds on my feet, and antiseptic alcohol spray everywhere else. My thinking is blurred. It takes longer to tog up and I'm not down to breakfast till 9 a.m., Rory waiting patiently. The hotel owner hovers at the door, an air of melancholy hanging over him. We are his only guests, Covid again, and I feel guilty that we didn't eat dinner at his hotel of peace, over which he has taken so much trouble since my last visit. A taxi arrives to shoot us back to Maricourt. Rory is carrying the water today, and our equipment has gone ahead to tonight's hotel in Bapaume. Relieved of the load, my back almost immediately starts feeling better.

Maricourt, even though not in my plan, proves the ideal place to start walking the Somme section as it is where the British trenches, the entire British war effort at the time indeed, started and ended, Britain's very own Kilometre Zero. The Somme snakes wildly just south of the village. In place of Switzerland is a soggy kilometre of marshy valley that rendered combat impossible until the French front line begins on terra firma to the south. We take a photograph together by a Western Front Way logo in front of the *mairie*, a nice boost, and we strut off on foot due west. A gentle breeze accompanies us to Carnoy, where we stop at a memorial listing ten villagers, three of them civilians who remained behind while mayhem erupted all around them. The most south-easterly of the battle's nineteen underground mines was detonated by the British here on 1 July 1916. They may have been small by comparison with the great mine detonated at La Boisselle on the Albert–Bapaume road, but the mines helped bolster British spirits even if they didn't materially damage the Germans much on the first day.

From here, we take a lane north-west through open country to Mametz. For the rest of the day we will be walking through territory the British gained along a 10-kilometre front on or soon after 1 July. We continue west to Fricourt along the Rue de la Libération, skirting just south of Mametz Wood. What liberation? 'The road through Mametz is still under enemy observation,' wrote Mark Plowman in *A Subaltern on the Somme*, 'so we turn sharply to the right to go around the back… Mametz Wood is nothing more than a small collection of thin tree-trunks standing as if a forest fire had just swept over them… All that remains of the village of Fricourt is a pile of bricks.'[4]

Siegfried Sassoon was here too. In his diary he wrote famously: 'The morning is brilliantly fine – after a mist early. Since 6.30 there has been hell let loose… 9.50 Fricourt half hidden by clouds of drifting smoke: brown, blue, pinkish and grey.'[5]

Captain Arthur Irwin was in the thick of those colourful drifting clouds that morning: 'We had come down from 800 men to something under 200… All my best chaps had gone… I think the attack should've been called off until the wire had been cut.'[6] 'Isn't it wonderful?' Private Arthur Burke of the Manchester Regiment recalled the colonel saying, as he watched his men mount the ladders that morning to go over the top. Burke wrote home about the brutal combat that followed when they reached the German lines: 'Then the hand-to-hand fighting started. It was Hell… In one dugout there were about twenty-five in there and we set the place on fire and we spared them no mercy, they don't deserve it.'[7]

The Volksbund military cemetery in Fricourt reminds us how severely the Germans too suffered, with no fewer than 17,000 buried here, less than half known by name. The metal crosses we see today replaced the temporary wooden markers only in 1966 following a Franco-German agreement. The remains of Manfred von Richthofen (the Red Baron), the great German fighter ace, were laid here till transferred in 1925, reburied in Berlin, and then at his family grave plot in Wiesbaden in 1975.

The Somme pushed the Germans, stretched already as they were fighting on both Eastern and Western Fronts, to the limit: 'the Somme was the muddy grave of the German field army and the faith in the infallibility of German leadership,' recalled one officer on German general staff.[8] Ernst Jünger captured how depleted the Germans became in the face of Allied superiority by late in the battle: 'Hundreds of British soldiers were running forward through a flat communication trench, little troubled by the weak gunfire we were able to direct at them.' It would have been far too dangerous, he wrote, for German soldiers to have operated so openly.[9] The near collapse of the German effort helps explain why British morale was still high at the end of the battle, despite all the losses, despite everything.

No British prime minister had visited an active battlefield before the First World War: not Waterloo, nor the Crimean War, nor Boer War. Indeed, not till 1878 did a serving prime minister, Benjamin Disraeli, even travel abroad, by train to Berlin, to the Congress of great powers to bring about enduring peace to Europe. Perhaps he should have stayed at home.

Wednesday 6 September 1916 was thus a historic day when Prime Minister Herbert Asquith, accompanied by future Cabinet Secretary Maurice Hankey, visited the Somme battlefield. Asquith considered the masterly Hankey 'the most useful man in Europe: he has never been wrong.' They travelled to the British GHQ at Montreuil on the eve of the big Somme push nine days later. It was a 'glorious hot day' as they were driven from Montreuil through 'the ruined town of Albert' to Fricourt, where they met Asquith's eldest son Raymond waiting for them on horseback at a crossroads. Their convoy proceeded along a 'broken shell-smitten road' to the centre of Fricourt where 'literally not one stone [was] left on another.' As if to underline the hazard of their trip, a German shell burst 100 metres away, resulting in a speedy ushering of the prime minister's party into a dugout, just as another shell was landing even closer. They waited 'some considerable time' in the dugout until 'the shell shower passed'. Never again would Downing Street minders let a prime minister be exposed to such imminent danger, though Churchill required firm restraining.[10]

Douglas Gillespie had dined with Raymond's youngest brother Cys, a friend since Oxford, at No. 10 in April 1914. His attention was caught by the picture display gallery of prime ministers erected on the principal staircase by Asquith's predecessor: 'Some of the portraits are very fine,' he wrote excitedly to his sister Daisy. 'Lord Rosebery looks the youngest of them all, except of course Pitt.' Rory and I look forlornly around Fricourt for traces of the dugout into which Cys's father was bundled. Today too is a 'glorious hot day'. Too hot. We are sweltering under the heat. Asquith was proud to be visiting the scene of recent fighting, and was lifted by meeting his beloved Raymond, looking 'so radiantly strong and confident that I came away from France with an easier mind'. The following evening, the prime minister sought solace from the strain, letting his hair down over dinner with Haig. 'You would've been amused at the Prime Minister last night,' Haig confided later to his wife. '[He] seemed to like our old brandy. He had a couple of glasses (big sherry glass size!) before I left the table at 9.30, and apparently he had several more before I saw him again. By that time his legs were unsteady...'[11] Indeed, as Simon Heffer writes in his book on wartime British politics, Asquith was 'exhausted... drinking heavily... [and] exhibited none of the raucous dynamism that made people admire Lloyd George'.[12]

Just one week later, on 15 September at 4 a.m., Raymond was preparing to lead an attack with the Grenadier Guards. Before going over the top at 6.20 and fixing their bayonets, his men were issued with sandwiches and rum rations. From their trenches near Ginchy, their objective was Lesboeufs, to the north-east of the battlefield. 'The ground in and around Ginchy was a battered mass of irregular ridges and shell holes, which overlapped and stretched away into the early morning mist. Direction became a matter of the greatest difficulty...' recorded the Guards' regimental history.[13] The prime minister's beloved son was soon shot in the chest as he led No. 4 Company. He lit a cigarette as if to make light of it to his men, and died on a stretcher being carried back to safety.[14] His gravestone in nearby Guillemont Road Cemetery carries Shakespeare's words from the Epilogue of *Henry V*: 'Small time, but in that small most greatly lived, this star of England'. Why do those words always send shivers down my spine?

His brilliant record as a scholar and Fellow of All Souls College Oxford had already marked him out, but Raymond's death elevated his status to the stratosphere: 'he went to his fate cool, poised, resolute, matter of fact, debonair,' wrote Churchill; his father 'then bearing the supreme burden of the state would proudly have marched by his side.'[15] The news reached Asquith's home in Sutton Courtenay, Oxfordshire on 17 September. '[He] opened the door and we stood facing each

Prime Minister H. H. Asquith visits the Somme in September 1916. Here he observes men setting explosive fuses. © Imperial War Museum

other,' his stepmother Margot wrote. 'He saw my thin, wet face, and while he put his arm around me, I said "terrible, terrible news". At this he stopped and said: "I know… I've known it… Raymond is dead." He put his hands over his face and we walked into an empty room and sat down in silence.'[16]

Does having the sons of national leaders fight in war cloud their objectivity, or demonstrate patriotic commitment? Asquith certainly was never the same man again, and within three months had been swept from power by Lloyd George. What of their colleagues around the cabinet table? The Labour leader Arthur Henderson had three sons in action. David, fighting on the Somme at High Wood, within 2 kilometres of Raymond, was killed on 15 September too, caught up in the same Battle of Flers-Courcelette.[17] What of Conservative leader, Andrew Bonar Law? Charles, his older son, was reported missing in Gaza in April 1917: after weeks of worry, a report came from the Vatican that he was on a list of prisoners, for his father only to be told later that the word 'not' had been omitted and he had, in fact, died. Jim, another son, was also killed, shot down in September 1917.[18] This second loss hit him particularly hard: for a long time, he could not work, till he went to France to ease his grief. Asking to see a plane like the contraption Jim flew, he was shown one riddled with bullets. Up the old man clambered into the cockpit where he sat in silence for three hours.[19] His adored wife, Annie, had died aged forty-two in 1909, so he was alone with his torment. 'Night seems to have descended upon him,' wrote his biographer Robert Blake. 'All those dark clouds which were never far below the horizon in his thought came rolling up, obliterating light and happiness.' He rallied to become prime minister for seven months in 1922–3 before succumbing to cancer, dying in office at the age of sixty-five.[20]

What happened on these rolling hills through which we are walking moulded the thinking of interwar prime ministers Stanley Baldwin, Ramsay MacDonald and Neville Chamberlain, each of whom sought to avoid war again at all costs. While only two British prime ministers fought in the Second World War (Ted Heath and Jim Callaghan, both strongly pro-Britain joining Europe), four had fought in the First World War, with similar profound impact. 'It's no use, you are arguing against the casualties on the Somme,' Churchill's doctor, Lord Moran, told American planners in 1942–3 who were pressing for an early invasion of northern Europe.[21] Clement Attlee, one of the last British officers to be evacuated from Suvla Bay after the failed Gallipoli campaign in 1915, was also scarred by the loss of life. As prime minister after 1945, he determined to build a more compassionate Britain for those who had suffered in the Second World War than Lloyd George had managed after 1918. Anthony Eden fought at Delville Wood just by Ginchy, while Harold Macmillan, the final of the four PMs, was severely wounded on the same day at Ginchy that Raymond Asquith was killed. A bullet cleaving the air a centimetre or two away from its chosen course, and Churchill, Eden or Macmillan might have been killed, and Raymond Asquith survived.[22]

Does first-hand experience of war make for better and wiser leaders? I wonder, not least because I have spent twenty-five years and more observing prime ministers close-up. Might Blair and Cameron have been less hasty to intervene in the Middle East, or Johnson to end international alliances, had they seen war this devastating? Does experience of war paradoxically make us more set on finding peace? One would hardly recommend the young going off to war to become gentler people. Besides, conflict can brutalize and disturb the balance of minds. Sometimes, as with Hitler or Putin, aggression feeds aggression, and makes them coldly indifferent to the suffering of others. I remain confident, though, that walking the Western Front Way with those from other countries and observing 'where war leads' (in Gillespie's words) will help build a more peaceful world, one step at a time.

We have walked out of Fricourt due north avoiding roads, skirting Contalmaison, where large numbers of volunteers from Edinburgh, Northumberland, Grimsby and Cambridge fell on 1 July. A memorial

The Welsh at Mametz Wood (1917) by Christopher Williams.

cairn erected in 2004 commemorates the 16th Royal Scots, which was famous for the high number of footballers and fans from Scottish clubs who fought in its ranks. Mametz Wood is visible just to the south. Lloyd George hung in Downing Street a graphic painting of Welsh soldiers fighting hand-to-hand within the wood, by artist Christopher Williams, which he commissioned. How could anyone not have been deeply affected by this painting that reveals, not glorifies, war?

Looking across the two fields that separate us from the village, it is hard to conceive that the gentle undulating soil saw such horror. Just beyond Contalmaison lies the hamlet of Bazentin-le-Petit. 'I got the MC all right,' wrote an excited Siegfried Sassoon on 14 July from there. 'Our second Battalion are near by – Robert is with them.'[23] Sassoon was referring to author Robert Graves, wounded in multiple places a few days later by German shrapnel. Graves recalled he 'felt as though I'd been punched rather hard between the shoulder blades.'[24] He was expected to die. So dressing-station medics were surprised to find him still alive on the morning of 21 July, too late to stop his death being announced in *The Times*, and a message of regret sent to his parents. He pulled through to live to the age of ninety, his feelings vented in his bitter *Goodbye to All That* in 1929.

I ponder how the Somme forged the artistic imagination of so many writers. '"There are dead things, dead faces in the water," he said with horror. "Dead faces!... They lie in all the pools, pale faces, deep deep under the dark water. I saw them: grim faces and evil, and noble faces and sad... But all foul, all rotting, all dead."'[25] These are the words of Sam Gamgee and Frodo in *The Lord of the Rings*, surely inspired by the war. J. R. R. Tolkien fought on the Somme between July and October 1916 close by the Albert–Bapaume road. Along it rattled British tanks up to the front, which found new life in the 'iron dragons', his monstrous creatures made of iron and bronze.

As the road rises again, we glimpse for the first time the mighty Memorial to the Missing of the Somme on Thiepval Ridge designed by Edwin Lutyens. The names of 72,000 British and South African[26] soldiers are carved into it, 'names... to whom the fortune of war denied the known and honoured burial given to their comrades in death'. We gaze across at it, the red bricks clearly visible, as are the French and the British flags fluttering from poles at the top, in recognition of the joint offensive. What I love about Lutyens is the way his buildings emerge organically, like the most satisfying food and wines, out of the local soil. Many a cold winter evening did I spend with school groups under his bountiful arches at Thiepval, while by candlelight students read poetry and obituaries of those from their schools who fell fighting, their names chiseled above us on the monument. Just as the soldiers experienced in the trenches, whatever spot we found to settle, the bitter wind would seek us out.

It was questions from students that first made me think deeply about the war, far beyond the details of military history they were required to know. Adolescents, I found – to my surprise perhaps – probed more deeply and genuinely than university students. Fear was one topic that intrigued them, imagining how young people often no older than themselves felt when facing the possibility of death. Unlike the regulars who had trained for war, the New Army at the Somme had no idea what they had let themselves in for. Terror was common. 'Imagine you are securely tied to a post, being menaced by a man swinging a heavy hammer. Now the hammer has been taken back over his head, ready to be swung, now it's cleaving the air towards you, on the point of touching your skull, then it's struck the post, and the splinters are flying. That's what it's like to experience heavy shellfire,' wrote Ernst Jünger of his experience on the Somme.[27]

The army's response for handling fear was to drill the recruits to think collectively and obey orders without hesitating, to exhort them with the nobility of the cause; or scare them with the consequences of cowardice or desertion. Officers were advised to clench their fists and 'strike out boldly' as they went over the top. 'Channelling', deflecting fear by diverting the focus elsewhere, was a technique that worked for some: Osborne deploys it by evoking walks in the New Forest with young Raleigh before they go on a joint raid in the most poignant scene in *Journey's End*. If all else failed, numb the mind with rum for the men, whisky for officers.[28]

Thick, dark, strong (80 per cent alcohol) rum was reintroduced to the BEF in September 1914 as a daily ration to give 'Dutch courage'. It arrived at the front in brown ceramic jars marked with the initials 'SRD' (standing for 'special rations department' but colloquially 'soon runs dry').[29] Before going over the top, soldiers were given a double ration. Rum was the Swiss Army knife of the day, used for disinfectant, pain relief in the absence of morphine, a calorie-rich food supplement and as a release from tedium and cold. 'Had it not been for the rum ration I do not think we should've won the war', blurted out Lieutenant Colonel James Rogers in 1922 to a Parliamentary committee. A soldier recalled his overriding memory of the war: 'pervading the air was the smell of rum and blood'.[30]

Nosh not liquor is at the forefront of our minds as Rory and I emerge from farm lanes plumb on top of Le Tommy Café on the Albert–Bapaume road close by Pozières. After substantial plates of eggs, sausages and chips, washed down by Orangina, we are in much better humour to re-engage with the war. We begin at the quirky museum attached to the café, overflowing with military hardware found nearby and overlooked by large war photographs on the walls.

Pozières, the highest point on the Somme battlefield, was of enormous importance to both sides. To the Germans, it protected their stronghold at Thiepval, so they defended it with dogged determination when repeatedly attacked from 1 July. British gains in the first two weeks of the battle had almost all been to the south of the Albert–Bapaume road: if Pozières fell, the Germans would be vulnerable to the north of it as well.[31] Edward Bridges, son of poet laureate Robert, and later Maurice Hankey's successor as cabinet secretary, saw action here at 1.30 a.m. on 18 July. In the same elegant handwriting he later used to record the minutes of Churchill's War Cabinet, he penned in his war diary: 'The enemy opened fire with a heavy barrage of 15cm shell, chiefly shrapnel, all along the trench, causing considerable casualties.'[32] On 23 July, the Australians achieved what many thought beyond them: they captured the village. For two weeks, the German threw everything at trying to recapture it. By the end of the Battle of Pozières Ridge on 7 August, all that remained sticking up above ground was a German concrete blockhouse, which the victorious Australians predictably named 'Gibraltar'. All else was ruin.[33]

We explore the Australian memorial commemorating those who fought in France and Belgium from 1916 to 1918 and the Tank Corps memorial. This too is an obelisk, featuring four models of tanks, one bearing bullet scars from the Second World War. Their first use in battle on 15 September came during the Flers–Courcelette Offensive. Some forty-eight were ordered to advance with the infantry, of which twenty-eight broke down, and of the twenty remaining, only three had not stalled or been destroyed by evening.[34] The case for the tank had nevertheless been made. A sensation was caused at home by a press report describing the brave new world of modern warfare; a radio message from a British aircraft flying overhead reported: 'Tank seen in main street Flers going on with large numbers of troops following it.' A decade before, radio barely existed: the twentieth century had truly arrived.[35]

We pause at the Pozières Memorial to the Missing with the names of 14,720 who died on the Somme between March and August 1918. We don't enter – am I becoming blasé about death, or inured to it? Our path takes us to the east of the busy Roman road past a low brick edifice with fresh geraniums placed on top commemorating composer George Butterworth who died on 5 August 1916 aged thirty-one 'within sight of this memorial'. At the bottom are the words 'Great in what he achieved, greater still in what he promised'. We listen to his folk songs on my phone as we walk along the road named after him through Martinpuich, razed to the ground by shells before being taken by the Scots on 15 September. Butterworth's setting of A. E. Housman's *A Shropshire Lad* provides a perfect musical accompaniment to the tranquil rebuilt village and rolling fields.

Over the next hill-brow, we pick out the Butte de Warlencourt, much as the troops did, and set our sights firmly on it. This marks the furthest point of the British advance when the battle ended in November 1916. We decide it is a good place to end our walking day too. This tactical strongpoint is a chalky 15-metre hill towering above the nearby Roman road, used earlier as an observation point in the Franco-Prussian War of 1870–71, and invested with great symbolic significance by both sides in this war. 'That ghastly hill,' wrote Charles Carrington, 'never free from the smoke of bursting shells... It shone white in the night and seemed to leer at you like an ogre in a fairytale.'[36] Enveloped with trenches, barbed wire, dugouts and gun emplacements, it was a hill of death, the Somme's equivalent of the Butte de Vauquois. Wave after wave of British attacks were launched against it in October 1916. Briefly taken on 5 November, it was swiftly recaptured in a counter-attack by the powerful Prussian Guard. 'The Butte de Warlencourt had become an obsession,' wrote Lieutenant Colonel Roland Bradford, 'everybody wanted it.' The temporary capture on 5 November, he said, had been of 'doubtful value... hardly worth the loss which we would suffer.'[37] Rory and I stop in front of his memorial, learning about his extraordinary short life.

Bradford was no armchair cynic. He had won a VC earlier in the Somme and was presented by George V with the medal in an open-air ceremony in Hyde Park in June 1917. On his return to his men, he ordered the hymn 'Abide with Me' to be sung every night. The song became the regimental hymn of the entire Durham Light Infantry until the regiment was dissolved in 1968. On 10 November 1917, Bradford became at twenty-five the youngest brigadier general in the modern history of the British army to lead a combat formation. Twenty days later, he was dead, killed during the Battle of Cambrai. On hearing the news, his men spontaneously broke into 'Abide with Me'. His brother George was also awarded the VC, the only time in the war two brothers received the great distinction. George too was killed in action, as was a third brother, James. One can only wonder about their parents.[38]

By the end of the battle, German forces were under simultaneous strain from the Brusilov Offensive on the Eastern Front, with troop numbers stretched beyond the limit. This explains the decision in early 1917 by Falkenhayn's successor Hindenburg to order a retreat to a defensive line of carefully prepared concrete bunkers and trenches, known to the Germans as the Siegfried Line, and the Hindenburg Line to the Allies. This move, called Operation Alberich, made a mockery of the sacrifices and glacial gains of the Somme.[39]

The scorched-earth policy entailed destroying all communications and buildings, but leaving the British free, bar booby traps and snipers, to walk across abandoned front-line German trenches to the open land beyond all the way to the Hindenburg Line. DON'T BE MAD, ONLY WONDER! advised a mocking German sign left in the ruins of Péronne.[40] The celebrated Sam Mendes film *1917* was set against this precise backdrop. It recounts the perilous mission of two lance corporals charged with delivering an urgent message to stop a futile attack on the Hindenburg Line.

* * *

A taxi speeds us the 6 kilometres from Warlencourt to another Hôtel de la Paix, this time in Bapaume, an important frontier town since the Romans, and where a French army was defeated by the Prussians in January 1871. Four decades later, from 1914, it became a German stronghold. The Allies never came close to taking it back during the Somme. When the Germans elected to abandon it in 1917, they left a time bomb in the town hall which killed two local French representatives and nineteen Australian soldiers. The Germans returned the following year, taking the ruined town back in the Spring Offensive, and clung on to it tenaciously until repeatedly attacked by Australian and New Zealand forces in August 1918.

After breakfast the following morning, I hobble on flip-flops haltingly to the town's CWGC cemetery which contains just eighty-four Australian graves, and twenty-three German. It is hard to say why the smaller cemeteries can be more affecting. Rory's arrival has certainly given me a new burst of life, allowing me to power ahead yesterday, and I want to turn it to advantage. I spend a long time in the shade of the trees searching for peace and meditating to the sound *ma-ra-na-tha*, an Aramaic phrase meaning 'come Lord'. Meditating can bring me a sense of profound unity in which all striving and worry disappear. But not today. I am desperate to find some interior space to immerse myself in during my pilgrimage of peace, but find myself constantly dragged back by the pains and anxieties I am experiencing.

We return to the Butte by 10 a.m., posing by a sign on the main road declaring *LIGNE DE FRONT 20 NOVEMBRE 1916*. With another day cut short yesterday because of my feet, we have to go due north, with Arras our target this evening. It means sacrificing the plan to walk along the banks of the Ancre to Serre, the northern point of the battlefield, at the opposite end to Maricourt. Needs must, but I'm very sorry not to be walking that stretch. It is where I begin tours of the battlefield, leading parties past the Hawthorn Ridge and the Newfoundland Memorial Park, through Hamel, Thiepval and Ovillers before stopping at La Boisselle and on to Albert for rum and rations. A week's history can be packed into just a few hours in this gloriously tragic procession. Through these villages thirty years ago my co-author David Walsh and I organized a walk to raise money for Leonard Cheshire's disaster relief fund, a forerunner of the Western Front Way.

Starting a Somme visit in a cemetery has always seemed right, and at Serre one is spoilt for choice, including Serre numbers 1, 2 and 3. Soldiers in the 'Leeds Pals' fought here, including Horace Iles, who was fourteen when he joined up. The battalion, made up of volunteers from the northern city, was formed in September 1914 but landed in France only in March 1916. That May, Horace was invalided home. His family tried to persuade him to disclose his real age to stop him returning. He didn't want to let his mates down, he protested. 'For goodness sake Horace, tell them how old you are... you are only 16. You have seen quite enough now: just chuck it up and try to get back,' wrote his older sister Florrie to him on 9 July. 'If you don't do it now you will come back in bits and we want the whole of you.'[41] She was too late. The letter was returned to Florrie marked 'Killed in Action'. Buried in Serre Road No. 1 Cemetery, he survived just moments on 1 July. Of the 750 in the battalion who went over the top that day, only forty-seven walked away when relief came, with 248 killed and the rest wounded or missing.[42]

Was the Somme worth it? Rory and I debate, as we trudge away from the battlefield. For the Bradford and Iles parents? For the million families who lost loved ones, or had them return home battered in mind or body? It took us just 20 kilometres to walk the length of the entire battlefield yesterday: 30,000 paces, thirty-three casualties for each pace. I imagine a million souls hovering lightly above the ground behind us. Usually, I feel a deep peace when I leave the Somme. Not this time.

My father was too young to experience the Somme, but not too young to hear it. Born on 29 May 1916, just a month before the madness started, he was living with his Ukrainian parents and four siblings in, as described by the 1911 census, a 'two room' dwelling in East London. Did the reverberation of those shells, cannonading along the Somme Valley, out across the Channel, over the mudflats of the Thames estuary and through the cranes, gantries and davits of the Port of London, form, in the early hours of a hot summer night, some of my father's first memories?

Just when I thought the answers to my questions were beginning to clarify, the immensity of what happened on the Somme tells me I have much further to travel.

11

Artois

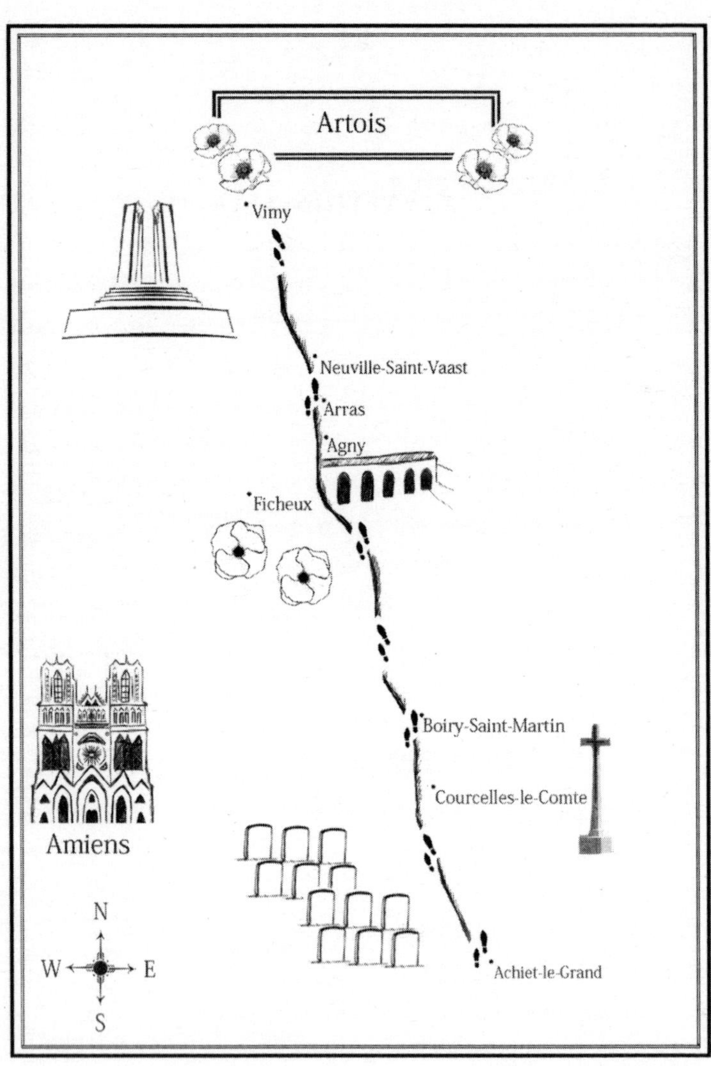
Artois
Vimy
Neuville-Saint-Vaast
Arras
Agny
Ficheux
Boiry-Saint-Martin
Courcelles-le-Comte
Achiet-le-Grand
Amiens
N
W
E
S

MY PATH FOR THE next two chapters takes me to a less-travelled part of the Western Front, between the two iconic battlegrounds of the Somme and Ypres. I've been looking forward to this section precisely because it is new to me, and there's much flag waving to be done for the Western Front Way. My chief worry, with just nine days to reach the Channel and complete the walk, remains whether my body will take me there before it's engulfed by enemies of its own. To maximize my chances of success in my own 'race to the sea', every superfluous load has been jettisoned, planned detours along the route scrapped, and Iron Man pretensions shelved, with taxis arranged to carry my rucksack to each new destination. After these, I have no other cards left to play. I'm becoming immune to pain and sleep-deprived nights. I am not remotely disturbed by what the medics would not totally rule out, rabies. Only Covid or – a new concern – sepsis can do for me.

I will be leaving behind me the bucolic villages and small towns I have walked through since Soissons to journey into a markedly different landscape. Picardy's expansive farmlands yield to industrial towns; the Somme's chalk hills and hamlets to the plateaus, coal seams and slag heaps of central Artois. White for black. Green for grime. Artois formed part of the Spanish Netherlands until the Thirty Years War, when Cyrano de Bergerac, no less, helped capture it for France. Since the treaty of 1659, Artois, while retaining its Spanish influences, has remained solidly in French hands, though every invading army, from

Marlborough and Wellington to Bismarck and Hitler, saw fit to trample unabashed across it.

Prosperity arrived in the second half of the nineteenth century with the mass mining of coal; so, by the First World War, the area was prosperous, supplying energy to industry across northern Europe. Béthune, Lens and Douai were among the towns that rapidly expanded. This was France's 'black country', supplying two-thirds of all national coal needs, while depositing slag heaps, railways and canals liberally in its trail. Fighting was so heavy here in 1915 precisely because the French government needed to seize back its industrial base and the coalfields from the German invaders.[1] Rebuilt after 1918, and again after 1945, the region went into slow decline in the late 1960s, as in Britain, with strikes foreshadowing closures and stagnation. There is evidence aplenty of this still as I walk through its heart.

Thrillingly, my route will take me at last to the battlefields near the Belgium border where Douglas Gillespie fought. 'We still have brilliant September days,' he wrote on this very day 106 years ago. 'A keen strong north wind today which makes the distances clear; better weather for the artillery, which is very important here.'[2] I feel myself drawing daily closer to Douglas's life, as he himself, though he could not have known it, was drawing daily closer to his death.

Fighting came to Artois mostly in the war's odd years, 1915 and 1917, in contrast to the major set-piece battles in the even years elsewhere on the front. Encounters took place here during the 'race to the sea', notably at Arras which successfully denied the historic city to the Germans, leaving behind 40,000 French dead in their national cemetery at Notre Dame de Lorette. Three battles of Artois were fought in 1915, including at Vimy Ridge. The year 1916, a quiet one in Artois, saw the British replacing the French in the trenches after they were redeployed south of the River Somme. All hell let loose in 1917 with the Battle of Arras from 9 April to 16 May. Presiding over the southern part of the sector was General Allenby, known as a hard man, though he cared deeply about his only child, Michael. Every night, before going to bed, he asked the officer in charge of casualty lists for the day: 'Have you any news of my little boy?' Upon hearing the words 'no news' he went to bed reassured. Not for long.[3] Michael died of wounds that July in Belgium, aged only nineteen.

All this lies ahead of Rory and me as we set out from the Butte de Warlencourt along farm lanes soft underfoot, with scant clouds high against a warming sky. 'Are you going to be OK?' asks Rory solicitously as we stride forwards. 'Think so,' I respond without thinking, anxious to reassure him, and feeling guilty I am letting him down. After an hour, we pass a brick-and-mortar memorial to Private Christopher Augustus Cox VC. A stretcher-bearer throughout the Somme, he was in action again in March 1917 just to our north at Achiet-le-Grand. Mid-attack, when his fellow stretcher-bearer was shot, he continued alone, carrying on his muscular back to safety several wounded. Second Lieutenant Sydney Chapman observed him: 'in front of Hill 130 in the front wave attending to the wounded. He showed absolute contempt of the volume of machine gun fire and heavy artillery... I found he had similarly treated six others, two of whom were wounded a second time while he was carrying them.' Cox survived the war and served in the Home Guard from 1939.[4]

What motivated men to be stretcher-bearers, often out in the open above the trench line? In place of weapons, they carried medical supplies and identification, which did not stop the enemy targeting them nor indeed the patients they were carrying. Before the First World War, wounded had been left till the end of the battle to receive the paltry medical attention on offer. By 1914, medical science was teaching that the earlier the wounded could be attended, the less the damage to their organs and limbs, and the higher the chance of survival. Many volunteers opted to serve as stretcher-bearers after 1914, and a fresh supply followed the Military Service Act of January 1916 which introduced conscription. Any able-bodied men not willing to fight thereafter had to register as Conscientious Objectors (COs), some 16,000–20,000 doing so.[5] Some became stretcher-bearers, but many more ended up in the 'Non-Combatant Corps' working in the kitchens and transport. A hard core who refused to wear uniform at all were imprisoned. The response to COs from the public and jingoistic press was unsympathetic: they were portrayed as weak physically, lacking in moral courage or effeminate.

Before serving, stretcher-bearers attended a ten-week course learning how to negotiate their way along communication trenches and in No Man's Land, how to administer morphine and keep patients awake, to splint limbs and dress wounds, as well as how to dispense day-to-day advice, including the management of feet, frostbite and body lice. A high proportion of stretcher-bearers were killed or wounded. It was a common experience too for them to find their patients dead when they handed them over.[6]

Regimental Aid Posts were the first line of care for the walking wounded, located usually in a dugout or at a trench corner some 200 metres behind the front line. Here a Royal Army Medical Corps (RAMC) doctor would be available with bandages and field dressings, as well as with brandy, cocoa and biscuits. Stretcher-bearers would bypass them in most cases to deposit their patients at Advanced Dressing Stations (ADS) situated in destroyed buildings some 400–600 metres behind, which offered a wider range of medical care. Triaging would take place here by members of the Field Ambulance before the wounded were taken on to Casualty Clearing Stations (CCS). As the war progressed, they benefited from improved surgical care and more nurses. Catering for some 200–500 patients, CCSs could still be vulnerable to enemy fire, though situated well behind the front lines.[7] Infection was a major cause of death, with no antibiotics for treating blood poisoning. High numbers died too on stretchers waiting to be seen. When battles were raging, the medical help available was swamped many times over. CCSs would often be located near railheads, so those who survived them could be taken on to the much better resourced base hospitals.

This puts my own ailments in perspective. Who cares about bloody blisters? Well, two medical friends tell me I should, specifically looking out for telltale signs of sepsis, a quick-developing condition when wounds become infected, which requires immediate medical attention. Long known as septicaemia, this often-fatal disease was little understood in the war. Body wounds and trench foot were frequent causes, but no reliable treatment was available to the soldiers contracting it at the time. But for the advent of penicillin, my own father would have died from it in North Africa in 1942. Before I left England, I hadn't even contemplated sepsis; but now it's featuring big-time. Rory says a close friend developed it in hospital, not entirely reassuring. Beth, my colleague at the National Archives Trust, tells me a friend nearly died of it when a mosquito bite became infected. Indeed, a series of friends I speak to by phone that morning all gleefully relay horror stories with sepsis. When we stop for lunch at Achiet-le-Grand, I nervously inspect my feet. There's no hiding the fact – the sides and soles of both my feet are still a mess, and there are definitely deep red lines around the outside of two of the blister wounds, one of the telltale signs. So while tucking into a pot of raspberry yoghurt with disconcerting dark crimson red lines in it, I decide to go that evening to A&E in Arras to have them checked out.

We press on northwards through this sleepy area of France while I eagerly try to engage Rory in some 'channelling' conversation. At the French necropolis at Courcelles-le-Comte we pause to learn about the *poilus* who died in a desperate struggle to deny the village to the Germans in late 1914. Most lie in the ossuary, but thirty-nine were selected to be buried in a decorative cemetery laid out on three sides of a square. An annual ceremony takes place in early October to commemorate those who died across south Artois. Did French soldiers fight with more determination than the British because they were protecting their own country, families and homes? we wonder. Absolutely not, would be the stock reply; but it's difficult to imagine that British soldiers would not have had an extra vim if they were fighting in trenches in Kent, in Warwickshire or Aberdeenshire.

Consider the fighting that returned here near the war's end in the Hundred Days Offensive in 1918. This time, the British, not the French, were in the action. The Paris–Arras–Lille railway passes over our route, and a battalion of the Royal Scots were charged with capturing a key crossing point during the night of 22–23 August 1918. Hugh McIver, a runner who had already been awarded the Military Medal and Bar, repeatedly carried messages between observation posts. While under heavy fire he captured a machine-gun post single-handed, alerting a British tank which, in the confusion of battle, had opened 'friendly fire' on its own troops. He was killed nine days later; the VC he was awarded is on display at the Museum of the Royal Scots in Edinburgh Castle. Whatever thoughts were driving him on to acts of extraordinary bravery that night, it's hard to imagine he could've given even more had he been fighting to protect his beloved Scotland.[8]

On we press, transfixed as we come over the brow of a hill by the sight of brilliant sunlit fields under a brooding indigo sky. We whip out our phones for photographs, but when the inevitable rain follows, I'm unable to whip out my waterproof clothes with the same alacrity because they are not there: alas, overly exuberant bag-pruning this morning meant they have gone ahead by taxi to Arras. After five minutes, I am wet to the bone. Just in time, Rory produces a waterproof bag into which I place my passport, Covid pass and money. Along the waterlogged farm track we trudge for thirty minutes until the cloudburst has spent its fury. The drenching leaves me strangely elated: it's only water, I think, it will soon go away. I walk on in silence with a fresh inner strength.

NON AUX ÉOLIENNES À FICHEUX (no wind turbines in our backyard) shout a number of angry posters as we walk through the two villages of Boiry. I saw virtually none before Reims, but increasingly they have scarred the countryside since. The two drenched figures (one more so than the other) spark into life. 'I suppose they're necessary if we are to have clean energy,' Rory says. 'But would you be happy living under the shadow of one?' I reply. We don't resolve that conundrum, but it's excellent channelling. As we approach Arras, our route is barred by a high earth bank thrown up by a new bypass. We try to scramble up the incline, but the rain has turned the earth to mud, and we need to make a long detour. Sodden and squelching, for these two bedraggled walkers the extra kilometre is a frustration.

Sassoon's poem 'The General' was written about the Battle of Arras in April 1917. As Rory and I trudge towards Arras, packs on back, we cannot but hear: '"He's a cheery old card," said Harry to Jack / As they slogged up to Arras with rifle and pack.'

Were the generals in the Arras battle, so castigated by Sassoon, deserving of his obloquy? Lessons had been learnt from the Somme the year before: the initial artillery bombardment was condensed and better targeted, shells' reliability had been enhanced, and a 'rolling barrage' introduced to protect the advancing infantry. More light machine guns, rifle grenades and accurate maps were on offer. 'Everything that was possible to be needed [was] in the front line ready for the attack,' opined Charles Ward of the Middlesex Regiment.[9] 'We had really got the German artillery right down,' Kenneth Page of the Royal Field Artillery concurred.[10] Perhaps Harry and Jack's trust in 'the General' was not entirely misplaced. For even though there was to be no breakthrough at Arras, significant advances were made, at least early on. Might Sassoon have had any qualms about his poem if he knew that Allenby, a prime suspect for his ire and by now commanding in Palestine, broke down in tears in public when told about Michael's death, and promptly read out a poem by Rupert Brooke for solace?[11]

'Our success is already the largest obtained on this front in one day,' trumpeted Haig to George V in a written report, reminiscent of a headmaster trying to impress his governors.[12] He was not wrong in his assessment; by Western Front standards the first day of the Battle of Arras had been a remarkable success. But, as with the war's preceding offensives, the advance then slowed, the German defence recovered, and dreams of a breakthrough evaporated.

We walk to Arras via the outskirts village of Agny, the scene of intense fighting on the first day. Tucked away down an unprepossessing alleyway is the CWGC's Agny cemetery with 408 graves. It takes time to locate one in particular among the uniform headstones. Poet Edward Thomas. His odyssey has affected me deeply since as a student I read the memoirs of his widow Helen, written to assuage her grief, *As It Was* and *World Without End*. After Oxford, Thomas scraped together a life as a writer and critic who revelled in the countryside. His poetry took off under the encouragement of his friend Robert Frost, his poem 'The Road Not Taken' inspired by their long walks together. It prompted Thomas to join up in 1915 at the comparatively old age of thirty-seven. He bade farewell to Helen and their three children in rural Essex in spring 1917 before he left for the front. Every time I take a party to the cemetery, I stand by his grave and we read Helen's description of that final parting: 'I stood at the gate watching him go. He turned back to wave until the mist and the hill hid him… Panic seized me, and I ran through the mist and the snow to the top of the hill, and stood there for a moment dumbly, with straining eyes and ears. There was nothing but the mist and the snow and the silence of death.'[13] Members of our party recite his poems too, not least his two four-liners 'In Memoriam' ('This Eastertide call into mind the men / Now far from home…'), and 'The Cherry Trees' ('The cherry trees bend over and are shedding… Their petals, strewing the grass as for a wedding / This early May morn where there is none to wed'). Joanna loved Thomas almost as much as Gerard Manley Hopkins. I can see her now on one of our final visits, the cherry tree in the cemetery shedding its blossom, reading the poem dressed in her sapphire-blue coat and scarlet French beret, a tremor barely perceptible in her limpid voice.

Their marriage was not always easy. Neither was ours. Like Helen, Joanna would have been happier if I had not had such a restless spirit.

'We cannot say why we love people,' Helen wrote in her memoir, and I know not either. 'There was never any pretence between us, all was open and true,' as it was between Joanna and me, though I hope against hope I was kinder to her, always aware as I was of her vulnerability and the fierce need I felt to protect her. 'If we love deeply, we must also suffer deeply; for the price for ecstatic joy is anguish. And so it was with us to the end,' Helen wrote.[14] And so it was with us, until I was unable any longer to protect her, to the end.

The Battle of Arras opened at 5.30 a.m. on 9 April 1917, Easter Monday. 'I thought what a funny time to start an offensive, Easter time,' recalled Private Victor Polhill of the London Rifle Brigade. 'It seemed all wrong to me.'[15] Edward Thomas's diary was never written for that day, so we don't know what he thought. Did he hear the shell coming towards him? Helen was later told that he had been killed smoking his pipe from a shell landing nearby compressing his organs, while leaving no outward mark on his body. Only later did it emerge that he was killed much more messily, shrapnel passing through his chest.[16]

We proceed into Arras in sombre mood; we could identify with Private Clark who recalled: 'I tell you we were glad to get a rest and had had nothing but a few biscuits during the last four days, and the drop of tea we got at Arras was the best I've tasted in my life.'[17] Our own drop was somewhat stronger when we arrived at L'Hôtel de l'Univers, a former Jesuit seminary. The monks might have approved.

Prudence suggested I should carry through with my intention to have my blisters checked for sepsis. After an hour in *accidents et urgences* at Hospital Center d'Arras, hospital number three of the walk, and with no indication how much longer I had to wait, I ask at the reception when I might be seen. 'It could be four hours, could be longer,' was the gist of the reply. With so many coughing and wan faces all around me, I decide to quit Covid Central and walk back untended. My instinct is I will be fine; but I'm losing confidence in my instincts, and don't know if I'm being *têtu*. Back at the hotel, which is being much more Covid-cautious than those I stayed in further south, a minimalist dinner is on offer, but it more than suffices as we plot our route for the next day.

Up early the next morning for interviews on the twentieth anniversary of 9/11, the day that did not end history, then down for a simple breakfast of croissants and preserves wrapped in cling film, and we are off. 'How can you not fall in love with Arras?' Rory asks, as we walk along cobblestones in the beautiful morning light. A wool town since the Romans, it flourished in the Middle Ages, producing tapestries for the English market: Polonius is killed by Hamlet behind 'an arras', i.e. a tapestry. We wander around the Grand Place and the smaller Place des Héros, as I have done so often, with their seventeenth- and eighteenth-century Flemish-Baroque gabled buildings, badly damaged in the war but meticulously restored, brick replacing wood. Deep below us lies a labyrinth of sophisticated tunnels dug by expert colliers, containing hospitals, guardrooms, canteens and dormitories, a subterranean metropolis beneath a medieval city. The tunnels were around 20 kilometres in total, and some parts led directly to the front line to the east. 'Surely not that long?' Rory takes some convincing that they were really that long; so did the soldiers.

A short walk takes us to the Arras Memorial, commemorating 35,000 who died in the sector with no known grave. Despite the busy arterial road close by, it is always quiet here. The flowers and lawns in the cemetery accessed down Lutyens's wide steps, with over 2,500 gravestones, are always beautifully tended. 'I had the inescapably powerful feeling that we were looking at the graves of our children,' said Wellington College parent Nick Parkhouse. Standing by the Stone of Remembrance looking down over the graves one Friday evening at the start of one trip, he read to our party the supreme passage from John Donne's 'Meditation XVII': 'No Man is an island entire of itself... if a clod be washed away by the sea, Europe is the less... Never send to know for whom the bell tolls; it tolls for thee.' Words that could have inspired Gillespie's dream. Nick read the poem twice, actually, in successive years. Once with Helen, his doctor wife, present; the following year, alone, her life like a clod suddenly washed away by her sudden death.

Walter Tull is one of the more surprising people to have their names carved in the stone walls of remembrance. He had played football for Northampton Town and then Tottenham Hotspur before the war. Arriving on the Western Front in November 1915, he was commissioned as an officer in May 1917. Nothing exceptional in that, apart from his father coming from Barbados. The 1914 *Manual of Military Law* specifically excluded those not of 'pure European descent' from being appointed officers in favour of commands being given just to 'natural-born subjects'.[18] This regulation notwithstanding, Tull became the first black officer in the British army to see action in war (though two had served in the RAMC), fighting in both Italy and France. He proved an unusually popular and resourceful officer until his death aged twenty-nine in the Spring Offensive of March 1918.[19] His commanding officer wrote that 'the Battalion and Company have lost a faithful officer, and personally I have lost a friend'.[20] We look at his bare name, just ten carved letters to mark such a life. Ten letters.

Close by is the Arras Flying Services Memorial, commemorating the 1,000 airmen killed on the Western Front who have no known grave. We look at the globe on its summit, with a band around it denoting the line of travel of the sun each 11 November. Royal Flying Corps pilots' average training time was just fifteen hours of flight. I had not realized till recently that an absurdly high proportion were killed before even seeing action – from their own flying errors or technical faults with the planes. Improved aerial reconnaissance maps for the infantry demanded for battles like Arras came at a high price. For optimum results for camera lenses of the time, pilots had to fly slowly and low over enemy trenches and strongholds, easy targets, not least when the Red Baron and his elite Jagdstaffel 11 (Fighter Squadron 11) prowled the skies.[21]

Walter Tull in 1917.

The Arras cemetery reminds us how quickly what had begun so optimistically on 9 April turned into the traditional story of stalemate and fiasco. The daily British casualty rate in the Battle of Arras was 4,000, higher than in any other battle in the war, including the Somme. It resulted overall in 125,000 German casualties to 160,000 British, a third of them Scottish, their greatest concentration of the war.[22] When the fighting stopped, bar the successes at Vimy Ridge and on the first day, the line had moved little. The benefits of a coordinated attack with the failed Nivelle Offensive were a chimera. 'No doubt exceedingly important strategic objectives lay behind the British attack,' German commander Erich Ludendorff carped. 'But I have never been able to discover what they were.'[23] Families losing loved ones on the Somme or Passchendaele at least could say they had died in a battle that people had heard of at home. But killed at Arras? What was that…

The city of Arras at large hasn't had a fine record in wars over the last two centuries. Adjacent to the cemetery are the walls of the fortress designed by Louis XIV's great military engineer Vauban. His fortifications proved rather more successful at Verdun; here, they failed to prevent the town being occupied by attackers in 1814, 1815, 1870 and 1940.

The Gestapo commandeered the fort during the Second World War, executing over 200 members of the Resistance. A concrete post marks the spot today. Whatever the weather, it is always cold and dank here. No single place so chills those on my trips, adults as well as children.

It is already 11 a.m., and we need to be moving. Vimy Ridge, two hours away, is our target by lunchtime. 'We're still having beautiful weather... Sunny days and misty mornings,' wrote Gillespie on 11 September 1915.[24] 'How the hell did they cope?' Rory asks as we trudge across early autumnal fields. An average of 144 days of combat was the maximum length American medics in the Second World War estimated infantry could bear before cracking.[25] That makes Rory's question all the more pertinent – because in every way conditions for troops fighting in Europe were far worse in the earlier war. Even today, psychiatrists do not know what precisely causes a military breakdown – noise, fear, lack of sleep, loss of comrades. Called 'shell shock' then, and post-traumatic stress disorder (PTSD) now, it rendered those who suffered from it paralysed by fear and exhaustion. Up to 10 per cent of officers were reporting symptoms of nervous shock by the end of 1914. That surprised me, because these were not volunteers but hardened regulars.[26]

The term 'shell shock' was coined by psychologist Charles Myers in an article in the *Lancet* in 1915. Explanations given for the syndrome included the physical impact of exploding shells on brain and body, the psychological toll on men unable to process emotionally extreme and unfamiliar experiences, and a concern that the soldiers were wilfully seeking a passage home. This last explanation sadly won the day with the increasingly worried military and politicians. With up to 40 per cent of casualties on the Somme described as having shell shock, their fear was it might rise to epidemic proportions. The order came down in 1917 that the term 'shell shock' was to be banned by the army, and even forbidden in medical circles. Magic! The Battle of Passchendaele had only 1 per cent of British soldiers reporting the condition shell shock. But the longer the war continued, the more the suffering. By 1918, twenty-one military hospitals were devoted solely to those with mental problems. Three years after the war's end, 65,000 men were still diagnosed with them. This figure scratches the surface – estimates of those severely traumatized by the war are many times higher. My grandfather, who we meet again in the next chapter, was just one of them.[27]

As enlightened medics realized, multiple problems arose because the men's experience of the war was so utterly removed from their pre-war daily lives, be they privates or colonels. Enforced separation from loved ones was distressing and disorientating, and in some encouraged the formation of intense male relationships and confidences. Mostly these close relations were platonic, but the removal of society's conventional structures sometimes enabled homosexual acts to take place between men, even though severely outlawed.

Understanding the full extent is all but impossible as fear of discovery drove behaviour underground, but we know at least 230 British soldiers were court-martialled, convicted and sentenced to prison for homosexual offences during the war.[28] Edward Brittain, brother of Vera whose groundbreaking *Testament of Youth* was published in 1933, had received the Military Cross on the Somme before being killed on the Italian Front. The year after her book's publication, Edward's commanding officer revealed to a stunned Vera that her brother was being investigated by Military Police for homosexuality.[29] Shortly after being forewarned by a fellow officer, he was killed by a bullet through the head, going recklessly ahead of his men. Was it effectively suicide, driven by his horror of imminent court martial, imprisonment and family disgrace? More than likely. More than likely too he was not the only tormented soul driven by the same fear to the same lonely end.

* * *

Author and publisher J. R. Ackerley might have been one of them if his war had gone differently. He led his men into action in early May 1917 outside Arras. But wounded and captured by the Germans, he became a prisoner of war. Realizing his homosexuality while in captivity and far away from military regulations, he later wrote about the experience in his play *Prisoners of War*. E. M. Forster helped his literary career develop, though, unlike his patron, Ackerley made no secret during his lifetime of his sexuality once his parents died. He himself played a vital part in developing the careers of several young writers, including W. H. Auden, Christopher Isherwood and Philip Larkin.[30]

Robert Graves hints at a deep bond with a friend David Thomas killed on the Somme in his poem 'Goliath and David'. Many of the war's poets including Sassoon and Owen had gay inclinations. Never before had men been thrown together, day and night, front line and in reserve, eating and drinking, with no front doors to retreat behind. Ironic that I'm writing this during Covid lockdown when we are forced apart as never before: in the war, people were thrown together as never before. Fear drove them together then; fear drives us apart now.

The war wasn't all high drama with men charging over the top when whistles were blown. Set-piece battles were the exception to the rule of soldiers' predictable daily routines. Private Walter Nicholson captured it perfectly: 'Trench fighting goes on throughout the war, but a battle comes like a hailstorm, mows down a field of corn, and is over for a year.'[31] 'Stand-to' for an hour before dawn kicked off the Tommies' day. Sentries, working parties and those lucky ones who had been asleep rapidly smartened up to be inspected by an officer, before an issue of rum and breakfast. The day now began in earnest: soldiers not on sentry duty were given chores accompanied by much grumbling, filling sandbags, repairing and cleaning trenches and fetching supplies from the rear, before 'stand-to' at dusk. At night, new trenches would be dug, working parties to repair the wire and observers would go out over the top, seeking cover when Verey lights cast their bright green glare, while others rotated between sleeping and sentry duty.[32]

For all these duties, never before had the men enjoyed so much free time, opportunities for talking and joking, games and smoking. Work in the fields and factories back home had been far more relentless and solitary. Trench life was similar for the Germans: 'We met for coffee in the dugout of one or the other of us every day, or sat together in the evening over a bottle or two and smoked, played cards, and comported ourselves like soldiers of fortune. Those pleasant hours in the dugout outweigh the memory of many days of blood and dirt and exhaustion.'[33]

For those who could afford it, cocaine and opium, regarded as being as harmless as tobacco, were freely available over the counter at pharmacies in Blighty. Their widespread use led to moral panic, expressed by the *Daily Chronicle*: '[Cocaine] will drive, unless the traffic in it is checked, hundreds of soldiers mad.' The Defence of the Realm Act 1916 made all non-medical possession of cocaine an offence, requiring a doctor's prescription for use.[34] Morphine remained in use widely to kill pain and in euthanasia. A soldier just beyond Vimy in May 1915 who had 'no eyes, no nose, no chin, no mouth – and he was alive' was administered 'a fourfold dose.'[35]

As Rory and I approach Vimy, the ground rises beneath us. Far below are the tunnels along which the troops proceeded to the front line safe from enemy fire, ensuring no repetition of the waste on the Somme when some units (famously the Royal Newfoundland Regiment) had to advance out in the open because the communication trenches were clogged, to be mown down before they reached their own front line.

The Canadians prepared their attack at Vimy in 1917 meticulously, the soldiers being shown precise models of the battlefield, assigned very clear objectives and tasks, and trained for several weeks beforehand. With thousands of pieces of artillery deployed, vastly superior in numbers to the Germans, and use of the new '106 fuze' to ensure shells detonated, the preliminary bombardment and rolling barrage proved invincible.

'Chaps, you shall go over exactly like a railroad train, on time, or you should be annihilated,' warned General Julian ('Bungo') Byng, the Canadian Corps commander. Early success was then pressed home, and within five days, the ridge had been captured, including Hill 145, its highest point. As we walk to the Canadian memorial which sits on it, past the preserved trenches and small museum, we pass countless shell indentations from the week-long preliminary barrage, as in a Paul Nash painting.[36]

The Vimy monument, designed by Canadian architect Walter Allward, speaks to me more than any of the other large memorials along the front, with limestone pylons, representing Canada and France, pointing to the sky. Allward's task was of course simpler than that of Lutyens at Thiepval or Reginald Blomfield at the Menin Gate in Ypres, whose creations had to find space for 72,000 and 55,000 names of the missing respectively. Allward needed room to engrave the names of just 11,285 Canadian soldiers who died in France with no known grave, which he did at the base of the memorial.[37] The architects required the names in the top rows to be readable by families looking up from the ground. Achieving this task makes Lutyens's Thiepval, admired by many, seem almost lumpy: it has majesty and presence, but not the timeless artistry of his Cenotaph in Whitehall.

Allward includes twenty symbolic figures, the largest of which, Canada Bereft, stands between the two pylons. Head bowed in grief, she represents the sorrow of all Canada at her lost sons. The power of the monument has played its part in the widespread belief that, at Vimy Ridge, the Canadian nation came of age. A similar story is told about the birth of Australia and New Zealand at Gallipoli, and used to be told about South Africa at Delville Wood on the Somme.

The permanence of this monument contrasts with the transitory nature of those who unveiled it in July 1936. Edward VIII presided over the ceremony in his capacity as King of Canada, in the presence of President Lebrun of France. Edward had abdicated before the end of the year, while Lebrun was swept away along with the Third Republic four years later, to be replaced, in another echo from Verdun, by Pétain. The month before, on 2 June 1940, Hitler had visited Vimy Ridge, charging the world's press to photograph him strutting on the monument's steps.[38]

Four years later, in September 1944, it was Field Marshal Montgomery who stood victorious at Vimy. Shot through the lungs by a sniper during the 'race to the sea' in late 1914, he had been a staff officer at the Battle of Arras, where he became understandably critical of the disregard of soldiers' lives shown by the generals. As a commander in the Second World War, he insisted on meticulous preparation before battle and heavy firepower to minimize casualties, exactly as the Canadians executed at Vimy.[39] Just a week before his visit, British tanks had driven through Arras as part of the great armoured charge across France that had followed victory in Normandy – the rapid breakthrough that British Great War generals dreamed about but only partially achieved during the Hundred Days Offensive of 1918.

How different was the limited progress in 1917. 'When we reached

Field Marshal Montgomery at Vimy Ridge in September 1944.

the top of the ridge, a remarkable panorama unfolded itself. We could see all the red-brick mining villages around Lens,' recalled Canadian George Hancox.[40] Rory and I survey that same view from the monument on top of Hill 145, looking out on a clear September afternoon over the slag heaps and mining towns, and across the plateau towards the hills around Ypres, seeing almost to the English Channel. At the same moment, a thought comes to us jointly: we are looking out over the terrain where Gillespie fought – and died.

Here at last, the place where the story of my walk was conceived. Perhaps answers will begin at last to flow.

12

Forgotten Flanders

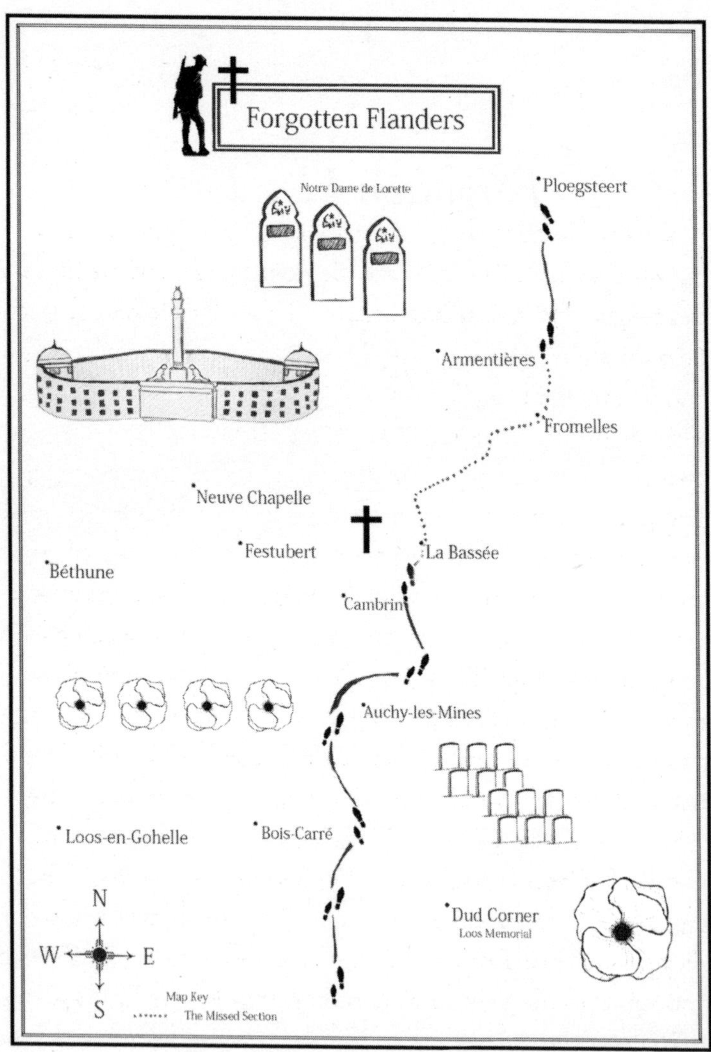

Forgotten Flanders
Notre Dame de Lorette
Ploegsteert
Armentières
Fromelles
Neuve Chapelle
Festubert
La Bassée
Béthune
Cambrin
Auchy-les-Mines
Loos-en-Gohelle
Bois-Carré
Dud Corner
Loos Memorial
N
W
E
S
Map Key
The Missed Section

An excited call from Tom Heap, great-nephew of Douglas Gillespie, just as we approach the front-line area where his great-uncles fought. The family has discovered a stash of letters in an attic written throughout his short life. He reads me some extracts over the phone. 'The best of luck,' Douglas writes to brother Tom with perhaps a touch of envy on 4 August 1914. 'It is a pity we can't go in as a unit,' he continues, because 'the war may be over' by the time he too joins. 'Dear Mother,' he writes three weeks later, bemoaning his poor eyesight, 'I have received a note from the War Office to say that I am physically unfit for military service – so that's an end to that.' Except, as we know, it wasn't. The letters reveal Douglas to be a diligent son, writing words to his sister that are ageless: 'Of course if I stay in this country it would be easier to keep daddy in retirement happy somewhere in reach of London, for I can see that will be the great difficulty for mother if he does retire.' Everyday irritations fill his letters, as when he is stuck waiting near Beaconsfield for Cys Asquith, the prime minister's son, to arrive for a walk: 'but he is late as always.'[1] A more rounded view of Douglas emerges from Tom Heap's extracts than from the letters selected for publication in 1916. But I still am little closer to understanding why he came up with the walk, or what he hoped to achieve by it. I arrange with Tom to come up to the family home after my return and to see the letters in depth. Perhaps then I will comprehend.

Over the next two days, I'll be walking across the flat plain between Vimy Ridge and Messines Ridge to the south of the Belgian town of Ypres.

This is French Flanders, ceded to France with Artois in 1659, still partly Flemish-speaking, and continuously fought over throughout history. The land this side of the border town of Armentières was heavily industrialized in 1914, full of coal mines, slag heaps, stolid buildings and brick stacks. The battlefield was soon scarred with ruins and mining detritus. It has been transformed since, the trenches and shell holes filled in, the historic towns, villages and industries rebuilt, but with no battlefield heritage sites or museums until recently to tell the story about what happened here. Only the ubiquitous CWGC cemeteries. Where once stood No Man's Land, now stand E. Leclerc and Carrefour supermarkets plying their trade beneath the towering pyramids.

* * *

'Forgotten Flanders', French Flanders, the subject of this chapter, contrasts with Belgian Flanders into which I will be walking once over the border. Belgian Flanders is proud of its war history, a memory of it almost every kilometre. But here, it is as if the land wanted to forget all that happened on it, turning its back defiantly on the old century. The French themselves did not fight here after the 'race to the sea', which might explain some of the indifference. But not the indifference of the British, who did. Who now has heard the names Armentières, Aubers Ridge, Festubert, Loos and Neuve Chapelle, the British battles of 1915? The families of those who were killed certainly did, over 50,000 in total. There's another reason why the battles are so little remembered: they were all largely failures, the fruit of a flawed strategy and a stubborn reluctance to learn. An added reason for anger: idealistic 25-year-old Douglas Gillespie perished on the first day of one of these battles, Loos, the biggest battle the British army had fought up to that point in history, and one of war's most foolish.

We finished the last chapter standing on Vimy Ridge. We now travel back in time two years. From the battle there in 1917 to late 1914 and to 1915. The popular view of the war, of willing innocence crushed by wilful incompetence, of 'lions led by donkeys', was born in these fields and in these battles. Well did historian Lyn Macdonald title her book on the year 1915, *The Death of Innocence*.[2]

The 'race to the sea' had been fought by the BEF, largely made up of 'Regulars', full-time army soldiers who had enlisted before war broke out. But a new breed of men was baptized into death in life on these plains. First up were the 'Territorials', established in 1908 as a volunteer adjunct to the Regulars, but with roots back to the yeomanry first established to combat Napoleon. Initially seeing action in late 1914, the Territorials filled the gap between the near destruction of the BEF Regulars and the arrival of Kitchener's 'New Army', the brainchild of the imperious War Secretary himself. He sought 500,000 volunteers to fight on the Western Front to be ready by mid-1916, hence Alfred Leete's famous recruitment poster of the moustachioed Kitchener pointing his gloved finger straight ahead. Unlike many, he believed that the war, once the central European powers mobilized, would never be over by Christmas, hence the need for large-scale manpower on the front. He fought for his New Army to have its own divisions, and for their training to be sped up so that they would be ready to fight in the Dardanelles in August, and at the Battle of Loos in September 1915. The New Army's 'Pals Battalions', comprising men from a particular locality who served together, came into their own on the Somme, ready for glory. Kitchener never lived to see his brainchild's decimation on its battlefields: setting sail from Scapa Flow towards Russia in early June, he died when his ship hit a mine west of the Orkneys, standing to the end erect on the quarterdeck.

The Territorials had swelled the five divisions of the BEF in August 1914, and, with the New Army, to sixty divisions by the summer of 1916, some 2 million men in arms. Into the trenches in Artois vacated by the French flooded these new recruits, many of whom had never travelled far beyond their local parish.[3]

Kitchener didn't lavish the same attention on his New Army's strategy or munitions. The Germans, who had neither need nor intention to attack, dug in securely, finding the flat plain as easy to defend as the British found it difficult to advance. But advance the British were determined to do, even if they had no clear or worthwhile strategy. The experienced German soldiers with superior machine guns simply mowed down line after line of infantry. British shells were deficient in quantity and quality, an issue which came to a head after *The Times* revealed a catastrophic lack of shells at the Battle of Neuve Chapelle in March 1915. The crisis it sparked prompted the formation of the coalition government, with Asquith remaining as prime minister and Lloyd George promoted to a new post, Minister for Munitions.[4]

Were lessons being learnt on the battlefield? British failures in March to May 1915 (Neuve Chapelle, Festubert, Aubers) revealed a common pattern – early gains halted then reversed due to poor intelligence and lack of support. The British response was to plan another battle fought in these fields using exactly the same tactics which had thrice been seen to fail. Thus in ignorance was Loos conceived. Having roundly condemned the Germans for their use of gas at Ypres in April 1915, the British then based their hopes on it in September. It largely proved a failure. John French, commander of the BEF, who had leaked a document on the shortage of shells in the summer to discredit Kitchener, was himself replaced by Haig at the end of 1915 after the debacle. Yet not after Loos were the lessons learnt; on the Somme, the High Command would make many of the same tactical mistakes again.[5]

Nor did 1915 see better news elsewhere. On the Eastern Front, the Germans delivered a crushing victory over Russia, throwing the Tsar's armies into a 'Great Retreat'. Meanwhile, the daring if high-risk Gallipoli campaign on the Dardanelles Straits took precious resources from British attacks in Flanders. On 16 September, Gillespie was distraught to learn that his tutor at Oxford, G. L. Cheeseman, had been killed at Gallipoli: 'To me, he was very much more than my tutor... He was the most loyal and honest friend... He will always haunt those rooms at New College where I have talked with him so often far into the night.'[6] Gallipoli proved another total failure in a bleak year, the British Cabinet ordering total withdrawal in December 1915. Churchill, the originator of the plan but by no means solely responsible for its conduct, withdrew in shame from public life for the trenches, where we meet him again later in this chapter.

We wrench ourselves away from the magnificent view from the Vimy Memorial, a decision eased by the gathering storm clouds suggesting it is time to move. Down the hill we speed on our way, through Givenchy-en-Gohelle and never-ending Lens to Loos-en-Gohelle, not once passing any indication of the war bar one solitary town memorial. We arrive at four at La Maison d'Ingénieur in Loos, a delightful, quirky hotel run as a cooperative. The 'house of the engineer' had been built by a prosperous colliery owner on a plot which fortuitously was too far behind the lines to suffer shell damage. Unblemished, it stands in its full nineteenth-century splendour.

Rory leaves tomorrow: it is our last evening together and in the high-ceilinged dining room, over the best home cooking of the trip, we discuss the progress towards realizing the Western Front Way. 'Do you think we will pull this off?' I ask, as I munch through a vegetable stew from the commune's garden. 'Look, after all this, we bloody well have to.' Rory has poured so much of his time and imagination into the walk, all but putting his career on hold for it. He got in touch first in early 2016 when the walk was aired, mad keen on the vision, and joined us on the pioneering trip that summer with his father, who died of cancer soon after too, another bond between us. 'I reckon it's going our way at last. Come on, we're both too invested to let this fail.' Years of lobbying are beginning to pay off, we agree, glacial though it's been to persuade the French of the benefits of a walking path. A cycling route, in contrast, they are lapping up, with enthusiastic backing of the French cycling body AF3V. Perhaps this should be our way forward in

France, we wonder over a particularly deep red Rhône, and piggyback the walking route on to it? We clink our near-empty glasses and toast Belgium, where the path is mostly marked out with signposts. Back up in my room, a doctor friend tells me by phone he can't decide whether the photographed blisters I sent him are becoming infected: if my temperature rises in the night, I should immediately check myself into the hospital.

The next morning after Rory leaves, Laurence, one of the hotel owners, offers to drive me to the infirmary. The only way I will complete this walk is if I have my blisters and wounds professionally treated, so I accept his invitation with gratitude. Two hours later, and after a lot of 'ooh la LA's, the nurse finishes bandaging my feet properly for the first time since Lou's deft care in Saint-Jean. Before she lets me go, she insists that the doctor sees me again. He looks grave. 'You risk long-term damage to your feet if you keep walking,' he tells me in faultless English. I had been fearing this, postponing the moment by evermore Compeed and Nurofen. 'Can I walk 15 kilometres a day as long as I do it slowly, please?' I beg. 'I am sorry. I don't think that's a good idea,' he responds. He sees I am crestfallen. But with a Gallic shrug and 'You should be resting,' off he sweeps. I take stock. I look imploringly at the nurse. She glances down at me on the bed, wanting to support me but unwilling to contradict him. So I reason to myself: he hadn't said an outright no. And I really don't think that 15 kilometres will do me any harm. In my mind, the 15 kilometres is 20, or 25. And if I really can manage 25 kilometres a day, I'll be able to finish on time.

Out of respect for his advice, nevertheless, I decide to walk only 15 kilometres today, a long way short of my planned destination, Armentières. After fond farewells back at the hotel and a lavish tip, to say nothing of a tipple to see me on the way, the comrades come out to wave me off. A farewell hug with Rory; in fact hugs all round. In my next life, I will be a comrade.

I'm back on my own. It's a warm Saturday morning, and I listen to music as I set off walking, adjusting to the solitude. I miss Rory, but I soon re-establish my rhythm. I knew I had to walk this year on my own so I could be single-minded: 2016 had fallen short in part because it was a constant carousel of new faces and I spent too much time worrying about their enjoyment. Solitude has helped me focus and, perhaps, to think. As I come down the hill under the thundering A21 towards Dud Corner Cemetery and the Loos Memorial, my phone vibrates. It is Rachel Sylvester, chair of *The Times* Education Commission, an idea I took to the paper in May, born from years of frustration seeing our education system infantilize and limit the achievement, joy and creativity of students and teachers: for the first time ever, we now have a holistic inquiry from early years to adult education.

'It's not great news, Anthony. I've got cancer,' Rachel blurts out. I stop in my tracks and prop myself up against the cemetery's perimeter wall to steady myself; sad and upsetting news always shakes me. 'They say they've caught it early and the outlook is very positive.' 'That's very good. They absolutely would not say that if they were not a hundred per cent certain,' I respond, having experienced many such consultations with Joanna. 'The medics never once told us less than the truth, however hard it was to hear,' I tell her. Rachel and I talk it all through. She wants to mull over the impact on our work together. After the call ends I wander around the cemetery lost in thought. I cannot hear news of cancer without becoming emotional. The tears come to my eyes and sting, as can happen when one hasn't cried for some time.

I'm the only person in this vast 2,000-grave cemetery, named after the pile of unexploded ('dud') shells left at the end of the war. It is enclosed at the sides and at the rear by the memorial, a 5-metre-high wall carrying the names of 20,638 British and Commonwealth soldiers mostly killed at the Battle of Loos. The architect, Herbert Baker, was the third in the British trio, alongside Edwin Lutyens and Reginald Blomfield, responsible for many of the memorials and cemeteries on the front. Baker was responsible too for the War Cloister at Winchester College, a spacious roofed quadrangle believed to be the largest private war memorial in Europe. Dedicated in 1924 in the presence of Prince Arthur, third son of Queen Victoria, it was one of the final public events in the headmastership of Montague Rendell, to whom Douglas wrote his famous letter.

There it is. Panel 125 to 127 of the Loos Memorial. 'Alexander Douglas Gillespie. Argyll and Sutherland Highlanders. 4th Bttn attd 2nd Bttn. Died 26 September 1915, age 26.' The date of his death is wrong.

I am numb. Here it is indeed, but I feel nothing. I need time to process it, and instead let my attention be caught by another name carved nearby, that of the youngest man to be awarded the Victoria Cross during the First World War, Private George Peachment, killed like Gillespie on the opening day of the battle, 25 September, aged eighteen years and four months. Here too are engraved the names of three rugby internationals who had played their last game: Walter Dickson (Scotland), Douglas Lambert (England) and Richard Williams (Wales). Recorded as well is the man who poet laureate John Masefield described as the greatest poetic loss of the war, Charles Sorley, best known perhaps for the lines in his final poem recovered from his kit: 'When you see millions of the mouthless dead / Across your dreams in pale battalions go.' It's no disrespect to Sorley to suggest that Wilfred Owen was the greater poet. Owen, though, had written little of value by the time he was twenty, Sorley's age when killed; so who knows how he too might have blossomed?

Musing on his 'mouthless dead', I leave the cemetery to continue into the town of Loos, blasted into the sky during the two-week battle in 1915. Undistinguished post-war architecture bequeathes it little sense of identity, nor can I find physical indications that five times in history this most unfortunate town came close to obliteration. The collapse of jobs is the latest blight, with 1,000 homes recently pulled down because the owners had moved elsewhere. I pause in Loos's centre, as gaunt faces staring straight ahead walk by, reflecting that something is not right in this unreal city. The British cemeteries and the slag heaps (now a UNESCO heritage site) sit uncomfortably alongside the anonymous architecture. A town without roots, like a person without roots, is no town at all.

New light industries are showing the way forward, as does the creation on the centenary in 2017 of a Canadian Monument at Hill 70, marking the successful capture of the hill in August 1917 by the Canadians in a bid to relieve pressure at Passchendaele. I wonder whether the years to come will see fresh commemorative initiatives across French Flanders – and will people want to visit them if they do?

At last I find my way out of the town and into open farmland. For the rest of the day, I'm going to be walking close to the British front line along the entire 15-kilometre length of the Battle of Loos. My gravel path takes me past harvested fields due north, but to my disappointment with no visible evidence of the fight. After an hour, I see the Bois-Carré Cemetery off to my left, and walk through wheat stubble to it. Most of the dead here date from fighting in 1917, with a small number of graves from the Second World War when, during the BEF's retreat to Dunkirk in April 1940, a Casualty Clearing Station was set up in the cemetery. Back on my track after 100 metres, I see another cemetery, Lichfield Crater, off to the left. With just fifty Canadian burials, it is a tenth of the size, made up of one large grave, formerly a British trench. It typifies the British commitment to keep bodies where they were first buried, unlike the French who in 1922 removed 800 graves from a cemetery opposite to the mighty necropolis at Notre Dame de Lorette.

Half a kilometre on, I cross the D39 near St Mary's Advanced Dressing Station Cemetery, marking an objective reached on 25 September 1915. One of the graves belongs to a former Wellington College student, John Kipling, son of Rudyard, killed on the third day of the battle. Some 707 Wellingtonians altogether died in the war, a number of mouthless dead exceeded only by the alumni of Sassoon's and Sorley's alma mater Marlborough and by Eton College. John Kipling's name, recorded on one of the many memorial boards in Big School, attracted much interest when I was the head at Wellington. I would have placed his father firmly on the 'difficult parents' list that difficult parents never imagine we keep. Certainly, the way Rudyard worked the system to allow his short-sighted son to join the Irish Guards in September 1914, shortly after his seventeenth birthday, suggests that he would have been no pushover. A hundred years later, he would have been bullying me to get his son into the top college at Oxbridge. Pushy parents, now as then, almost invariably do more harm than good to their children. The worst even lead them to the same tragic fate.

Not till 1992 did official recognition come that this grave before me was indeed that of John Kipling.[7] Little is known about how battle-scarred soldiers responded to orders from seventeen-year-old Master Kipling with no experience of war; little is known too about how he was killed after last being seen advancing towards the German line, possibly with a head wound. Did the need to prove himself make him reckless? Did guilt explain why Rudyard came to France to tour base hospitals and interview survivors, desperately seeking to discover what might have happened? Most seventeen-year-olds I have known at school were more children than adults, their whole lives ahead of them. As I walk away, still simmering, I feel a deep sorrow at the parental egotism which led young John to be thrown down the throat of this ravenous war. The loss of Kipling's youngest child propelled him to shape what became the CWGC, and to pen two of its key iconic and moving inscriptions: 'Known unto God', on all unidentified graves, and 'Their Name Liveth For Evermore' on cemeteries' Stones of Remembrance, from the Bible's Ecclesiasticus. Kipling came wondrously close to Gillespie's vision too in the speech he wrote for George V delivered at the CWGC cemetery at Terlincthun outside Boulogne in 1922: 'I have many times asked myself whether there can be any more potent advocates of peace upon earth than this massed multitude of witnesses to the desolation of war... we cannot but believe that the existence of these visible memorials will eventually serve to draw all peoples together in sanity and self-control.'[8]

Reflecting on the many contradictions of Kipling, I walk along grassy farm tracks towards the rebuilt village of Auchy-les-Mines. En route, I pass by the site of the Hohenzollern Redoubt (named after the Imperial royal family of the Kaiser, indicative of its prestige), which was known as one of the strongest positions on the entire front line. Falkenhayn had ordered it to be built to strengthen positions behind the German front line, on a slight rise that had a view over the entire battlefield. It became a skilfully constructed nest of trenches, observation posts and machine-gun positions, protected by belts of dense barbed wire. Even the British official history said the repeated attacks on it, towards the end of the battle, 'brought nothing but useless slaughter of the infantry'.[9] Little remains today, just a slightly raised patch of scrubland a short way off the path.

I have now reached almost the northern end of the battlefield, very close to where Gillespie fought. 'Your attack will find particularly favourable ground between Loos and La Bassée,' said French commander Joffre when urging the British into action. This is the ground I have walked over today, and I can tell you, there's nothing favourable about it, nothing whatsoever. John French was so worried about the lack of any protection for attacking British soldiers, and how the slag heaps and plentiful buildings provided cover for German machine guns, that he asked Kitchener to reconsider. Press ahead, the great man wrote back, 'even though by doing so we may suffer very heavy losses'.[10] Indeed.

Almost everything that could go wrong went wrong. The artillery did not cut the barbed wire. The 150 tonnes of poison chlorine gas blew back into the British trenches. Gas masks the soldiers wore meant they couldn't see or communicate. When the British battalions advanced, as French foresaw, German machine guns were ready to greet them. Most of the attacks on the northern part of the battlefield failed completely, though some success had been achieved in the south of the front.

The following day, two New Army divisions were sent to reinforce the positions that had been taken. They were shot to ribbons: 'Barrels burning hot and swimming in oil, they traversed to and fro unceasingly; one machine gun alone fired 12,500 rounds that afternoon,' recorded one German unit diary. Of 10,000 British soldiers who advanced on 26 September, around 8,000 became casualties. After the two-week battle came to a predictable end, some 60,000 British and some 30,000 German casualties were left in its wake. German soldiers subsequently nicknamed the area 'Leichenfeld von Loos' – the corpse field of Loos.[11]

Few have captured the utter futility of Loos better than Robert Graves. Platoons, he wrote, had been ordered to advance side by side. When one officer whistled for the advance to continue: 'He jumped up from his shell-hole, waved and signalled "forward!" Nobody stirred. He shouted: "you bloody cowards, are you leaving me to go on alone?" His platoon sergeant, groaning with a broken shoulder, gasped "not cowards, sir. Willing enough. But they are all F-ing dead."' (Swearing, with 'fuck', 'shit' and 'bloody' the most common, was everyday language amongst men and officers freed from the conventions of polite society, as a coping mechanism and sign of virility.)[12] Graves was struck how on the night of 25 September, the Germans let his own Royal Welch Fusiliers go out into No Man's Land to collect the dead. He watched morbidly transfixed as they were brought back, their bodies frozen in rigid positions, some 'bandaging friends' wounds, crawling, cutting wire'. It brings to mind the dead at Pompeii.[13]

My 15-kilometre limit today has been reached, maddeningly on the cusp of where Gillespie was killed near Cambrin at the far end of the battle. This is torment. To have come so far but to be unable to see where Douglas fought seems very cruel luck. What should I do? I debate the options. I could start back here tomorrow morning? But then I will risk not reaching the North Sea. I am too tired to think it through now, and decide simply to cut north-east to La Bassée and call a taxi to Armentières. As I enter the town, I cross

The damaged cathedral of Armentières in 1918.

the Aire–La Bassée Canal which Gillespie referred to so often in his letters, and which until early 1915 had marked the divide between the entire British and the French armies, till the floods of Territorials and New Army soldiers allowed the British to stretch all the way down to the River Somme.

Herbert Baker's Indian memorial at Neuve Chapelle is one of the sites I have been looking forward to seeing, and is another I must miss. It commemorates the 4,700 Indian soldiers who died in the battle, of the 140,000 who served on the front; and the British Indian army itself, established after the 1857 rebellion and wound up on independence in 1947.[14] With the BEF stretched to the limit, they were sorely needed, playing a crucial role in the First Battle of Ypres, and manned a large part of the British front till the new recruits arrived, including half the attacking force at Neuve Chapelle.[15] At the end of 1915, the Indian Corps redeployed to the Middle East, though some labour and cavalry companies remained in Belgium and France (as we saw at Nancy) until November 1918. The memorial was opened in 1927 by Conservative minister, India Secretary Lord Birkenhead. Watching from the crowd was Kipling whose poetry breathed Empire. And yet, despite its apparent permanence, the mighty Raj had just twenty more years before final dissolution.

My taxi is waiting for me outside La Bassée's *mairie*. Exhausted, disappointed and masked, I slump down into the back seat. It is market day in Armentières, the streets full of stalls and customers, and I must walk the last half a kilometre to the Hôtel Joly. The unexpectedly jolly patron is sitting on a dining-room chair on the street outside his hotel amidst the swirl of market stalls. He springs up and proudly shows me through to the garden-room suite which, truth to tell, has probably seen better days. It is Saturday evening and a big day for the town, so I'm not surprised that the restaurant he booked for me ('the best') turns out to have lost the reservation. Several *désolés* and bowings later, I make my departure.

It gives me an opportunity to walk through this most beguiling town whose prosperity since medieval times has been based on beer and fabric. In October 1914, it was the site of the ferocious Battle of Armentières. The Allies clung on to it, but as the war ground on, it acquired a louche reputation for ale, profanity and fornication. All three were brought together in the song popular with soldiers, 'Mademoiselle from Armentières', or 'Inky Pinky Parlez Vous' (which acquired multiple lyrics, several referring to creaking bed springs). Here, as in no other town on the front, the 'Tommies' (named after 'Tommy Atkins', slang for ordinary soldier) had free rein to pursue 'Jane Shores' (rhyming slang for prostitutes). In April 1918, the Germans eventually took the modern-day Sodom or Gomorrah, having showered it in mustard gas (a more deadly gas than chlorine, and first used in 1917). So thick was it that they couldn't inhabit the town for two weeks. When finally forced to retreat, they blew up buildings of value, including the belfry which had somehow survived four years of bombardment. By the end of the war, three-quarters of Armentières was in ruins, and all public buildings and churches were rubble. I marvel at the tasteful rebuilding at the hands of architect Louis Marie Cordonnier, using Flemish gables and red brickwork.

I awake refreshed in my titanic garden suite to the sounds of bells summoning the town to church this Sunday morning. Over breakfast, I decide I cannot go back to La Bassée: I have to press on and try to manage 20 kilometres today to add to the 15 kilometres yesterday. It will still make it touch and go, whereas retracing my footsteps, even to see the hallowed Gillespie ground, will be fatal. Decision made, I walk around eating my croissants (I am alone) and look at framed interwar menus on the wall from when the Hôtel Joly was the last word in elegance in the entire region. The town festival dinner was held here in November 1931, a riotous seven-course banquet concluded by *gâteaux Armentièrois*, washed down by Morlant champagne. It rather outguns the salmon tart and banana washed down with Orangina I consumed in my room last night. While waiting for the taxi to take my rucksack to Ypres, I chat to the patron about my best route out of the town. Dare I say, my French is becoming a bit more fluid? I can't wait to try it out on Sarah; I hope it will impress her, though I am far from confident. Leaving as the bells chime 9 a.m., I zigzag my way through Armentières's empty streets, making for the border. The lack of new building is hardly surprising: the town, which touched 30,000 in 1914, is still far below that size.

On the Avenue Léon Blum, I pass a small rock monument with a plaque bearing the words '*En Hommage à nos Libérateurs. 6 Septembre 1944*'. Armentières had no sooner been rebuilt after the war than it was pulverized again in the Second World War, to oust the Germans who had captured it in May 1940. I reflect on the fluidity of forgotten Flanders as I cross the unmanned border into Belgium past an empty building telling us in big red letters RÉPUBLIQUE FRANÇAISE. BUREAU

DES DOUANES. 'Hoy,' a group drinking coffee outside a café shout loudly after me, pointing back down the road from whence I came. I imagine I've broken some protocol on face coverings, or failed to have my Covid documents checked. But when I approach them, they tell me I had dropped my glasses on the pavement. Yet again, I am overwhelmed by the kindness of strangers.

I find a quiet bench to sit down and reflect. I have made it to Belgium. Just 100 kilometres more to go and I'm still going. I had long imagined this border-crossing moment but, now it is come, as when I saw Douglas's name yesterday, there is no elation. I speak to Sarah and share my thoughts. Does missing that 15-kilometre chunk of the walk yesterday mean I can no longer claim that I have completed it? But it's more than mission credibility. I have lost my bounce and am cross with myself that I didn't build in any rest days. I've been walking non-stop now for thirty-two days – bar the wedding trip to the Dordogne, delightful but hardly a rest. I've allowed no time for my body and mind to recover and it's caught up with me – my feet, guts, back, spirits and sleeping are not in great shape. I'm cross about something else too. I agreed long ago to speak about my recent book on the 300-year history of the Prime Minister at a literary festival on Friday 17 September, the entire reason for my hurry and the pressure I have been putting myself under. The organizers declined understandably to let me appear online after the walk had to be postponed. My talk has to be *in person*. So I have no margin for error. I have to make it to the English Channel by Wednesday 15 September latest. That's just four days away.

I decide to keep on the busy N365 direct to Ypres due north from Armentières, so am delighted to find a broad strip of tarmac by the side of the road to keep me away from passing traffic. Safe from cars it most certainly is; but not from cyclists. I am now in Belgium, and the first difference I note is their sheer volume and attitude. They take a very dim view of this figure walking along their cycle lane. I continue to use it but am on constant tenterhooks looking in front and behind me in case the swarming hornets approach.

After an hour, I am at Ploegsteert. A metal cut-out of Churchill, cigar in mouth, stands by the side of the road announcing he fought here. In January 1916, following his demotion after the Dardanelles, he was given the rank of lieutenant colonel and put in charge of a battalion from the 6th Royal Scots Fusiliers. This was a quiet section at the time, chosen perhaps because he had the least chance of causing injury to himself, and possibly those under his command. In February, he wrote to his wife Clementine: 'I have now had two officers hit out of five in my HQ mess and there is no doubt that we are rather a target.'[16] He took part in thirty patrols into No Man's Land, a task often considered too risky for a lieutenant colonel. A fellow officer recalled, 'He never fell when a shell went off; he never ducked when a bullet went past with its loud crack. He used to say after watching me duck, "it's no damn use ducking; the bullet has gone a long way past you now."' His men regarded him as utterly fearless.[17]

The novelty for this restless man soon started to wear off, though, and he became maddened that further advancement was denied him: 'how powerless I am! Are they not fools not to use my mind – or knaves to wait for its destruction by some flying splinter?'[18] He had remained an MP, and in early March 1916 he was back in England on leave which he extended to twelve days to attend the House of Commons. Pushing for swift progress with the tank, very much his brainchild, was one of his crusades. Soon after his return to Ploegsteert, he agitated to be back in action on the battlefields of Westminster, and when in May his regiment was merged, he was granted permission to return to politics.

On my left, I pass the Ploegsteert Memorial to the Missing commemorating more than 11,000 United Kingdom and South African forces who died in the sector without any known grave. Hyde Park Corner Cemetery directly opposite had been a prominent junction in the war just to the north of Ploegsteert Wood. One of the eighty-three British burials I seek out in the cemetery is that of Ronald Poulton Palmer. To aficionados, he was the illustrious captain of England rugby who won a famous Grand Slam in 1913–14, crowned by his four swerving tries against France. Of the twenty-seven rugby internationals killed in the war, they rank him unquestionably the greatest. Concealed to me, until I saw Hugh Salmon's play *Into Battle* in the autumn of 2021, was a richer dust. I am thinking of his deep compassion, displayed in his commitment at Oxford to the Christian clubs for working boys and later in his concern for workers at the Huntley and Palmer biscuit factory in Reading. 'What he hated most… was the artificial barriers that hold people apart,' spoke William Temple, later Archbishop of Canterbury, at his memorial service in Oxford in May 1915.[19] I hear an echo in those words of another 25-year-old idealist born weeks earlier, who met his end nearby.

Less than a month before his death, Palmer took part in a friendly football match behind the lines. I don't know what he would've thought of the game that took place near here that first Christmas Day, but I doubt he would have disapproved. Widespread if not universal fraternization occurred along the front on 25 December 1914, with agreements to bury the dead, exchanges of drinks and cigarettes, photographs and the occasional football match. I visit the official UEFA memorial opened in 2014 by its then president, Michel Platini, no doubt valuable instructionally for visitors, if of questionable historical veracity. Some embarrassment may have been caused by Platini receiving a four-year ban for ethics violations soon after, but nothing can take away from the magnificent eruption of the human spirit here as elsewhere on the line in the war's first Christmas.[20]

I reach the London Rifle Brigade Cemetery in Ploegsteert. Just twenty-two of its men buried here died fighting in the sector, but a plaque in the entrance commemorates the 1,922 from the Territorial Force who died in the war. Sarah's grandfather fought throughout the war with them, a coincidence that warms her, and survived. My own

In search of the track near the Belgian border.

grandfather, Wilfred Willett, nearly didn't. When war broke out, he immediately broke off training to be a doctor at London Hospital to enlist. He was a keen shooter at St Paul's School, so the London Rifle Brigade (LRB) was his natural regiment. First, he decided to marry his sweetheart, Eileen Stenhouse, who he had met at the May Ball at the end of Cambridge, and whose aristocratic Scottish family disapproved of the Willetts' background in commerce (building!). So they married in secret and then he joined the regiment for training at Crowborough in Sussex. Before embarking from Southampton to Le Havre on 5 November, he found a cottage nearby for them to spend their last night together. 'I could think of no words to comfort her that did not seem forced,' he later wrote. 'As soon as I had blown out the candle, I could feel her tears dropping on my cheek… the night was full of sorrow and neither of us slept.'[21]

After a long train journey via Abbeville and Saint-Omer, he arrived in Belgium. Gillespie made a similar journey, the train wheels propelling them forward to a similar fate. On 22 November, Wilfred's battalion moved to the village of Ploegsteert, where they billeted – the brewery just to the south of this cemetery provided their first bath for a month. I don't know when my grandfather, a second lieutenant in No. 2 Company, went into the front line with the regiment to relieve the regulars battered after the First Battle of Ypres. But on 13 December, a Sunday like today, his life pivoted. As the regimental history records: '2nd Lieut. Willett [was] wounded in the head while gallantly going to the help of a man who had fallen victim to a sniper...' Noticing his batman wounded in No Man's Land, he used the medical knowledge he had already acquired to go over the top to assist him, without a moment's hesitation for his own safety. As the history continued: '[He] was unable to take any further part in the war.'[22]

A bullet in Ploegsteert a hair's breadth closer to Churchill's head would've changed world history. A bullet a hair's breadth further away from Wilfred's head would've changed my family's history. Exploiting all her family's aristocratic connections, Eileen acquired a pass from the War Office to cross to France before Christmas to bring him home, a rare mission for a wife, but she was fiercely determined and had a clear intuition that he would die if left in a base hospital. Once back in England, she helped nurse him to health, and fought the doctors who, thinking he would die or be a vegetable, sought to conduct exploratory operations on his brain. Her persistence and love bore fruit, but a full recovery and return to his beloved medicine proved impossible. For a long time, it looked as if he would be unable to have any children. Historian Joanna Bourke opens her seminal book *Dismembering the Male* quoting his memoirs in the Imperial War Museum: as he cradled Eileen that last night, he wonders, 'Should I ever sleep with her again? Or should I be limbless or faceless next time? I would meet her in heaven but in what state?'[23]

After months of torment, they did manage to have children: my mother, another girl and a boy. This idealistic man who wanted to serve mankind as a doctor, survived, unlike Palmer and Gillespie, but he never recovered his self-esteem, his happiness or his life. His span was foreshortened, his days embittered, his chosen career over, making it a misery for him and those who loved him. I grew up inside that story, the novel *Wilfred and Eileen* by Jonathan Smith and the television series that followed, and it can be difficult to separate what's real from the myths all families pass on.[24] But my mother's lifelong sense of foreboding and constant anxiety I know to be a truth; and all because of what happened right here in these woods all those Sundays ago.

A truth too that I inherited these debilitating personality traits, and have never been able to transcend them. If only I could, 107 years later, summon up from the depths all my troubling thoughts and leave them here, right here, in these woods, with the same sounds of birds, where they originated. That would make it, for me at least, a path to peace.

13

Ypres Salient

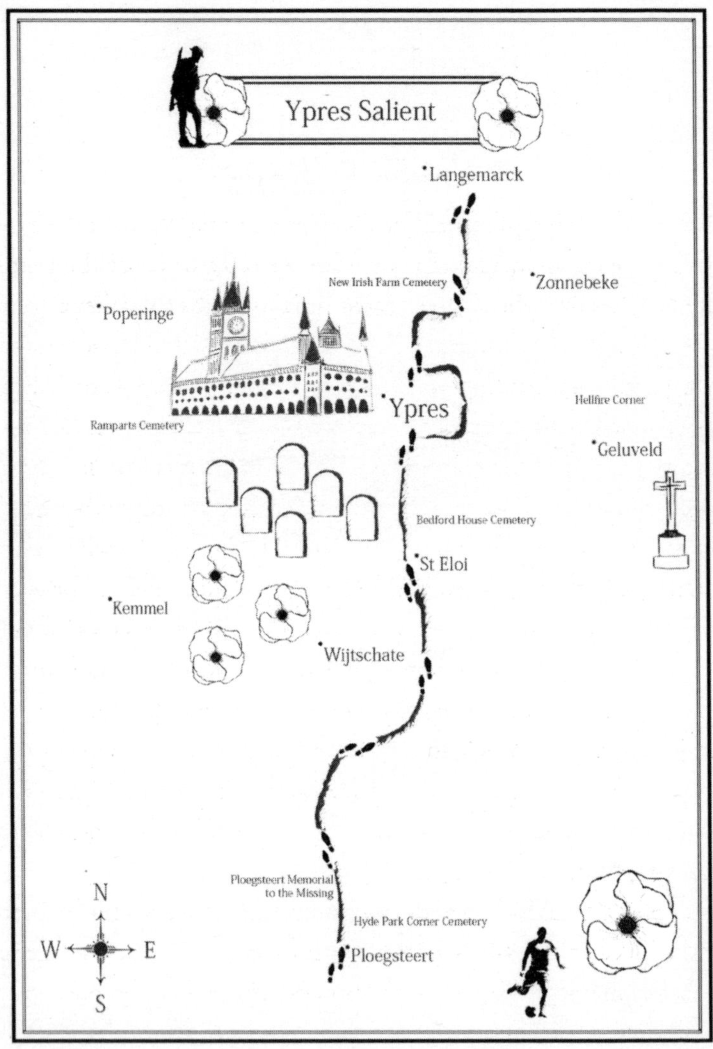
Ypres Salient
Langemarck
New Irish Farm Cemetery
Zonnebeke
Poperinge
Ypres
Hellfire Corner
Ramparts Cemetery
Geluveld
Bedford House Cemetery
St Eloi
Kemmel
Wijtschate
Ploegsteert Memorial
to the Missing
Hyde Park Corner Cemetery
Ploegsteert
N
W
E
S

I'VE MADE IT TO my favourite of all towns and cities. At last I let myself feel some emotion, looking out from the ramparts near the Menin Gate in Ypres over the Kasteelgracht moat towards the salient: to the south, the hills of Messines; to the east, Zillebeke; and Passchendaele to the north-east. Turning back towards Ypres, I gaze over a townscape little changed in 400 years – a blaze of gables, brick chimneys and tiled rooftops framed by the majestic spires of the Lakenhalle (Cloth Hall) and the Sint-Maartenskerk (St Martin's Cathedral). Ypres's deep hold over me started in 1984, more than half my lifetime ago when I first visited, and I saw, half-saw, Wilfred Willett in the stillness between Cloth Hall and cathedral. Few places on earth have been more fought over nor seen a higher concentration of casualties. Yet, unlike so many of the dejected places I have passed on my journey, it has sprung back magnificently, as thriving and exquisite today as ever in its long history. The courage, human ingenuity and imagination that have gone into making this transformation possible continue to inspire me, as they do all who visit.

A quarter of all British and Commonwealth soldiers who fell in the war died here in the salient around Ypres ('Wipers' in the parlance of the British infantry).[1] Whereas the Somme, the war's only comparable British theatre, saw fighting rage for four and a half months, here the fighting continued over four and a half years. 'A more sacred place for the British race does not exist in the world,' said Churchill in 1919.[2] This indeed is the British Verdun, the town that could never fall, the only major town in Belgium never to fall into German hands. Had it done so, nothing would have stopped German forces from advancing over the flat countryside to seize the channel ports of Calais, Boulogne and Dieppe. And had they fallen, the war really would have been over for Britain, and hence for France, which could not have survived alone. The challenge of defending this bastion was all the harder because the Germans surrounded it on three sides and on higher ground, so their artillery could rain down shells at will on the town and defensive positions beyond the city walls. Salients jutting out into enemy territory, as we have seen on the walk, can only be defended at great cost, if at all.

Not everyone was convinced of the salient's cardinal importance. 'There is no doubt that the Salient at Ypres is simply an inferno. It is not war, but murder, pure and simple,' thought soldier Morgan Crofton in June 1915. 'Why we don't give it up now, God alone knows. As a strategic or tactical point Ypres is worthless. The town is a mere heap of rubble, cinders and rubbish. Not a cat lives there now, it is the abomination of desolation.'[3] Sentiments shared by many, and not just among the rank and file.

Crofton's reference to cats was apt; they have long been a symbol of the city. Cats dealt summarily with any pests over the winter amongst the wool stocks in the Cloth Hall. Every May, the medieval town would celebrate the gruesome Kattenstoet festival, when, once the wool had been sold, and the cats' mission accomplished, they were hurled from the top of the tower. The festival still takes place, but in a more genteel age, only soft toy cats now plummet artlessly from it.

With the textile industry at the height of its influence in the fourteenth century, the population of Ypres approached 100,000 and it vied with Bruges and Ghent to be the dominant city in Flanders. The Cloth Hall completed in 1304 was its proudest building, followed closely by the Cathedral of St Martin, completed later in the fourteenth century. Boats on the River Ieperlee would pull up at the west front of the Cloth Hall to deliver and collect their wares. In the 1670s, up popped the irrepressible

Vauban, building his thick walls, moats and frontal fortifications; for a time, they dwarfed the city with their gargantuan size. But in the mid-nineteenth century, Ypres began to lose some of its prominence within Flanders as the waters receded. The River Ieperlee was placed underground so boats could no longer dock at the Cloth Hall. At the same time, the town was decommissioned as a fortress, with military defences demolished and moats filled in, replaced by a park for families. Very civilized. No one envisaged this innocent and exquisite town becoming the centre of the world's first industrial-scale war.

First-time visitors to Ypres are taken aback, as in Albert, when they realize almost everything they are seeing has been rebuilt. In November 1918, the town was a smouldering, forlorn and dangerous place. Gradually, the unexploded ordnance was cleared, and the inhabitants gingerly crept back to live in temporary huts and eke out a living. Pilgrims and tourists started to flood across the Channel from 1919, some hoping against all reason, like New Yorkers amongst the wreckage of 9/11, to find their loved ones. Others wanted to see where they had fought and died, or to return items that they had 'rescued' from the ruined churches. Still others came as tourists: cafés, restaurants and small hotels soon began to sprout up all over the salient. Museums too, as at Sanctuary Wood/Hill 62 to the south of the Menin road, where a local farmer decided to leave a section of the British trench system as he found it. What a good thing he did, because it is hard today to imagine what the labyrinth of interconnected trenches must have looked like before his fellow farmers cleared the debris and filled them in to resume their lives and the more easily to forget. Not all wanted to remember.

The debate all along the Western Front – nowhere fiercer than here – was whether to rebuild towns in modern style, to reconstruct them exactly as they had been before being destroyed, or to build a new town nearby. Churchill was prominent in arguing that Ypres should be left in its decimated state as a permanent memorial, like the French *villages détruits*. Eventually, with the support of Belgian King Albert, the restoration lobby won the day, and the medieval city soon began to rise again from the ashes, guided by whatever original architectural drawings and pre-war photographs could be found. St Martin's Cathedral was thus restored before the Second World War, but with a spire rather than the pre-1914 square tower, as were the cobblestoned streets and the regal Grote Markt (marketplace). Reconstruction of the Cloth Hall began in 1928, a task only completed in 1967, just in time for the fiftieth anniversary of Passchendaele, and the release of *Sergeant Pepper*. The forerunner of the imaginative 'In Flanders Fields Museum' opened inside it, enriched by exhibits found when rebuilding the town.

When taking parties to the trenches, I begin on the ramparts, the ideal vantage point to explain the four battles of Ypres. The surrounding hills, like the rim of a bowl, can be clearly seen, as can where the front line of the salient pulsed backwards and forward. The First Battle of Ypres (19 October–22 November 1914) came at the end of the 'race to the sea' and was a German attempt to knock the BEF out of Ypres and cut off the Channel ports. It failed. The Second Battle (22 April–25 May 1915), renowned for the first mass use of poison gas, was a German attempt to control the high ground around Ypres, resulting in the British front line shrinking some 3 to 4 kilometres, making the town far more vulnerable. It failed to break the British line. The Third Battle (31 July–10 November 1917) was a British offensive designed to break through the German lines, and seize the German-held ports of Ostend and Zeebrugge, from where U-boats were wreaking havoc on Allied shipping. Known also as the Battle of Passchendaele, from the ridge on which the latter stages of the battle were fought, it was the costliest in terms of casualties. It failed. The Fourth Battle (7–29 April 1918) was part of the German Spring Offensive and aimed again to knock the British out of Ypres and advance on the Channel ports. And yes, it failed.[4]

But I'm getting ahead of myself, and must backtrack to my approach into the town on foot from the south. After Ploegsteert, I continued along the Armentières–Ypres road, detouring only to see a museum new to me, the 'Plugstreet 14-18 Experience', another fruit of the centenary, with a spectacular long sloping descent to the underground entrance, over which a glass pyramid lets light on to the galleries below.

Back on the road and avoiding cyclists, I spend an hour climbing gently upwards until I reach the village of Messines (Mesen in Flemish). Adolf Hitler served in this sector during First Ypres, carrying messages from a command centre near the ruined church to Wijtschate, a village closer to Ypres.[5] While not acting as a runner, he painted several pictures of Messines church. One, said to be his favourite, he had with him in Berlin: it now hangs in the local museum. As I stand in front of the rebuilt church this Sunday morning, I reflect how odd it is that Churchill and Hitler, the principal protagonists in the Second World War, both painters, should have fought so closely together here in the First.

A preliminary to the Battle of Passchendaele, the Battle of Messines Ridge (7–14 June 1917) was a short and unusually effective attack, knocking the Germans off the elevation. The British had long been preparing an assault here, and at 3.10 a.m. on the first day, detonated nineteen huge mines. Twenty-three had been planned, but four were aborted due to a combination of flooding, enemy tunnelling and collapsing shafts. One self-detonated in 1955, killing some cows. The other three are thinking about it.[6]

The craters have long been filled in and restored to farmland, but not at Spanbroekmolen, also called the Peace Pool, which lies across open fields to my west. Unlike the Somme's much-visited Lochnagar crater at La Boiselle, this one has filled with water. The scale of the hole never fails to impress: 75 metres across and 15 metres deep. A half-a-kilometre tunnel was dug from the British line, and 90,000 lbs of ammonal high explosive were packed into 1,800 waterproof tins in a huge chamber which was detonated just fifteen seconds behind timetable. But the Ulster troops had already climbed out of their trenches and several were killed by the falling earth in No Man's Land.[7] I like to finish trenches trips here on the tiered ground overlooking the crater thoughtfully created for visitors. We begin with a few moments of stillness, then the party recite poetry or read soldiers' recollections, and share their thoughts about what they have seen. If there is time, we draw or write. If a trip to the battlefields cannot provide an opportunity for creative expression, when can?

The Mont des Cats is clearly visible from Messines to my west, a small hill on the French–Belgian border renowned for its monastery and cheese. Gillespie visited it on 18 August 1915 just before his final leave home. You can hear his excitement: 'It was a marvellous sight, you might go here day after day for a week, and not get tired of it, for on a clear day you could see beyond Arras to the south... I could see the ruined Cloth Hall at Ypres quite distinctly, and the ruined Cathedral Tower, and I could even see the shells bursting over Hooge.'[8]

Messines too offers so much to see. I walk to the CWGC cemetery with its New Zealand Memorial, one of seven on the front, listing over 800 Kiwis who came here halfway across the world only to die with no known grave. ('Kiwis', the name given during the war by Australians to New Zealanders, was one of many to remain popular after 1918.) Samuel Frickleton was carried shoulder high through the streets of Auckland, cheered on by thousands who came out to greet the hero when he came home wounded in June 1918. One of eleven New Zealanders to be awarded the VC, his knocking out two machine guns at Messines became the stuff of legend in a country desperately mourning those who would never come home.[9]

A little further on is the Island of Ireland Peace Park, whose cylindrical Irish Tower design dates back to the eighth century. Its inside is lit by the sun only once a year, at the eleventh hour of the eleventh day each eleventh month. This was the last war that Ireland fought before the end of British rule, partition, and the creation of the Irish Free State in 1922. The site was chosen for this unified and unifying memorial because of the 36th (Ulster) Division fighting alongside the 16th

(Irish) Division. Rarely on my walk has the case for peace been more eloquently expressed than in the words inscribed on the bronze tablet: 'As Protestants and Catholics, we apologise for the terrible deeds we have done to each other and ask forgiveness. From this sacred shrine of remembrance, where soldiers of all nationalities, creeds and political allegiances were united in death, we appeal to all people in Ireland to help build a peaceful and tolerant society. Let us remember the solidarity and trust that developed between Protestant and Catholic soldiers when they served together in these trenches.'

As I walk away on the long straight road to Wijtschate often taken by that supreme racist Hitler, I contemplate these fine words. Why did it require a war on foreign soil to bring Ireland's Protestants and Catholics together, and why did a civil war then break out to drive them apart? How can people of different beliefs and backgrounds live peacefully alongside each other? We know they can. But countering the power of demagogues to whip up nationalistic and racial fervour can be extraordinarily difficult. Yet, this is exactly why Gillespie's path of peace must be created.

My son Adam calls. He has just completed his first week teaching at an academy school in London. 'It's not great, Dad. I think I'm still suffering the after-effects of Covid and cannot find my usual energy. It's frustrating.' 'Can you leverage down your expectations of yourself, give yourself time to bed down gradually in this new job?' I tell him I am having to compromise my own plans on this walk, missing out sites I had wanted to see, for the sake of a greater end, completion. 'I'll try,' he says. He'll be desperate to start flying, and I feel for him. But I know he will prevail, and I'm so proud of him going into teaching, not least into state schools which are so much harder than my own path in the independent sector. I am immensely proud too, as was Joanna, that all three of our children have been working in the public service. I try so hard to be a good father, but I find it difficult knowing how far to intrude. I wish I cared less when they are worried or unhappy.

I've arrived at Wijtschate, nicknamed predictably 'Whitesheet' by British soldiers, which had disappeared off the face of the earth by the time the British captured it during the Battle of Messines. The skeletal remains of Gordon Highlanders killed in December 1914 and left where they fell to rot had been a macabre curiosity of the sector, and only when the Germans were pushed back were they able to be buried.[10]

After another hour walking, with Ypres looming into sight, I'm at Sint-Eloois and crossing over where the front lines stood from mid-1914 to mid-1917. Because the land here is slightly raised and above the water table, it was suitable for mining, with some thirty-three high-explosive charges detonated close by. The constant churn of mine and shell explosions made the ground waterlogged, and with the drainage system destroyed, it made it almost impossible for infantry to attack. Nevertheless, that was exactly what British commanders decided to do on a bitterly cold late-March night in 1916 in the middle of snow and sleet. At 4.15 a.m., mines were detonated and the troops advanced, but in the darkness they became confused about their direction, and when the sleet turned to rain, the water levels in the shell holes, craters and trenches rose and rose.[11] This unholy concoction of rain, mud and mayhem foreshadowed the folly of Passchendaele. I try to ascertain from old trench maps where the front, support and reserve lines once stood, but find it impossible to grasp the layout or to imagine on this benign September morning what the St Eloi battlefield looked like, not helped by its preserved mine crater being closed. I can understand why the troops were confused.

Walking on towards Ypres, I pass Bedford House Cemetery on my right. Château Rosendal stood here before the war, an elegant country house in a wooded park surrounded by moats, whose sole misfortune was to be in the wrong place, just behind the British front line. While the house was being steadily destroyed by German artillery, the British used its deep and generous cellars as a command centre and Advanced

Dressing Station for field ambulances. Those who didn't survive were buried in a series of plots between the moats.

The task of creating the permanent cemetery fell happily to Wilfred Clement Von Berg. Although only an assistant architect at the CWGC's predecessor, the Imperial War Graves Commission, he had an imagination not possessed by all his seniors. Excited by the chance, and encouraged by Lutyens, he 'brilliantly exploited' (in the words of writer Gavin Stamp) the ruins, moats and the irregular features of the land to create the vast, irregular and rambling cemetery I walk around today.[12] One of the largest on the salient, with 5,139 graves, it is eclipsed in size if not presence by Herbert Baker's conventional Tyne Cot cemetery (11,961 graves). While Bedford House lacks Tyne Cot's view across the salient down into Ypres, it offers an idyllic space to understand the four years of fighting. Burials are from all four battles, and well over half are unidentified, which says much about the ground in which they were fought, with the soldiers drowning and losing their identities in the merciless churning waters of the Ypres basin.

That's it. I've had enough for the day. I walk the short distance into the city, entering it by the Lille Gate, before crossing the town to the Ariane Hotel. The relief on arrival is intense. I've only walked 22 kilometres, but it feels as if I have covered twice that distance. The receptionist remembers me from previous trips, and when I explain about my journey, asks if I would like her sister, a nurse who lives nearby, to put new dressings on my feet. 'Yes please,' I respond quickly. Up she comes and spends half an hour gently peeling away the gauzes, plasters and bandages. 'You must rest, Mr Seldon, spend several days here to allow your feet to recover.' 'I cannot do that,' I reply. She sees she will get nowhere and tells me at least to rest up at the hotel all evening. Guilt searches me out: it is the first night I've spent in Ypres and not walked to the Menin Gate for the Last Post ceremony at 8 p.m. Up in my room, I write an article for *The Times* about the walk and tune in to a recording of today's church service at Windsor to hear the new

The ruined Cloth Hall in Ypres during the winter of 1917.

preacher. Sarah was eager that I did so. Sure enough, her first question when we speak later that evening is, what did I think of the service? I like to make Sarah happy.

The day had clearly etched deep into my subconscious, because I dream that Sarah has invited Churchill and Hitler to dinner. I cannot place where it was, but perhaps in the Irish Tower. Reconciliation and forgiveness are the evening's themes. 'Do you feel remorse for the many millions of people who died and the lives you ruined?' I ask the German leader. He doesn't answer but looks at me incensed at the temerity of being questioned and as if he regretted his decision to accept this unusual invitation.

It is heaven to wake up in a clean room in such a beautiful hotel. For a moment, I have forgotten the walk, so it is with a feeling almost of resentment that I start my morning routine: a few yoga stretches while avoiding loosening the new bandages, then I pull back on my threadbare underpants and mud-stained trousers, put on my top and socks, both damp as usual from the previous night's wash, squeeze and twist my feet nervously into my boots, slap on insect repellent, measure out my water, and plan the route for the day. My boot soles, I note, are worn at a steep angle, pushing my knee joints outwards each step I take. Without physio Rupert's 'leg educators', the angle would have been even more intense. Only 100,000 more steps to take, I tell myself, just 100,000.

I'm meeting Geert Bekaert, the CWGC's regional director, at the Ramparts Cemetery by the Lille Gate. I've been too slow getting ready, so I bolt down my breakfast in seven minutes while perching on the very edge of my chair and trying not to get indigestion. I'm late, so I hop along across town in my angled boots, laces still undone flying off in all directions, while finishing a *pain au chocolat*. Hidden from sight, I tidy myself up behind a street corner but am still panting when I arrive at the cemetery. Geert is already there, dressed immaculately with a hint of Hercule Poirot precision, and after some photos, we talk about the prospects for the Western Front Way. The excellent progress being made in Belgium is largely thanks to him and his team. It makes me sad afresh that the same appetite for a permanent pathway doesn't yet exist in France; nor indeed the same appetite to embrace the memory of the war.

I love this cemetery by the water's edge, and the only CWGC graveyard to stand within the ancient walls of Ypres. Built by the old ramparts over what had once been dugouts, it contains 198 burials. The French established it, but after the war was over they moved their bodies to the national necropolis. Six New Zealand Maoris were killed by the same shell here on 31 December 1917, their headstones symbolically grouped together. Rose Coombs, author of *Before Endeavours Fade*, the bible of battlefield tours and beloved by all who visit the Western Front, had her ashes scattered over the grass in 1991. Reginald Blomfield designed it with much sensitivity, with the grass bleeding down into the moat. Most of all, I love being here on an early spring or autumn evening, with the town's lights playing on the water, and the birds singing in the trees above us. It is the perfect place to finish off a first day in Ypres, after attending the Last Post ceremony at the Menin Gate.

I retrace my steps, walking back to the Menin Gate, marvelling at how much of Vauban's ingenuity and theatre remains, not least his protruding pentagonal walls into the moat. Along the top of the ramparts, he planted tall trees to provide cover for soldiers and for the buildings in the town behind, and to let smoke from muskets and cannons linger amongst the leaves to provide a smokescreen.

It is 11 a.m. and I have arrived at the Menin Gate, commemorating 55,000 British and Commonwealth soldiers killed in the Ypres salient with no known grave. The plan had been for the memorial to commemorate every single unknown soldier. But Blomfield's design afforded insufficient panel space for all their names to be engraved for the families to see, so an arbitrary cut-off date of 15 August 1917 was chosen. Those killed subsequently without identified remains are recorded on the memorial at the far end of Tyne Cot Cemetery. These numbered eventually 35,000. Total that up, and it's 90,000 lives ended on the salient, and that's just those with no known grave.

The Menin Gate wasn't part of the original thinking. After 1918, the British government visualized marking out a 'zone of silence' as a memorial in the area where the Cloth Hall and cathedral once stood. But it failed to persuade the Belgian government on the merits of the plan, after objections from local inhabitants caused a rethink. So the Belgians offered a site to its east instead through which British soldiers travelled out to the salient. The British were happy to accept the offer, even though more troops left for the front through other exits freer from enemy fire, including the Lille Gate. By 1921, Reginald Blomfield had finalized his plans for his barrel-vaulted classical design, with the main road passing intriguingly through its midst, and with the lion of Britain, but also of Flanders, atop.[13]

The Menin Gate at Midnight by Will Longstaff.

Six years in the construction, its opening in July 1927 proved controversial from the start. Lord Herbert Plumer, the victor at Messines, said in his address that the memorial had been erected for all those families who had experienced the 'deep void' of having no grave at which to mourn. But 'now it can be said of each one in whose honour we are assembled here today: "he is not missing; he is here."'[14] Sassoon would have nothing of it. In his poem, 'On Passing the New Menin Gate', he wrote:

Here was the world's worst wound. And here with pride
'Their name liveth for ever', the Gateway claims.
Was ever an immolation so belied
as these intolerably nameless names?
Well might the Dead who struggled in the slime
Rise and deride this sepulchre of crime.

One can understand Sassoon's bitterness. But I question whether his artistic fury took full account of the feelings of the families who travelled here, many of whom experienced comfort and solace from seeing their loved ones honoured in this way on such a grand official structure. I am an unashamed admirer of the monument, what it was attempting to do, and what it has achieved for approaching a century. This monument to death is a celebration of life, not least with the vehicles rumbling through it every hour of day and night, and because of the unsurpassed Last Post ceremony. The ceremony's origin lay in a spontaneous Belgian response of gratitude to the defenders of their country (the commitment to defending Belgian neutrality in the 1839 treaty, let's remember, was the reason Britain gave for declaring war in August 1914). So it was, exactly a year after the monument's completion, that the Last Post Association began in July 1928 what rapidly became a nightly ritual at 8 p.m. with local buglers playing the Last Post, followed by a two-minute silence. Every single night since it has taken place, with the exception of the Second World War when it continued at Brookwood Military Cemetery in Surrey, until Ypres was finally liberated in September 1944 by Polish forces and the ceremony was promptly resumed. Nowhere in history comes so close to attaining perfection.

Unruly school parties, casual tourists and hardened servicemen and women fall silent, swept up and transported by something they sense is far greater than they themselves, as the sound of the bugles ricochets and ricochets off the barrel vault, alongside the words of the Kohima prayer: 'When you go home, / Tell them of us who stay, / For your tomorrow, / We gave our today.' For a moment, perhaps longer, all are transported. Time stands still. It is profoundly spiritual.

Clever Blomfield. He solved the problem of every engraved name needing to be clearly readable by the bereaved, by devising a structure on several levels that visitors can climb through and between so as to be always close to the panels. I walk away from it to the Braille model of the monument which stands on a plinth on the ramparts. I close my eyes, marvelling at how it unveils itself like a symphony as I trace my fingers all over it. Replete, I can open my eyes and survey the monument in a new light.

As indeed did Australian Will Longstaff, an official war artist who attended the opening ceremony and heard Lord Plumer speak in July 1927. Unable to sleep that night, he walked round and round the gleaming memorial, when he claimed to have a vision of the dead of the salient ('steel-helmeted spirits rising from the moonlit cornfields') marching towards the battlefields. Soon after, he painted *The Menin Gate at Midnight,* which became one of the best-known representations of the war, not least because of the many Australians unable to afford the trip to Belgium, up to a million of whom travelled within the country to view the picture. Even though Longstaff eschewed any interest in spiritualism, his painting caught a popular mood obsessed with the paranormal. As I study his work, I can't help thinking that his painted spirits are on a journey. Life is a journey to death, his is a journey in death, while I am seeking desperately for this walk to be a journey to life.[15]

What right had Sassoon, has any of us, to be scornful? Mourners came here in the hope of making a mystical connection with those they loved, and some found comfort imagining them walking amid the moonlit cornfields, others that they lived on in some form of afterlife. The bereaved had choices when contemplating the departed, not unlike the planners when considering dead towns. They could see death as final, no afterlife, akin to those planners who wanted to leave destroyed towns forever in ruins to slowly rot into the ground. They could believe in a physical resurrection of the body, as do some Christians, akin to the planners who wanted the town reborn. Or they could believe in an afterlife but not in a bodily resurrection, as held to by many Indian soldiers who fought nearby, akin to planners who wanted to rebuild afresh in a new spirit. Allowing ourselves time to reflect deeply about the meaning of our lives and on what if anything follows death was something the soldiers understandably found hard to do at the time, and indeed is difficult for us to achieve in our busy lives. But this monument, this town, this walk, where unprecedented numbers of the young died before their natural time, compels us to think about such questions. I have seen people dying regretting that they found too little space to contemplate the meaning of their life and death. I think about Gillespie's own searching for meaning after Tom's death in October 1914.

It prompts me to reflect on it being such a male war. Where were the women? Might there have been peace in the world in 1914 if women had ranked among the politicians, military leaders and officials? Apart from the long-suffering mothers, wives and daughters at home, the men only saw French women at the front when being served drink and food in *estaminets* or sex in brothels, or British women in medical and driving roles. Olive Mudie-Cooke combined the latter two roles when, in January 1916, she went to France to serve as an ambulance driver with the First Aid Nursing Yeomanry (FANY). Over the next two years, she began to sketch and paint what she observed, especially wounded troops being evacuated. *In an Ambulance* is her painting portraying a nurse cradling a match to light the cigarette of an injured soldier propped up on an ambulance bed. After the war, she continued to paint till 1925 when, in her mid-thirties, she committed suicide.[16]

Her powerfully vivid work hangs in the Imperial War Museum, as does that of the far better-known artist who also portrayed injured soldiers, John Singer Sargent. Though he visited Ypres briefly in July 1918, his famous *Gassed* was painted in the studio, portraying a chain of ten soldiers blinded by chemicals with hand on the shoulder of the man in front to guide them. It won the Royal Academy's 'painting of the year' to wide acclaim in 1919, though some claimed it lost veracity by not being based on first-hand observation. Lucian Freud told art historian Martin Gayford the impact of the painting was diminished precisely because of this, with the artist demonstrably using the same models in the studio again and again. Virginia Woolf, no fan either, condemned it for being too patriotic.[17] If Mudie-Cooke had been male, might her work have achieved the recognition it deserved?

I am puzzled too by the government's enthusiastic encouragement of official war artists, given so many of their works became bitter and seemed to undermine the very propaganda purposes for which they were set up. The war artist scheme was established in the belief that government could shape art, to inform, commemorate and celebrate the most extensive war so far in British history. For its first eighteen months, the government had given little thought to works of art, but thinking changed after Eric Kennington exhibited his *The Kensingtons at Laventie* in April 1916 in London. The men he portrayed had endured four days in the trenches in arctic weather, and he created his sensitive painting on glass after he was invalided out of the army. Nothing about it would have given the government cause for concern, the opposite, and shortly after it was exhibited, the War Propaganda Bureau recommended an official government scheme be set up, with the first artists appointed in May 1916. The establishment of the Imperial War Museum by Cabinet in 1917, charged with collecting material including art which documented the war, provided another impetus. That year, a series of artists, including C. R. W. Nevinson and Paul Nash, were commissioned to go to the front to paint. The creation of the Ministry of Information under Lord Beaverbrook in early 1918 was another spur and resulted in still more artists being sent out, including Stanley Spencer and Wyndham Lewis.[18]

Thus did the genie escape the bottle. Angrier paintings, as with poetry, came after the repeated military failures in the war. Only much later did plays and film catch up. Paul Nash, had served in the trenches until 1917, and became a war artist after he was invalided out. 'I am no longer an artist, interested and curious,' he wrote to his wife from Ypres. 'I am a messenger who will bring back word from the men who are fighting to those who want the war to go on forever… It will have a bitter truth and may it burn their lousy souls.'[19] He was commissioned in April 1918 to produce a large painting of the front to hang in the never-built national Hall of

Remembrance. For his subject, he chose the Menin road, which had been etched indelibly into his memory. Two soldiers in the middle of the painting appear lost in the lifeless war-ravaged landscape, the road on which they are travelling having been swallowed up in the devastation of war. It was perhaps his finest work. Back in England in 1918, he worried away adding to it in the same studio as his brother John who was painting his own masterpiece, *Over the Top*, displaying soldiers from the Artists' Rifles advancing to their death in the snow in No Man's Land. 'It was in fact pure murder... It was bitterly cold and we were easy targets against the snow and daylight,' John recalled sixty years later.[20]

Too late, the government woke up to *The Menin Road*. Nevinson's caustically sardonic *Paths of Glory*, painted in 1917 and depicting two soldiers lying dead face down in No Man's Land, was exhibited privately to avoid government censorship. Not on display until March 1918, it had a brown strip of paper over the dead bodies displaying the word 'censored'.[21] In the same vein, Paul Nash painted *We Are Making a New World*, a dead war-scape with no soldiers, no life and no hope, portraying splintered tree shards and shell holes at Inverness Copse, near Hooge, a short distance along the Menin road. Incredible to think it appeared on the front cover of *British Artists at the Front*, published by *Country Life* in 1918.[22] Incredible to think too that here I am a hundred years later, in a still treeless landscape, with cars whooshing past me headlong into the new world we have made.

Many of the artists, on both sides, found it difficult to adjust. German Käthe Kollwitz lost her son in 1914, chanelling her depression into her work. Others like William Orpen and Paul Nash had breakdowns in reaction to what they witnessed. Nash painted landscapes subsequently and knew well Eric Ravilious, killed as a war artist in September 1942 flying out of Iceland. The book's cover is inspired by him.

I walk back into the town past 'Hellfire Corner', now a busy junction on the Ypres–Menin road, but then a congested crossing for ambulances, ammunition and troops on which enemy artillery was constantly trained. Believed to be the most dangerous spot on the entire salient, it was frequently mentioned in the satirical soldiers' newspaper, *The Wipers Times*, started in 1916.[23] The mocking tone of this publication is on my mind as I re-enter the town, thinking guiltily of my own ineptitudes on long-ago journeys. On my first trip driving a school minibus, I was anxious for my students to hear the Last Post ceremony but I didn't check where it was, drove to Menen 20 kilometres away, before realizing my error too late. On another early trip, one of the pupils picked up a shell from a crater in the Newfoundland Park on the Somme and managed to get it back through customs to his home before realizing the detonator was still live. On yet another I was invited by senior staff staying at the palatial Regina Hotel in Ypres to come in for drinks after the students had been sent off to their rooms. At 2 a.m., walking back across the Grote Markt to the unsalubrious Zweerd Hotel, I experienced for the only time in my life 'Cloth Hall spin', Ypres's own variant of bed-spin, with the whole Cloth Hall and indeed town rotating in agonizing slow circles. All of this, naturally, before health and safety took over school trips.

I walk past the Cloth Hall, now thankfully rooted back to the ground, to enter St George's Church. Opened in 1927 as the focal point for British commemoration of all who died on the front, it is bursting with ornaments, decorations and plaques to individuals and institutions. The small number of plaques from schools particularly caught my eye on my early trips, and in a minuscule way, I have tried over the years to encourage state and independent schools to put up commemorative panels to remember their dead. *Public Schools and the Great War*, the book I wrote with David Walsh, the person who first identified the Gillespie letter, was born here in this church, to examine whether the much-derided public-school officer class were the cowards and incompetents portrayed in many contemporary dramas. Alumni from public schools we found died at almost twice the rate of soldiers at large. Some were bullies and haughty, but the vast majority of officers in the trenches – like the Gillespie brothers, like Palmer and Willett – were not callous of their men; nor shirkers, as they found to their cost, from danger.

I return to the hotel via a pharmacy for more pills to settle my guts: I have either been swallowing too many Nurofen, or I've picked up a stomach bug: either way, it's draining. After a short rest on my bed, I take only the provisions I need for a short journey due north to Langemark. Walking out through the industrial zone, before long, I pass the New Irish Farm Cemetery, for those who fell in the Third Battle of Ypres. With 4,719 burials, it is a 'concentration' cemetery, gathering in the human remains from eighteen smaller graveyards. My brain is dizzy with fatigue and emotion as I walk around the headstones. I'm standing among the dead who stood here in the front-line trenches among the still living waiting for the whistles to be blown for the start of the battle on 31 July 1917, looking up to the Passchendaele Ridge to my east where it ended three and a half months and 500,000 casualties from both sides later.[24]

Most often, I've stood up on that ridge looking down back to here asking myself the same question: how could it have happened? The British plan to attack the Belgian ports from the land and neutralize the U-boat bases never had a realistic chance of being achieved. Much was claimed later for the battle bleeding the German army dry and destroying its morale. But three months after, it was the Germans who launched a blistering offensive against a depleted British army in March 1918.[25] It was British morale that was rock bottom after Third Ypres, not the Germans'.[26] Still more than the Battle of the Somme, which miraculously saw British morale still high at its conclusion, Passchendaele unleashed bitterness that has not dissipated to this day. Even Lloyd George later wrote that: 'Passchendaele was indeed one of the greatest disasters of the war… unutterable folly.'[27] For the rest of his life, he felt guilt for failing to stop the offensive.

The weather was one of the excuses offered by the army. August 1917 was indeed the wettest for seventy-five years. With the intricate local drainage system destroyed by war, and a water table just 35 centimetres below the surface, the battlefield was soon a horrifying quagmire.[28] 'Figure to yourself a desolate wilderness of water-filled shell craters, crater after crater, whose lips form narrow peninsulas along which one can at best pick but a slow and precarious way. Here a shattered tree trunk, there a wrecked pillbox, sole remaining evidence that this was once a human and inhabited land. Dante would never have condemned lost souls to so terrible a Purgatory,' recalled a lieutenant colonel in the Royal Artillery.[29] The Third Battle of Ypres was a cruel and shocking affair. Two years on from the Battle of Loos, and casualties were still terrible. Tuesday 25 September 1917 was a particularly bloody day during Third Ypres with a major German counter-attack on the Menin road. Was it for this that Gillespie died?

What else could Haig have done? his defenders ask. A good question: leaders, as I know from my own writing, are too often blamed when no better options were on the table. But here, such options *were* available. Haig could have brought in more methodical and successful commanders earlier, like Plumer and the Canadian general, Arthur Currie, rather than leaving the battle's opening stages to aggressive cavalryman Hubert Gough. When Currie became involved from mid-October, he chose well-supported mini assaults which consolidated territory gained in place of ambitious attacks aimed at breakthrough. To achieve the objectives at Passchendaele, he said, would cost 16,000 casualties: the final figure was 15,700, with 4,000 of them dead.[30] Haig should have ended the battle much sooner, in early October, when it was clear its stated objectives of reaching the Channel ports would never be realized. Continuing the battle into November when the only possible gain was capturing a worthless ridge which would be retaken by the Germans three months later was inexcusable. Haig recovered some of his reputation in the Hundred Days Offensive that ended the war, and his state funeral in

January 1928, an honour he shared along with Nelson, Wellington and Churchill, saw an outpouring of emotion nationally. Churchill, though, could not forgive him, telling him in 1926 he remained 'a convinced and outspoken opponent of our offensive policy at Loos, on the Somme and at Passchendaele.'[31]

Fighting during the *Dritte Flandernschlacht* (Third Ypres) was often just as unpleasant for the Germans. Their defensive tactics were often clever, yielding ground while fiercely defending and counter-attacking elsewhere. Edmund Blunden wrote that 'German dead, so obvious at every yard of [the Somme] were hardly to be seen [on the salient].'[32] But as the battle went on, resisting the British blows became ever more costly. German commander Crown Prince Rupprecht wrote that Passchendaele was 'the most violent of all battles fought to date', but saw it as a German victory, telling his men, 'Despite the employment of immense quantities of men and material, the enemy achieved absolutely nothing.'[33] He was right.

Rupprecht has been something of a ghostly companion on the walk. He commanded German forces in Alsace and Lorraine in 1914, then on the Somme in 1916, and at Passchendaele in 1917. He was one of the better German commanders, but realized by early 1918, even before the Americans arrived, that Allied material superiority doomed the German cause.[34] After the war, he came to loathe the Nazis, and was exiled to Italy. Rupprecht lived long enough to return to his beloved Bavaria in 1945, even campaigning unsuccessfully for a restoration of the monarchy, and died there in 1955. He was buried in the uniform of a Bavarian field marshal, a vestige of a bygone army he'd led into France in the summer of 1914, half a lifetime before.[35]

I walk on, leaving behind Haig's legacy to the approaching autumn rains. I'm walking along farm tracks, perfectly flat, with cyclists swarming periodically past me, zigzagging my way across old front lines from each of Ypres's four battles up towards Langemark. As I pass cottages and farms, the smell of burning wood floats towards me, indicating that the summer is passing. The air, the soil, the plants seem damp. A chill is in the air. I pull in my jacket tight to my chest and walk on along rutted tracks till I come out at Langemark, in German hands until October 1917, then briefly a British town, until the Germans reclaimed it in March 1918.

As I walk, my thoughts return to the first autumn of the war. It was here, at Langemark, that the First Battle of Ypres climaxed in late October and November 1914. German forces repeatedly tried to break through to Ypres and beyond, but the BEF with its 160,000 regulars prevailed. Those left walking at the end were exhausted; the others had been killed or wounded. It proved a major defeat for the Germans. At Langemark, inexperienced German infantry suffered dreadfully as they advanced into the iron rifle sights of the more experienced British and French soldiers.[36]

The battle came nevertheless to be portrayed as a triumph for German national spirit, of idealistic youthful students betrayed by incompetent leaders. 'With feverish eyes each one of us was drawn forward faster and faster over turnip fields and hedges till suddenly the fight began… from the distance the sounds of this song met our ears, coming nearer and nearer… "Deutschland, Deutschland Uber Alles"'.[37] So wrote Hitler in *Mein Kampf*, even though he did not fight at Langemark. The song was not the German national anthem at the time: that was 'Heil dir im Siegerkranz', sung to the tune of 'God Save the Queen'. But the nationalist song suited post-war myth-makers better than the genuine one about the, by then exiled, Kaiser. Nor was it true that all of the casualties were young students; only some 15 per cent were, research suggests.[38] But this didn't stop the far right after 1918 promulgating the myth of the heroic young Germans, marking the battle on 'Langemark commemoration day'. When the Nazis took power in 1933, they exploited the myth further, and after 1938, every member of the Hitler Youth paid a compulsory fee known as the 'Langemark Pfennig'.[39]

In the German cemetery in Langemark, a section is reserved for the students who died. As I enter, I'm greeted by the 'comrades' grave', containing the remains of 25,000 German soldiers. Altogether, 44,000 are buried here. So this is where the path of peace has led me, to a mass grave and a mass fiction.

The lies that were spread about what happened here in 1914 helped propel Germany into another, even more destructive war in 1939. As I stand here, Vladimir Putin is spreading untruths to justify his war in Ukraine. Gillespie's dream may have been idealistic; but what alternative have we than to build friendships, starting with the young, across national borders, joined together by a reverence for truth?

In the mass grave at Langemark amongst all the German dead lie two British casualties, Private A. Carlill (aged nineteen) and Private L. H. Lockley (also aged nineteen). Both had been prisoners of war who had perished in the final two weeks of the war.[40] What better way to commemorate 'the silent witnesses from both sides' who lie side by side here than for us, the living, to walk side by side to build a better world?

14

To the Sea

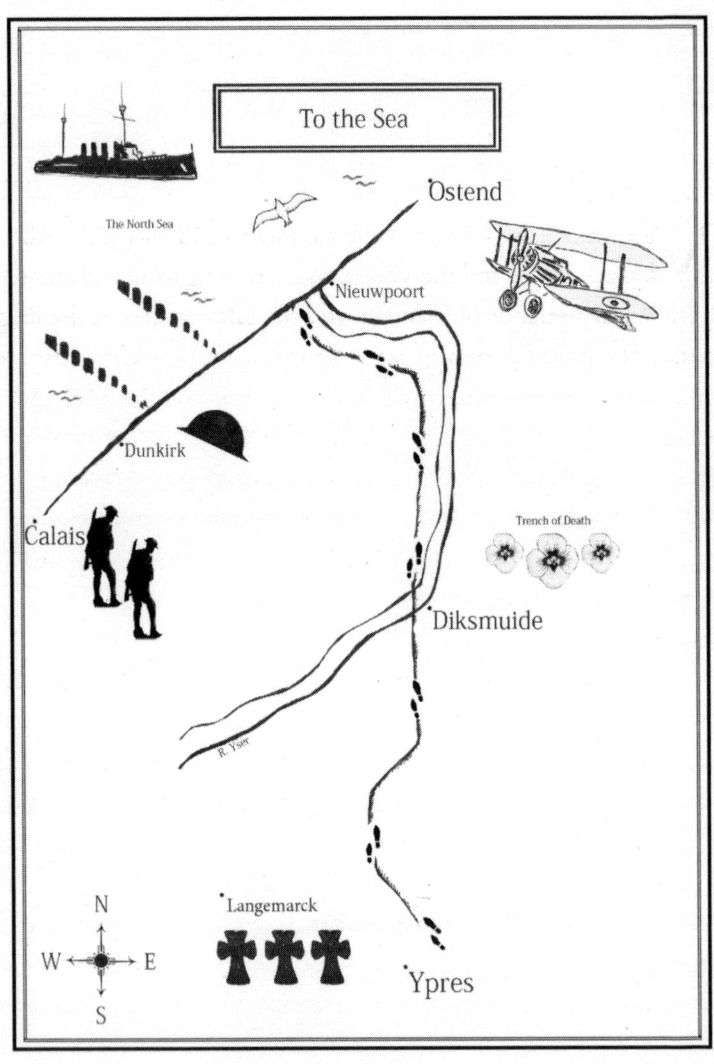
To the Sea
Ostend
The North Sea
Nieuwpoort
Dunkirk
Calais
Trench of Death
Diksmuide
R. Yser
N
W
E
S
Langemarck
Ypres

MY WALK BEGAN AMIDST the mountains and hills of the Alps, the Black Forest and the Vosges and is coming to an end among the fresh-water wetlands of Flanders and the salt marshes of the Belgian coast. The lofty Rhine was my inspiration as I took my first steps; with many rivers my companions in between – the Meurthe, Meuse, Aisne, Marne and Somme – the humble Yser, my seventh and final river, will now gently guide me to my journey's end. I started walking from Kilometre Zero in high summer along an elevated plateau and finish, thirty-eight days later, in the gathering autumn below sea level. My head was full of questions then, and as I approach the finish, I still have many answers to find before I can rest.

When William of Normandy left for England in 1066, entwining Britain and France for the next millennium, he set out from the Somme estuary. The land to the north of Diksmuide where I will be walking was then a similar-sized delta. The Yser that flowed into it, at just 80 kilometres, is the shortest of my seven rivers. Arising in France due south of Dunkirk, it flows north-east across the border into Belgium, then travels due north and out into the sea. Sea-going ships in the Middle Ages would sail all the way up to Diksmuide, transferring their textile cargo to smaller boats to travel by the Yser or the Ieperlee Canal to Ypres. In the centuries that followed, the local people gradually reclaimed the estuary from the sea, as they did in Holland, by creating polders which drained land below sea level with dykes, drainage canals and windmills to pump out excess water. Such reclamation work created vast tracts of fertile arable land where once the estuary had been, with the newly landlocked Diksmuide becoming a leading agricultural town in Flanders, and Nieuwpoort, 15 kilometres west, the new maritime gateway. For four years, the First World War put the clock back a thousand years, with the estuary, rising and falling with the North Sea's tides, fleetingly reborn.

Back at the Ariane Hotel I pack up my possessions and climb into my walking garb. Goodness, I'm weary of this routine. Before I leave Ypres, I pop out to the hospital for the Covid test needed for my return travel form, then catch a taxi back to the German cemetery to resume. As I set off from Langemark on a warm Tuesday morning, I sense the sea in my nostrils. For the rest of the walk, I will be back in territory rarely visited by the British, and unknown to me. What joy.

I imagined a gentle amble today through arable farmland but am pulled up short. For years, I've championed the value of paper maps over satnav, but on this walk I've had to admit defeat. Knowing exactly where I am on a route has made a real difference; the main downside is electronic maps don't distinguish between a farm track and a busy autoroute. For the first ninety minutes, indeed, it's landed me on a busy road with lorries screaming past. To distract myself, I listen to the news. It is mostly bleak: rows over the continuance of lockdowns, Cabinet minister Michael Gove appointed to 'save Christmas' and North Korea firing another rocket, so Kim Jong-un can remind the world of his presence. I'm following the news less and less, nor am I tuning in to podcasts and radio programmes as I had imagined: yesterday, I listened to the quiz show *Brain of Britain*, becoming depressed that I knew so few answers. I forge on along my noisy road, bad news in one ear, bad traffic in the other, through a hamlet incongruously called Madonna. Soon after I find a track skirting fields, mostly cabbage, not very exciting, with grind of agricultural machinery and long views over flat countryside for kilometres in every direction.

We've not heard much about the Belgian army, but it is in these unprepossessing cabbage fields in 1918 that it had its finest hour. Following the fall of Antwerp in October 1914, over 90 per cent of the country was in German hands. The remaining Belgian army and the royal family, together with thousands of refugees, were crammed awkwardly into a tiny corner in the very north-west, cheek by jowl with its troops responsible for manning the Western Front north of Langemark to the sea. The troops had been heavily involved north of Diksmuide in late 1914, as we shall see, but for the following four years, this north-western tip of the Western Front was as calm as the Alsace tip, with 'the daily communiqué from Belgian headquarters its own version of "All quiet on the Western Front"'. All the while, secret negotiations had been taking place with Germany about the restoration of Belgium's status after the war. Hopes of such a German guarantee help explain Belgian refusal to let its army be placed under general Allied command. Some of its Dutch-speaking Flemish soldiers questioned too why they were fighting and dying under an unrepresentative (and French-speaking) governing elite.[1]

But in late September 1918, the Belgians overcame their qualms, or saw the way the wind was blowing, and finally let their army join forces with the British in attack. Saturday 28 September was its bloodiest day of the war with over 1,000 Belgians killed. The next day, its troops seized Zonnebeke and Passchendaele, pushing on well beyond Ypres. Three weeks later, they reached the Dutch frontier at Sluis, liberating the entire Belgian coast.[2] By late October, the war was all but over. We saw earlier how a much-prized pair of boots (very significant to me) was passed on from soldier to soldier as they died in Erich Maria Remarque's famous novel: in its penultimate paragraph he describes how its hero Paul Baumer was finally killed in October 1918, 'on a day that was so quiet and still on the whole front, that the army report confined itself to the single sentence: "All quiet on the Western Front"'.[3] I was brought up on stories of the liberation of Western Europe from the Nazis in 1944–5, but the ending of the earlier war is new to me, and I marvel at the history as I walk through the scene of this earlier liberation.

With the entire country either in German hands or a combat zone, Belgium suffered far more intensely from the war than France, which had very large swathes physically unaffected. An estimated 70,000 Belgian houses were destroyed, and a further 200,000 damaged.[4] Large cities like Antwerp and Louvain suffered extensive destruction. The latter's historic library was rebuilt with American money after 1918. Germany honoured its promise under the Treaty of Versailles to replace the books burned in its attack in August 1914, for them only to be destroyed again by its artillery in 1940.

Some 320,000 Belgians fought in the war, of whom nearly 40,000 were killed, a third of them from disease.[5] Civilians suffered terribly too, with 8,000 dying from fighting, atrocities and illness.[6] The soggy Flanders terrain became quickly contaminated by dead bodies, and was responsible for many deaths from infection. But so too increasingly was the Spanish flu, which began to take its toll at exactly the point in late September 1918 when the Belgian army re-entered the war in earnest, which I learn about at exactly the point, 14 September, that Boris Johnson unveils England's winter plan for Covid. The flu epidemic caused sufferers to develop a deep blue skin, and bluish froth around their nose and mouth, culminating in them drowning in their own body fluids. Death would usually occur within a few hours of contracting the illness; those who survived the first few days often died subsequently from pneumonia bacteria. The virus had travelled to Europe probably from the mid-United States via the AEF. The Port of Brest in Brittany, where large numbers of US troops landed, had the highest incidence of the epidemic in all of France. The disease acquired its moniker 'Spanish flu' only because Spain, as one of the few major European countries to remain neutral in the war and hence unaffected by press censorship, gaily reported the growing epidemic. The world's attention was even more concentrated on Spain when King Alfonso XIII was seriously ill with it (he survived, and remained king until the declaration of the Republic in April 1931).[7]

The illness, unlike Covid, was particularly prevalent amongst twenty- to forty-year-olds, a phenomenon still not fully understood. It did not help that this was precisely the age of those in military service, crammed together in trenches, billets, ships and barracks, ideal 'super-spreading' locations. The effect of flu on the troops on both sides, ground down by the fighting, was devastating. But it did not turn the tide of the war, as Ludendorff later claimed when he blamed the pandemic for the ultimate failure of his grand offensive. Germany was on the run by August 1918 before the pandemic made its full impact felt.[8]

Dorothea Crewdson, a British nurse at Étaples, complained on 27 October 1918 that 'I have 13 flu-ers filling the atmosphere with germs [but] it makes a change from the everlasting dysentery, which we're getting very tired of'. A month later, she recorded: 'It seems a weird complaint too, for the virulent forms are so rapid and complications develop before you know where you are... I wonder if the experts will really discover what the complaint is. The latest theory, I believe, is it is a form of swine fever.'[9] In the absence of any firm understanding of the pandemic, rumours, then as now, spread rapidly. The social media of the day, more social than media, was gossip: theories amongst the soldiers were rife. Some asserted the pandemic had been caused by the typhoid vaccination that had been compulsory for all British servicemen. Others said it was due to the use of biological warfare by the Central Powers. Conspiracy theories abound whenever health scares spread. I find it easier to understand the prevalence then than now.

Lloyd George himself almost succumbed to the illness when he visited Manchester in September 1918. After a rousing speech, he collapsed with the fever. For eleven days, he was bed-bound, closely guarded in a rapidly converted room in the Town Hall, cared for by doctors who used a respirator to help him breathe. As his biographer

Kenneth Morgan confirmed to me,[10] some of his close team didn't think he would pull through. With the war still in a precarious state, the gravity of the illness was hushed up.[11] Had he died, Churchill was a possible replacement. Luck in timing is a vital attribute for a successful prime minister.[12] Churchill in 1918 would have been a disaster – for him and for the country: when his hour did arrive, he was ready.

Two hundred miles south of Manchester, Philip and Masha Margolis were less fortunate than the man they were so proud to call their prime minister. They had freshly emigrated from the town of Pereiaslav near Kyiv in the Ukraine (then in Russia, as Putin would have it be again), and the 1911 census places them in Whitechapel in London's East End, his occupation 'worker'. They had escaped from persecution, pogroms and poverty, but in London's East End, with Jews and Christians divided by streets, as my uncle Cecil Margolis recalls in his memoirs, fighting and brawling was commonplace among the young.[13] They eked out a life converting the downstairs room into a haberdashery shop, despite the family business suffering from periodic burglaries; but they felt safe at last from mortal danger. Safe, at least, until the epidemic struck. Even before Lloyd George caught it, they did. Then, as during the pandemic, relatives could not see loved ones close-up, so the older children waved a final goodbye to their parents in London Hospital from a safe distance.[14] They died on 16 and 21 July 1918, and are buried in Edmonton Jewish Cemetery. As soon as the funerals were over, household goods piled up in the front room were auctioned off to raise money, and the three boys, aged four, ten and twelve, were dispatched to an orphanage in Norwood in south London where they were given the numbers 45, 82 and 126. My Aunt Bess, after running away from foster homes, was taken in by relatives.

Abraham, the fifth and youngest child, escaped being given a number but posed a different kind of problem. Born on 29 May 1916 in a midwife's home in the Spitalfields' Petticoat Lane (the family joked he was the only bargain to emerge from that shopping thoroughfare), he was only two when his parents died. Too young for the orphanage, he was 'fostered by one Jewish couple after another',[15] until eventually adopted by a stable couple, Marks and Eva Slobodian, Russian émigrés who may or may not have known his parents Philip and Masha. Tragedy struck again when Marks, listed in the 1921 census as a 'boot repairer', died soon after, leaving young Abraham (now Arthur) with his stepmother who scrambled to make a life for him. My father was deeply shaped by the experience. Without the war, the flu would not have spread as it did, and he might have been brought up in a secure loving family with brothers and sisters. As it was, he only learned he had siblings when aged twelve. The story is that his brothers found out where he was living and wrote 'Abraham is our brother' in chalk in large letters for him to see on the street outside. The shock of discovery helped induce his lifelong stutter. As with all families, sifting truth from myth is difficult, but though I cannot confirm this, it seems quite likely.

I think of my father often, overhearing hushed voices in the night talking about him, wondering whether he was wanted, and from where his next meal was coming. In restaurants, I remember he would scoop up his bread roll and slip it in a paper napkin into his pocket, 'just in case'. He was a wonderful man but the early traumas scarred him for life and cannot but have affected my brothers and me.

So the war was indirectly responsible for the death of my father's parents, and it ripped the life and dreams out of my mother's parents. I think of my parents as I shuffle through the flat landscape, nervously pecking on the roll I had secreted into my pocket at breakfast. In the distance I can spy the IJzertoren (Yser Tower), at 85 metres commanding the plateau from here to the sea. Despite being quite astonishingly ugly, the four-sided concrete tower with square cross atop encapsulates the quest of my walk. Built in 1928–30, it commemorates Belgian soldiers killed in the war, doubling up as a monument to Christian pacifism. The noble aspirations of this tower, however, were soon overshadowed when it became a symbol of Flemish nationalism, a movement of the

The British ambassador and defence attaché on the path beyond Diksmuide.

right which sought to break away from the rest of Belgium. During the Second World War, Flemish nationalists collaborated with the Nazis in the hope of bringing this about. These deep divisions continued after the war when in March 1946 two former members of the Belgian Resistance blew up the tower as an act of reprisal. A new, slightly taller monument was rebuilt in its place with the words 'never war again' in the three Belgian languages (Dutch, French and German) and in English on its base. Inside is a United Nations peace museum. The search for peace goes on and on: will it be resolved, I wonder, as long as militaristic ambitions trump wider friendship within and between nations?[16]

I arrive in Diksmuide in the early afternoon. Here I really can sense the proximity of the sea, though I find it impossible to register that the walk is almost at an end. My hotel won't let me in yet. No point in standing still, so I propel myself to explore. I notice that the town, unlike the carefully restored Ypres, was rebuilt after 1918 in a blend of traditional and modern styles. I go in search of a pharmacy for a shaver and deodorant to make myself presentable for a special ceremony to take place tomorrow, splashing out on a crisp white shirt while I'm about it. Feeling suddenly overwhelmed and extraordinarily tired, I make for the St Nicholas Church off the Grote Markt. As I sit in a pew, I am flooded with uncontrollable emotion, so dip my head down below the sight-line in embarrassment. Despite its violent history, raised first from its rubble after 1918, and again after a fire following shelling in 1940, it radiates a peace as I find deeply spiritual places can. I leave lighter and calmer, ridiculously happy to see a sign advertising the Western Front Way outside the tourist office.

The Pax Hotel is now open if not staffed. I walk around trying to spot somebody and decide to wait in the bar, happy with the appropriateness of the hotel's name for the last night of the walk. A face appears, and I'm shown up to an enormous room on the second floor, where large earplugs on the sideboard make me wonder how much peace the hostelry really knows. I will find out soon enough and, meanwhile, prop myself up on my bed and spend two hours working through the infernal travel locator forms to allow me to re-enter Britain the next day. I keep imagining that, like a soldier on the last night in the trenches before leave, a terrible occurrence will prevent me getting home. Like many soldiers on the front too, I have read a new gospel chapter every day, and finish John before dinner. I take Gillespie's diary down to the brasserie opposite the hotel, which I read in the empty dining room. One hundred and six years ago today Douglas was staying in billets in 'rather squalid cottages beside a grimy canal' near to La Bassée. Going out for a long walk, he was nearly arrested as a spy, and found a pretty swamp: 'with long reeds and marsh plants, and I disturbed a kingfisher from a trunk tree which had fallen across a ditch.'[17] Four days later, he is back in the trenches. He has eleven more days to live. I have less than twenty-four hours to go. I decide that I must come back out to

France again. I need to complete that missing leg and find out where he died. That surely will provide the remaining answers I have failed to produce so far. Perhaps a descendent of his kingfisher will guide me.

I awake to glorious sunlight streaming in through big plate-glass windows. It is my last day, Day 38, just assuming I can complete the 20 kilometres to the sea, and my travel documents will suffice. For a final time, I spray myself with antiseptic and insect repellent, put plasters and bandages over my blistered and raw feet and toenails, and squeeze my clean body into semi-clean clothes which have known only travel soap for too long. I sniff them extra carefully before doing so, and spray on a precautionary additional squirt of Lynx deodorant, just in case: because today is a big day.

Today will start with meeting Martin Shearman, the British ambassador to Belgium, and his defence attaché, Group Captain Justin Fowler, as arranged by Rory and the team, who will walk with me all day. My new companions are already in the dining room sipping coffee when I come down. Over breakfast, we plan our route. The almost indescribable relief of being able to rely on others for directions, and having company, catches me by surprise. I hadn't realized quite how lonely I had become, nor how heavily I had let the daily grind of decisions bear down on me. We are soon out on the road and crossing over the Yser, Martin in trainers, casual grey trousers and an elegant dark top; Justin in full combat gear looking as if he could repel the entire Russian army single-handedly. The diplomat, the soldier and civilian: a snapshot of the British state in action.

Just past the Yser Tower we pick out the dyke path on the west bank of the river, passing – renewed joy – one of our VIA SACRA WESTERN FRONT WAY signs on a wooden post. After a kilometre, we arrive at the Dodengang ('Trench of Death') nestled into the dyke. After 1918, the Belgian government designated twenty-five special war sites to be maintained in perpetuity. But even before the visitor guides had been printed, some had been ploughed over by farmers desperate to forget the war and return their land to productive agriculture, while other sites were seized by builders to erect dwellings for returning Belgians forced away by the war.

The 'Trench of Death' would have met the same fate, but for an early example of crowdfunding when 100,000 Belgian francs were raised from the public to deviate a planned new road and preserve the site intact. Like at Vimy Ridge, concrete sandbags almost too perfect have been constructed, with very precise traverses and dugouts. Truth inevitably became embellished about this site in a quest for renown and visitors. 'Thousands' of Belgian soldiers were claimed to have been killed here in a desperate bid to keep out the Germans from the small part of the country still independent. 'The Belgian army launches several attacks against German machine guns,' declares a sign at the entrance. 'These assaults invariably end in blood baths... An incredible number of lives are lost every day.' The First World War needs no embroidery, but who can begrudge it here? It is an excellent visitor location.[18]

The Dodengang or 'Trench of Death'.

Martin and Justin are diplomatically tolerant while I babble on like a man rescued off a Pacific island after half a lifetime alone. As we thread our way through dykes, ditches and fields, we talk about Belgium's politics and economy, the Foreign Office and the RAF (Justin's army garb, I learn, was deceptive). We're soon at a site called 'Petroleumtanks' where the Germans crossed the river in October 1914 during the 'race to the sea', attacking the Belgian army along a 35-kilometre stretch of the Yser and the Ieperlee Canal. The Allies called this the Battle of the Yser; to the Germans it is 'Erste Flandernschlacht' (the First Battle of Flanders) and part of the First Battle of Ypres. On the night of 17 October, Belgian regimental commander Arsène Bernard watched over his men as a comet traversed the sky. He wondered if his family, trapped in Brussels when it fell under German control, were watching the comet too: 'perhaps our gazes met up there', he wrote.[19]

The next morning, the Germans, sensing that Calais and Dunkirk were within their grasp, launched a ferocious attack bolstered by the giant siege guns with which they had crushed the Allies in Antwerp. If they took the Channel ports, they reasoned rightly, British supplies would dry up, the soldiers would sooner or later have to stop fighting, and Paris might even fall. The Germans had not anticipated the Royal Navy firing on their positions from warships lying just off the coast. The guns slowed up but could not stop the German advance westwards and, on the night of 22 October, they erected a temporary bridge over the river. Having established a bridgehead on the dyke on the other side on which they planted their machine guns, some 20,000 men crossed under the cover of darkness. With the Germans making swift progress on the west bank of the river, the Belgians retreated east to the embankment of the Nieuwpoort–Diksmuide railway line, their final point of defence before the coast. A German attack on 26 October was halted by fresh French battalions but they proved no more successful than the Royal Navy in stopping the powerful drive forward.[20]

The Belgians had little alternative now but to play their ace card. The seventeenth-century military engineer Vauban makes his last appearance in our story at this point. Much of the Flanders canal network had been masterminded by him, but his crafty mind had anticipated this very threat, and knew that letting in the sea again would ultimately defend the Channel ports to the west from attackers from the north and east. The key was the sluice gates at Nieuwpoort which held back seawater at high tide and let fresh water flow out into the sea at low tide. Opening them would return again to nature a substantial part of Belgium that remained free. The chief lock-keeper, though, was not keen; only the promise of a decoration induced him to show sappers how to operate the gates. On the evening of 29 October, with the tide already rising and the wind blowing in from the sea, eight sluice gates were duly opened. Nearly 1,000,000 cubic metres of seawater surged forward. As American military historian Robert Cowley, who walked the Western Front from west to east many years ago, wrote, 'At first the only sign was the desperate agitation of the freshwater fish – the trout, carp, and pike that inhabited the canals and side streams – as the salt water took over… The Germans panicked as they felt the ground disappear under them… Guns sank in the mud and had to be abandoned. The water hid ditches and creeks, into which men plunged over their heads.'[21] By 31 October, almost all the land between Nieuwpoort and Diksmuide was under water, creating a giant lake some 5 kilometres wide, 15 kilometres long, and up to 3 metres deep.[22]

The Western Front had seen nature bent in some extreme directions, but nothing like this. 'A strange silence reined. The enemy, driven away by the most irresistible of the elements, had vanished,' wrote Belgian chief of staff, Emile Galet. It was a scene of utter desolation: 'bodies, human and animal, floated amid a flotsam of leather helmets, knapsacks, and cartridge boxes. Bloated corpses rising to the surface marked the line of yesterday's trenches.'[23] I am having to rely on my imagination because no trace of any of this devastation remains today under a benign sun and gentle breeze as we continue to weave our way through the many small canals and watery channels where once we would have been under the sea.

We are intrigued by a tiny memorial chapel by the side of our path erected in 1925 in memory of the 40,000 Belgian casualties in the war. Vivid stained-glass windows commemorate the action and act like a pictorial synopsis of the last five weeks. Then, through the trees, as if on cue, we make out the spire of Our Lady Church in Nieuwpoort. I have sensed and smelt, and now I can see, the physical ending of the walk. There's no time for sentiment, though, because we risk arriving late for the civic reception in the walk's honour at 1 p.m. in the old city hall. We thus pass speedily past the Ramscappelle Road Cemetery outside the town, symbolically of great significance as the last CWGC cemetery on the front, with the graves of British and Commonwealth soldiers killed on these very final few kilometres to the sea in mid- to late 1917. What were they doing here? Only later do I find out the extraordinary story.

From 20 June 1917, Belgian forces were temporarily replaced in great secrecy by British troops on this furthest section of the line for one of the most daring (if ill-conceived) plans of the entire war. The aim was to facilitate sea-borne landings of British troops on the Belgian coast as soon as their forces broke through in the Third Battle of Ypres. Back in Blighty, the Combined Ops boffins had been giving extensive thought to how to land troops from the sea. As specially trained units practised night-time manoeuvres, the army experimented with landing tanks from boats, the Royal Flying Corps explored how it could provide air cover, while the Royal Navy planned for its battleships and battlecruisers, which had been underemployed in the war, to launch artillery. Unfortunately for the boffins, the Germans had been preparing for just such an eventuality, and had been fortifying the Belgian coast east of the Yser since late 1914, a forerunner of the Atlantic Wall built during the Second World War.[24]

The British soldiers were deployed here thus on this Belgian-held toehold on the eastern bank of the Yser in anticipation of the link-up with the British landing and to establish an overland route to the bridgehead for reinforcement and supply.[25] German intelligence discovered what was being planned and executed a spoiling attack to ruin the British scheme. In early July, German artillery began to bombard the floating bridges the British had placed across the mouth of the river. Promised British artillery to defend against this failed to transpire. The Germans now unleashed their infantry, using flamethrowers and, for the first time in the war, mustard gas (an agent smelling like mustard causing blisters on skin and lungs). The German attack was devastating. Within just twenty minutes they had knocked out a large part of the British bridgehead, including the part closest to the sea. Operation Beach Party, as it was called, saw heavy British casualties, with 3,000 men lost, and was a humiliating defeat for Haig, who had argued wrongly that the German strength on the Western Front was waning.[26]

When no breakthrough of the salient line occurred at Third Ypres, the plans for an amphibious landing were permanently shelved. The strategy was criticized by one military analyst as a 'crack-brained' scheme, 'a kind of mechanical Gallipoli affair'. It was to be another twenty-seven years before the Allies on D-Day mastered how to pull off a successful sea-borne landing at scale on heavily defended enemy-controlled beaches.[27] The bodies of those caught up in this adventure lie still in the Ramscappelle Road Cemetery that I yomped past with my new official buddies, Martin and Justin, in the cause of arriving punctually for a good lunch.

Crack-brained the plan might have been, but it showed that somebody in London was at least thinking imaginatively. My emotions begin to surge as we go through the old city walls and walk into Nieuwpoort, entering just by the sluice gates that changed history and passing the Albert I Memorial. Albert was far more than a ceremonial monarch. When Belgium was invaded on 4 August 1914, he rode to Parliament to ask whether it wished 'to maintain intact the sacred gift of our forefathers'; the thunderous response came back 'Belgium would fight.'[28] He commanded the forces personally, took responsibility for the decision to open the sluice gates, and oversaw the final two months of fighting. His pledge to remain amongst his soldiers throughout the war led to him being widely admired, as was his wife Elisabeth, a duchess in Bavaria no less, and a friend of writers and artists. Her many acts included working alongside nurses, establishing the army's symphony orchestra, and serving as a go-between with the British government on her regular visits to London. The monument was dedicated in 1933. Within a year, Albert had fallen to his death, aged just fifty-eight, in a climbing accident in the Ardennes. Few at the time realized he would be the last Belgian monarch to exercise real power, and the last to be loved across the disparate country.

The ambassador's car is waiting for us outside the city hall. Hastily, we change into our civic weeds. I am a different person in my crisp white shirt; more presentable, but less comfortable and at home. Is my pilgrimage really drawing to a close? I feel self-conscious, an impostor, as civic dignitaries crowd around to congratulate me. Many photographs, speeches and chinking of glasses of sparkling wine later, my head is reeling. We sit down to eat a five-course lunch too rich to digest in the medieval hall. The day is not over. After coffee, we change back to walking clothes for the final 3 kilometres following the long harbour to the sea. Martin is a keen ornithologist, and points out cormorants, herring gull and oystercatchers as we stride along our watery way. It brings back to mind Jonathan Williams, my ornithologist saviour from Verdun. Wilfred Willett too, who took my mother on regular holidays to observe birds for his *Daily Worker* columns in similar landscape on the Norfolk Broads just 160 kilometres away over the North Sea. To mind as well a book that has mesmerized me all my life: Paul Gallico's 1941 novella *The Snow Goose*, set in the marshlands of Essex amidst 'the great saltings and mud flats and... tidal creeks and estuaries.'[29]

Suddenly, the land ends at an esplanade and the beach begins. Martin and Justin back away discreetly to let me walk slowly down to the sea alone, with the river mouth on one side and the beach curling round towards France on the other. This is where Continental Europe ends and then, out of sight over the sea, the Channel ports and home.

Here, I am in the midst of history, where 'ignorant armies clash by night'.[30] To my left, the beach where Henry V's troops departed for England and Saint George after victory at Agincourt. To my right, the Belgian ports of Ostend and Zeebrugge, the targets of Third Ypres. Not admitting defeat, they were raided in April and May 1918 by the Royal Navy and Marines, a strategic failure presented as a brilliant success in Britain. Further inland are the places that would have been so familiar to Marlborough's and Wellington's forces – Ghent, Oudenaarde, Waterloo. I can just make out the town of Dunkirk, from where the BEF scuttled in May 1940, portrayed again as a daring victory plucked from the jaws of defeat. To its south, Napoleon and Hitler marshalled their forces to invade Britain, gazing avariciously across the Channel from the French coast. As Kaiser Wilhelm II might have done if the line had not held...

I used to pretend to my students – shame on me – that the trenches zigzagged all the way across this beach and under the sea to the cliffs of Dover. Perhaps I was half right: the war continued even out there in the anonymity of the swirling waters of the North Sea. As an island, Britain could sustain its effort on the Western Front only by a constant stream of boats ploughing back and forth, day and night, every day of the year. I remember Dover Patrol as a board game from my youth. I didn't know at the time that it was based on a real Dover Patrol, created after the fall of Antwerp in 1914 to keep German submarines and surface warships out of the English Channel to protect British vessels, and to persuade the German navy to take the much longer and more dangerous route over the top of Scotland out into the Atlantic. Some

125,000 British supply ships crossed the English Channel in the war, of which a mere seventy-three were lost to German action.[31]

Now, out of nowhere, the thoughts and feelings cascade down upon me – Douglas and Tom Gillespie, how to realize the Western Front Way, what to do with the rest of my life, and how not to be defined by grief and regret. Some answers at least are becoming clear – Sarah for one. The walk has convinced me that I am ready to settle down with Sarah. But does she feel the same about me? The walk has pushed me to the limits of my physical and mental endurance and left me without the luxury of the time I imagined to answer all the other questions that filled my head as I set out from Kilometre Zero.

Suddenly, I feel cold and exposed in my thin clothes as an autumn breeze whips in off the sea. It is late afternoon and I have a train to catch to England. Then what? I freeze with fear. Here I am with the waves gently lapping at my boots, at the end of my walk, but is it the end of my journey?

I am momentarily paralysed, like Douglas must've been at the end. I cannot go forward, and I cannot go back. I am afraid to return to England so unprepared for what lies ahead. Sarah I hope might want me, but does the world want me when I have found 'nor certitude, nor peace, nor help from pain' on the path of peace?[32] This sea before me, no more than 50 metres deep, deeper than No Man's Land was wide, was once only a river. Why, my first river, the Rhine, flowed out here. The sea is thus my last river, my eighth, and I must find out how to cross it.

Now, all roads lead to La Bassée.

15

Epilogue:
La Bassée, February 2022

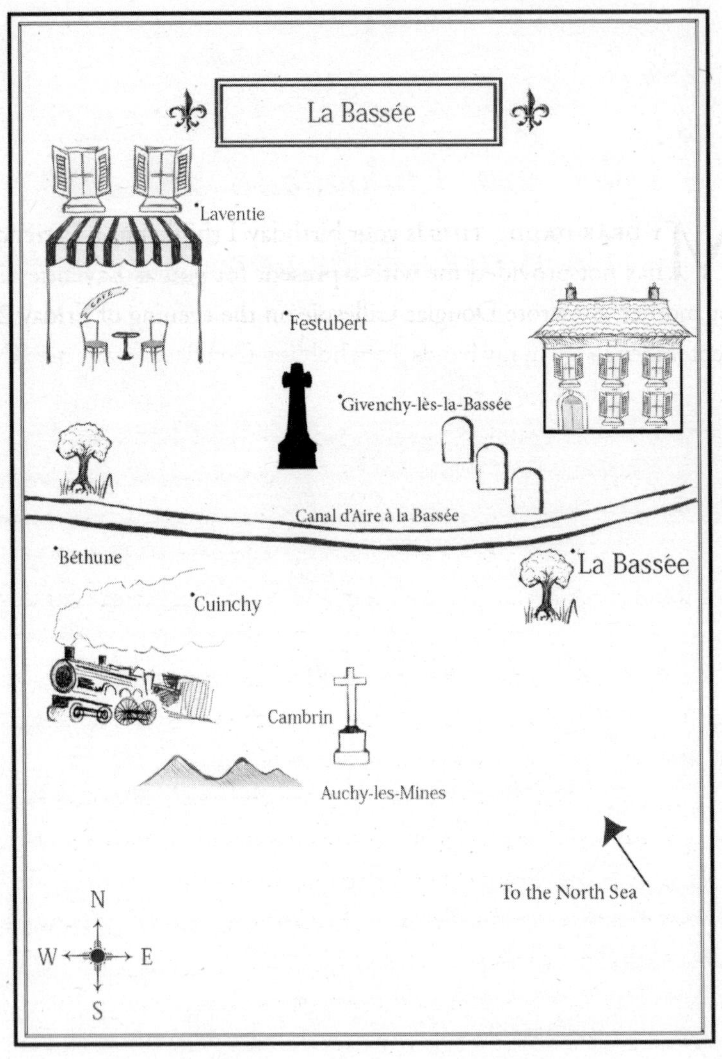
La Bassée
Laventie
CAFÉ
Festubert
Givenchy-lès-la-Bassée
Canal d'Aire à la Bassée
Béthune
La Bassée
Cuinchy
Cambrin
Auchy-les-Mines
To the North Sea
N
W
E
S

'My dear daddy, this is your birthday, I think, but this trench has not provided me with a present for you as Laventie did for mother.' So wrote Douglas Gillespie on the evening of Friday 24 September 1915. In my hands, I am holding Douglas's final letter. The holy text of the Western Front Way.

'Before long, I think we shall be in the thick of it, though if we do attack, my company will be one of those in front, and I am likely to lead it; not because I have been specially chosen for that, but because someone must lead, and I have been with the company longest.'

Could it be possible that we know somewhere deep inside ourselves when we are living the last hours of our lives?

'Tom himself will be here to help me, and give me courage and resource and that cool head which will be needed most of all to make the attack a success.'[1] A success. Did he believe that?

After my return from Belgium in mid-September 2021, I travel to a village near Cambridge to talk about my journey with Douglas and Tom's niece, Peggy Heap. She has invited her children: Tom (my companion on the Western Front Way campaign from the start), Alice and son-in-law Len. The discovery in the attic of the battered brown suitcase has thrown up a tremendous tranche of Douglas and his brother Tom's letters and memorabilia, lovingly preserved by their surviving sister Daisy, Peggy's mother. Great nephew Tom had read me a few morsels as I was walking to Loos, but they, like the published letters, portrayed the thoughts of a conventional man, not an idealist: diving deeper at last is the moment for which I had been yearning.

We talk together about how Douglas might have felt that evening near La Bassée, knowing that the next morning he would be leading his men into action on the first day of the Battle of Loos. He doesn't exactly help us.

'Anything one writes at a time like this seems futile, because the tongue of man can't say all that he feels. But I thought I would send the scribble with my love to you and Mother. Always your loving Bey' (as the family called Douglas).[2] His final written words.

I need to understand his last moments on earth. Did this brave man feel any trace of fear that still evening as he gazed out across a treeless No Man's Land towards the lights of La Bassée? Did his parents sense his bewilderment as they gazed that night out of the windows of Longcroft, the family home in Linlithgow, towards a moonlit Firth of Forth?

I have to return to France, to the area around La Bassée missed out on my walk, to see if I can discern any more about the author of the Via Sacra – to my mind the best idea that emerged from the war. I am fixated on the thought that if I can understand why Douglas came up with his vision, it will provide the key to finding my own peace and allow me at last to conclude my pilgrimage. Without that, I feel destined to walk on, forever searching.

This much we know. At 6.30 a.m. on Saturday 25 September 1915, Douglas gave the order to his company to fix bayonets. He blew his whistle and climbed up the ladder with his men and walked out into the anonymity of No Man's Land.

The Argyll and Sutherland Highlanders were in the first wave of the 19th Brigade's advance that morning. The company Douglas led, as he noted with pride, was in the vanguard. 'They went over the top in splendid order as if at training,' recorded the British official history.[3]

As he advanced into No Man's Land, did he, if only for a second, think of his plan for a tree-shaded Via Sacra? Did he worry that he himself might become one of the 'silent witnesses'? But unlike so many of his comrades, he is not silent – he talks to us down the decades as we try to enact his vision to help people across the world find their paths to peace.

Douglas's immediate path that morning, though, was far from clear. Because of the British use of gas, the secret weapon on which much hope for the battle had been pinned, his company had had to move back 30 or 40 metres to allow the chemicals to be released safely from the front line. 'The gas poured forth in great volume. But owing to lack of wind, it moved very slowly, and appeared to drift obliquely,' wrote Lieutenant Colonel F. Rowley in his report of the attack. It then began blowing back towards the British trenches.[4] As Douglas's men fumbled clumsily perhaps to put on their gas helmets, for this action was a novelty it being the first British use of gas in the war, it 'hindered both [their] sight and hearing'.[5] Several were killed before they even reached their own front line. But not Douglas. 'When the infantry finally moved out, advancing into clouds of their own gas,' said historian Nick Lloyd, 'they could make little progress against stubborn resistance.'[6]

Disaster compounded disaster. Smoke to mask the advancing troops had failed to materialize. Still Douglas pressed on. The *coup de grâce* of underground mines to disorientate the Germans had been compromised when a premature British attack gave away their timing. 'As the minutes ticked by, observers saw German heads and rifles [re] appearing over the parapet 80m away.'[7] Worse still, earlier mines in No Man's Land meant that the attackers 'were forced to tread narrow paths between the craters in single file, easy targets for enemy riflemen and machine gunners.'[8] As historian Andrew Rawson wrote: 'With the Highlanders forced to bunch together, the Germans could hardly fail to miss.'[9] For German snipers trained to identify and kill officers, it was a rich picking. Somehow Douglas managed to survive through all of this. But then his luck changed.

Loos's preliminary bombardment had failed to cut the wire along the line. What did Douglas think as he lay breathing heavily in a crater just in front of the German wire, knowing that most of his men had already become casualties behind him, and that 5 metres ahead lay unassailable German trenches crammed with battle-hot German infantry? Two months before, he had crawled out across No Man's Land and halted at the German wire. Instead of pressing on, he nonchalantly snipped off a piece to send back home as a souvenir. Why did this prudent lawyer not retreat this time too until a better-resourced assault could be garnered which might have at least some prospect of success? For a while he was transfixed, afraid to go forward and afraid to go back. As he weighed up the most important and lonely decision of his life, did thoughts of Tom cross his mind: the devastating impact on his parents of the loss of their only surviving son? Was he driven on by courage and heroism, or by fear of failure, his duty to God? We will never know. What is sure is the decision he took; having taken it, he managed somehow to find a way through the wire and to leap over the German parapet. With no one in support, only one possible outcome could ever have been possible.[10] All but suicide, I'd say, for a man with everything to live for. A blaze of bullets, hot metal gliding into hotter flesh, and it was all suddenly over.

Dum. Dum. Dum. Dum.

His parents awoke on the morning of Saturday 25 September in Longcroft happily unaware of any of this. They came downstairs to find the *Scotsman* on the breakfast table with only scant news from the front. Edinburgh's special fund for 'the relief of distress in the war' was the lead story that day. No whisper of the battle reached homes across Britain. But on Wednesday at 10.47 a.m., the Linlithgow post office picked up a wire from the War Office. The knock on the front door – these telegrams were always delivered personally – the anguished look between parents, the envelope ripped open. 'Deeply regret to inform you that A. D. Gillespie of A and S Highlanders is reported missing believed killed between 25–26 September. Lord Kitchener expresses his sympathy.'

When, ten months before, an earlier telegram had arrived with news from La Bassée about Tom, mention had been made that the King and Queen expressed their sympathy. Small consolation for the grieving parents and daughter. The day after the second telegram arrived, Thursday 30 September, the *Scotsman*'s headlines reported the news for the first time: BATTLE OF LOOS. SPLENDID WORK OF THE NEW ARMIES. SCOTTISH REGIMENTS IN THE FOREFRONT. HEROIC BAYONET CHARGES. As his grief-ridden parents read this, Douglas's final letter, the one I am holding, dropped through their letter box.

Two months later, another letter arrived at Longcroft, this time from the Red Cross with information from a Private R. Stewart 8564. He had witnessed Douglas jump into the German trenches at about 6.30 a.m. on 25 September. Stewart thought he 'must've been killed there because his body was later seen in front of the German trenches'. The Highlanders' attack had then been called off at 9 a.m., all surviving troops being ordered 'to withdraw as best they could'. If only Douglas had paused in front of the parapet a little longer.

The shock still seems visceral as we sit around the dining-room table at Peggy's home, the very table on which Tom and Douglas ate their meals every day, and on which are now spread out the letters and memorabilia they left behind. Will they reveal the origins of Douglas's idea of the Via Sacra? I still don't understand why he, apparently alone of all the soldiers who took part in the war, came up with such an inspired vision. No poet, nor artist nor philosopher dreamt it up. Nor any working-class author like W. H. Davies or George Coppard. Why then this upper-middle-class young man, educated at Cargilfield prep school and Winchester College, then New College, Oxford before being called to the bar?

The family have been sifting through the trove and point me to a letter from celebrated historian Arnold Toynbee recalling pre-war student trips together to Greece. Was it Toynbee, the future champion of international trade and cooperation, who during those holidays seeded the ideas in his mind? But how to explain Douglas's desperation to join up? 'I remember how Bey, in spite of his eyesight not being up to standard, pretty much forced his way into the front line,' Toynbee wrote. He wanted to be at the heart of this war; and he wanted to stop future wars.

They pass me a letter that Douglas had written to his sister on 26 April 1914, in which he reflects on the political turbulence in Britain over the previous five years: he would like to 'take some part in the big fight of Capital and Socialism which will fill, in one form or another, the next fifty years. If a man who stands halfway can be of any use, I would like to try.' So he saw himself as a peace-broker. More telling still is a letter he wrote to his mother on 30 July, just five days before the war broke out: 'Europe will be crippled for 30 years if a great war does come,' he foresaw. 'It might be worth paying such a price if it drove into the head of every man in Europe that the present armaments are insane – but that I'm afraid is just what a war won't do, because of the passions it will leave behind.'

Here it is at last. Even the phrase 'every man in Europe', which was to appear in his later letter envisaging the walk. He saw himself as a halfway man, standing between classes and nations, wanting not to accentuate difference but to find the common ground. We probe further into his psyche. His extraordinary sensitivity to and love for his friends lay at the heart of his life. The family point me to the poem he wrote after the death at Gallipoli of his close Oxford friend Isaac Balfour: 'A year last June we walked / The Highland hills, and bathed, and talked / Of everything beneath the sun…' In the final verse he imagines Balfour's spirit coming to him in Flanders and reassuring him, after Julian of Norwich, that 'all is well'. 'Isaac was the most lovable of men. He was in many ways my greatest friend,' he wrote to his parents. I talk to the family about this deep passion for friends, and how his love for others spread far beyond his own social circle.

Faith too provides a key to unlocking his mind. John Bunyan's *The Pilgrim's Progress* followed him in his kitbag wherever he went at the front. On his death, his bookmark was found in the page that ended: 'Then I entered into the Valley of the Shadow of Death... I thought I should have been killed there... but at last the day broke, and the sun rose, and I went through that which was behind, with far more ease and quiet.' Were these the final words he read, snapping the book shut as he readied himself to go over the top? I find Douglas's vision of former foes walking side by side to discover common ground, a pilgrims' progression, profoundly spiritual. I see him as a pilgrim, a man on a journey, wanting all people to join him on his tree-shaded path of peace.

My train back to London is summoning me, and I bid a fond farewell to this family whose lives have become so intertwined with my own. I understand more now about Douglas, his desire to reach out across class, across nation, and ultimately across No Man's Land. I too share that passion, the deepest impulse in my body being the desire to build bridges and unite rather than divide and destroy. Does that help explain why, on reading his letter, instantaneously I knew I had to help make his vision a reality? Only now do I see it. I share too Douglas's deep love of friends and family, and understand intuitively his desperate grief at the loss of Tom, Isaac and others close to him. I have always hated saying goodbye and feel deep pain at rejection and loss in any form, as in young love, or as with the loss of Joanna, inconsolable grief creeping up and all but overwhelming me when least expecting it. This acute vulnerability will always be a part of me and Douglas is helping me see it and learn to accept it through a century which is yesterday and which is now.

I returned twice to France after the walk. The CWGC have been tirelessly supportive of the path, and in October 2021, Sarah and I travelled out on Eurostar with new director-general Claire Horton and vice chair General Sir Bill Rollo to help build relations on the ground, and to walk the section to Armentières I missed. Local mayors and dignitaries greeted us wherever we went. Their concern is less international peace: rather, Gillespie's plan will bring tourists and vitality, and that is all part of it. We visit Neuve Chapelle, Aubers Ridge and Fromelles, scene of one of the most devastating losses in Australian history, a futile attempt in July 1916 to divert German attention from the Battle of the Somme. In 2007, a mass grave containing Australian and British soldiers was verified: the bodies have now been reburied in the new military cemetery which we visit. That evening, we drive up to Ypres for the Last Post ceremony at the Menin Gate with Claire reading and Bill laying a wreath, followed by a civic dinner in honour of the walk. Under Blomfield's barrel-vaulted arches, I sensed not Sassoon's rage but Gillespie's hope for a better world reverberating among those present.

Then in February 2022, I returned with Sarah and dear friends, John and Lou James, to see again where Douglas spent his last days alive. As our train sped us to Dover, we read about his train journey to Dover returning from leave at the end of August 1915, his last time in England. 'The Kentish country looked very green and sleepy and peaceful,' Douglas wrote as he approached the coast. Once at the port, he was pointed straight onto the boat: no Covid vaccination or travel locator forms for him. 'The channel was very calm,' he tells us. 'We had one torpedo boat running alongside of us the whole way.' Good that the Dover Patrol was doing its job. Would that the Channel was as calm for us. With Storm Eunice rallying, the sea was choppy: ferry services were suspended soon after we arrived in France.

Douglas jumped on a waiting train at Calais and slept all journey before arriving 'at my railhead about 5 o'clock on a misty morning' at what can only have been Béthune, then the major rail junction serving the army in northern France. We jumped into our waiting vehicle on the car deck and drove through the storm to Béthune. After a short wait in the town, Douglas was driven 10 kilometres to (he doesn't give the name in his letter) the small front-line village of Cambrin, close to the La Bassée Canal. The drive, he says, was 'quite pleasant after a night on the train, with the sun rising above the mist and corn-fields.'[11]

On our way to Béthune, we stop off at Laventie, where Douglas bought his mother her last birthday present, and where the poet Ivor Gurney drank 'vin, rouge-blanc, chocolat, citron, grenadine' in its 'small delectable cafés.'[12] We visit the memorial at Neuve Chapelle to the Indians who Douglas admired so much: 'splendid looking men, very tall, with great turbans and long black beards; they are fighting very well now.'[13] John and Lou had recently returned from teaching in India, and have a deep affection for the country which I share. We notice bullet marks on the circular lattice memorial, a relic of the fighting here during the BEF's retreat to Dunkirk in 1940.

We drive south past Festubert and Givenchy to La Bassée, leaving the car at the railway station through which for four years poured German soldiers and supplies off trains arriving from further east. Our scarves and hats are blown off as we walk head on into the gathering storm and rain along the Aire–La Bassée Canal to Cuinchy, and then to Cambrin. 'In the distance I could see mine heaps standing up everywhere… which are now used for observation posts by the artillery,' Douglas wrote. Slag heaps still dominate the landscape, but the brick stacks he described have long gone. His mind, as so often, turns to his younger brother fighting here in autumn 1914: 'It was through this part of the country that Tom marched and fought during his last days,' he wrote. 'It must've looked very much the same to him, except that the leaves would be turning, and that the villages and farms would still be occupied and untouched.'[14] To the end, Douglas loved nature. Was he sad or reassured to find himself fighting in the same place as Tom? Both, perhaps…

His mind turns to the chateau where Tom spent his last nights. We pass a possible pile near the canal, a likely suspect, but we cannot tell if it is the same building. Douglas had a jaundiced view of the canal itself, disappointed that it was too dirty for him to swim in. I tracked down a photo of the waterway almost drained of water, and I can understand why. Robert Graves, with the Royal Welch Fusiliers, took a dim view as well, berating 'Cuinchy-bred rats: they came up from the canal, fed on the plentiful corpses, and multiplied exceedingly'.[15] Fellow writer Edmund Blunden, though, found unexpected delight in it: 'We halted

The La Bassée Canal near Cuinchy during the First World War.

in the open by the La Bassée Canal, and many of us swam there in unexpected luxury.'[16]

The Cambrin Churchyard Extension is one of two CWGC cemeteries in the village and contains front-line burials up to February 1917. Most of interest to us inevitably are the seventy-nine graves from the Argyll and Sutherland Highlanders. We walk amongst the headstones standing above the mortal remains of those who, like Douglas, died on 25 September. He would have known these men, have read their final letters, touched them lightly on the shoulder and helped steady their nerves as they prepared to go over the top. His spirit if not his body is here: that lies out in the fields over the cemetery wall, towards the slag heaps, his remains blended into the mud and cabbages, his name engraved beyond on the weathered panel on the Loos Memorial with the wrong date.

Storm Eunice is at its most intense when we are in the cemetery, twigs and even small branches flying horizontally through the air, rendering it impossible to hear each other. Extreme weather which assaults our routines inclines us to look for deeper meanings. The roaring storm cannot disturb the dead, but it has snapped the white flagpole bearing the British flag. A little way off, the French and the United States flagpoles are still standing, their national banners stiff in the wind. The Union Jack lies squirming on the ground, like a Firth of Forth salmon breathing its last gasps. An intrinsic believer in the Union, Douglas would have been distraught at the fallen flag.

A broken Union, I hope not; a broken life, we know so; a broken vision, we must ensure not.

Had Douglas survived, he might have driven the Via Sacra forward himself. The family believe a career in politics after the war could have attracted him rather than returning to the bar – a perfect springboard for the walk's campaign, as he would likely have risen far up the ministerial ranks. He might of course have encountered indifference to his plan, or worse in a world not yet ready to listen. But he didn't survive to find out, and it is left to us to pick up the flag. This trip to La Bassée has given the mission fresh purpose and urgency.

Progress on realizing the walk has been swift. As I write this in April 2022, the route through Belgium has been fully marked and is open, and over three hundred communes are supporting it in France. Marking out the definitive route continues there as each month more paths are connected and signposted, avoiding the busy main roads I had to experience. France wants the walk to commemorate victims not just of war but of terrorism too. That's good. Diverse groups of young people, cyclists, walkers, military enthusiasts and pilgrims are hearing about Douglas and his idea. Because of the dedicated team bringing about the transformation, the Western Front Way is becoming a global beacon for commemoration, reconciliation and international collaboration, exactly as he envisaged. How appropriate too that Kilometre Zero, where I started my walk, is the term used by many countries globally, including France and Germany, Russia and China, as the precise location in their capitals from which all distances within their countries are measured. True of Rome's Milliarium Aureum, giving birth to the maxim 'All roads lead to Rome'. Would that all countries could fan out peace from their seminal marker points. For Gillespie's Via Sacra to become a universal Via Pax.

He wanted his plan to be a 'Via Sacra for every generation, but not I think a Via Dolorosa', a walk to enhance and deepen life, not to dwell on loss.[17] What is life if we do not savour it? He is asking us to reflect on just this. Did I do all I could to cherish the time I had with Joanna, and the children when still at home? To make the most of my privileged jobs? I fear not. I have talked a good game on happiness, set up organizations like Action for Happiness even to help spread it, while rushing too much: too many books and too much activity, with insufficient depth and connection. In the time that is left, I must live better, and more in tune with my ideals.

I set out in early August 2021 without a wife, a home or a job. The walk I hoped would help me resolve them all, if it really was to be a walk for greater peace. Well, reader, the experience of the walk and aftermath has helped me to move beyond my grief at the loss of Joanna, and to embrace the prospect of a new marriage with a whole heart. Sarah, to my utter delight, accepted my proposal. My father was so pleased when I decided to marry Joanna, who was Jewish. Sarah is a devout Christian and I think he and my mother would have loved her every bit as much. We were married in April 2022, and I was so grateful that Jessica and Susie agreed to be bridesmaids, and Adam best man.

We do not know where we will put our roots down permanently yet, but have bought a small house in the village of Bray, so at last I have somewhere to put my possessions and make a home. Not knowing where we will settle ultimately is exciting rather than a worry – as long as it is by or near water, and has an open log fire. Sarah is resigned to this quirk in her new husband. I have accepted work trying to build loving relationships at schools. Starting young will help build a better world.

* * *

While I am writing these final pages, the world is descending into chaos again with war in Ukraine. How could we have let this happen? The events, which will likely unfold for much longer still, give added urgency to Douglas's Via Sacra vision.

The armistice, 11 November 1918, fell on a Monday. We do not know how its announcement was greeted at the Gillespies' home. Most likely it was a sombre day, and when the clocks struck eleven, there was no rejoicing. When Tom had died, Daisy rushed home expecting it to be 'the hardest day of all'. But when her father met her at Edinburgh station, she was surprised to hear him talking about the 'wonder and beauty' of his last letter, and how they derived deep consolation from thinking, 'No one could have lost a son in a more beautiful way'.[18] In contrast, Douglas's death seems to have broken them, brave though the face was that they turned to the world. Daisy became the custodian of the memory of her deeply loved brothers. Peggy told me on my visit to Cambridgeshire that no one was allowed to look at their letters that she guarded: '*ne touche pas*', her mother said if anyone went near the shrine.

At the Rosery in Matfield, Kent, my own ancestors, Wilfred and Eileen, took the news of the armistice stoically. Wilfred was still ill from his head wound and coming to terms with not being able to resume his training as a doctor, unsure if he would be able to have more children. Eleven months later, my mother, Audrey Marjorie, was born.

In the East End of London, my father must have heard the sirens at 11 a.m., but aged just two and a half, would not have understood what the sound meant. Nor did local people, who thought it was to announce a Zeppelin raid. The young Arthur must have been disorientated after his parents had suddenly died, his siblings had disappeared, his home had changed not once but several times, and now he had a new mother looking after him. He prevailed, unlike so many orphaned at the time. 'The intellectual architect of both Blairism and Thatcherism,' the *Economist* said of him on his death in 2005.

My father, Arthur Seldon, outside his stepfather's cobbler shop in approximately 1923.

The soldiers had long vacated La Bassée and Cambrin by 11 November, which, like the towns through which I walked – Saint-Dié, Nancy, Verdun, Reims, Soissons, Noyon, Arras, Armentières, Ypres and Diksmuide – were smouldering, uninhabitable ruins, stripped of nature and life. Douglas foresaw this Armageddon: 'There are some villages and factories... where hardly one stone is left upon another, just heaps of brick and mortar... Sometimes you see a piece of an upper floor, which somehow has never fallen down, with the bed still perched on it...'[19] He could've been talking about Mariupol, Kharkiv or Donetsk today.

The soldiers who for four years had fought on the Western Front didn't hear the news of the armistice along the lines they had guarded. By 11 November, most were fighting further east as the front line advanced towards Germany. Relief, anger, joy, humiliation, fear and sadness were amongst the emotions that they felt. But for many of them, as for Ivor Gurney, the war did not end on 11 November: the dreams from the pit continued to taunt them, driving many to poverty, squalor, desperation and suicide. Only for the fortunate does peace come when war ends.

On 11 November, Adolf Hitler heard the news much further east while convalescing at a hospital in Pasewalk deep inside Germany. Partially blinded by gas near Ypres six weeks before, he said that news of the armistice brought on a new wave of blindness.[20] At that very moment, blindness made him believe that the war had been lost through betrayal, and only through another war could national honour be regained. A blindness and a betrayal fiction shared by Vladimir Putin.

In Russia, the armistice was barely noticed with the country deep into the bitterest and cruellest of civil wars, primed by the war that had just ended: 'Trench life for Russian soldiers... was an inhuman experience... Men were either brutalised or traumatised by what they saw.'[21] As Gillespie so clearly foresaw, the war would beget more war 'because of the passions it will leave behind'.

Juliet Nicolson's grandfather Harold was working as an official on armistice morning in Whitehall. At 10.55, he witnessed a hatless Lloyd

George emerging from No. 10 and, white hair flying, crying out, 'at 11 o'clock this morning the war will be over'. On the hundredth anniversary of that day, I chaired Juliet in No. 10 talking to today's officials about the armistice. At one point, she unfolded a rough sketch that Lutyens had given her grandmother Vita Sackville-West of a design he had drawn for a memorial in Whitehall. It became the Cenotaph.

As I finished writing this book, Lloyd George's successor in No. 10, Boris Johnson, was working to support Volodymyr Zelensky, the Ukrainian leader. My grandparents' home town, Pereiaslav, to the east of Kyiv, is in Putin's firing line. I see in the faces of those suffering grievously in that country the faces of my own children, for they share the same blood. Our relatives too were among those murdered by the Nazis at Babyn Yar in Kyiv in 1941: the memorial to 100,000 gunned down in a ravine was shaken by a Russian missile during the invasion. Europe is facing its greatest crisis since 1945, and the possibility of the Third World War. Should that happen, the First World War monument at Neuve Chapelle will no longer be marred by just a few bullet holes from the Second World War. It could be wiped off the face of the earth.

Amidst such mighty forces at play, Gillespie's gentle vision of a 1,000-kilometre path along the Western Front, with people of all nationalities walking side by side, learning from the silent witnesses 'where war leads', feels like a drop in the ocean. But it is a drop which is becoming a stream, a stream which will become a mighty river, a roaring sea indeed, like the North Sea where I ended my walk, and I for one am happy to devote the rest of my life to seeing Gillespie's magnificent roaring dream become a reality.

Blessed are the peacemakers, for they will
be called the children of God.

Matthew 5:9

Glossary

Allies – A loose term for the military alliance that fought the Central Powers. It included British, French and Belgian forces on the Western Front and Russia on the Eastern Front (until 1917). Other Allies were Serbia, Montenegro, Italy, Romania, Portugal, Greece, Hejaz, China and Japan. From 1917, the Allies included the United States of America. In this book, Allies/Allied predominantly means British, French, Belgian and US forces on the Western Front.

BEF – The British Expeditionary Force was the overall name given to the British forces that fought in France and Flanders during the First World War. Originally, it consisted of six divisions and 100,000 men in total sent in August 1914. By 1918, it had grown to a strength of five armies and over 2 million men. Over the course of the war, some 5 million men served in the BEF.

Central Powers – The military alliance that opposed the Allies during the First World War. These countries were a coalition of Germany, Austria–Hungary, the Ottoman Empire and Bulgaria.

Colonial – Both Britain and France were major imperial powers, and all brought forces from their overseas empires to the Western Front. These are mostly referred to in the text as 'colonial' forces.

CWGC – The Commonwealth War Graves Commission marks, records and maintains the graves and places of commemoration of British and Commonwealth military service members who died in the two world wars. The CWGC was named the Imperial War Graves Commission or IWGC from 1917–60.

Dominions – By the First World War, several parts of the British Empire were effectively self-governing, and these were called Dominions. The Dominions were Canada, Australia, New Zealand, Newfoundland and South Africa (Southern Rhodesia was also de facto mostly self-governing). All of these Dominions sent forces to the Western Front.

Flanders – A geographical and historical term for a region that is today part of northern France and northern Belgium.

Kaiser – The German word for 'Emperor'. Kaiser Wilhelm II was the German monarch throughout the First World War.

Machine Gun Corps – A corps of the British army that was formed in 1915 to train men to operate machine guns. Unlike regular corps, men in the Machine Gun Corps were dispersed all along the front.

No Man's Land – The area between the Allied and German front-line trenches.

'race to the sea' – A series of encounter battles fought between September and October 1914 as the French and German armies repeatedly sought to outflank each other whilst moving north, eventually reaching the English Channel. These manoeuvres ended with the Battles of First Ypres and Yser in October and November 1914. By December 1914, the line of the Western Front had been formed.

Organization (British)

GHQ – General Headquarters. The main British headquarters, answerable only to the War Office and the British government. Led by a commander-in-chief, of whom there were two during the First World War, Sir John French (1914–15) and Sir Douglas Haig (1915–18). Both French and Haig received the rank of field marshal.

Army – The army (i.e. First Army, Third Army etc.) was the largest organizational structure on the Western Front, and (in theory) any army had all of the paraphernalia necessary to fight major battles. By 1918, Britain had five armies on the Western Front. Commanded by a general.

Corps – The corps was, in effect, a mini-army, with an established headquarters, several divisions, its own artillery, Royal Flying Corps units, engineering units and logistical train. Its size tended to vary according to military requirements. Some corps generated a unique identity – for example the Canadian Corps was considered an elite unit – but most did not. Commanded by a lieutenant general.

Division – The division consisted of several brigades and could be around 10,000–20,000 men. The division was the largest unit that the ordinary soldier was likely to associate with. Divisions would have their own support units, like artillery, signals, and ambulance units. Commanded by a major general.

Brigade – The tactical grouping of battalions is called a brigade and could reach a strength of around 5,000 men. Commanded by a brigadier general.

Regiment – The regiment linked the battalions to a specific locale, usually a county, where they were based and from which they drew much of their recruitment. Traditionally, most British regiments have had more than one battalion and during the First World War most included numerous battalions. Examples of regiments include the Oxfordshire and Buckinghamshire Light Infantry, the Argyll and Sutherland Highlanders, and the Grenadier Guards.

Battalion – The battalion was around 1,000 men and made up of several companies. Commanded by a lieutenant colonel.

Company – A company is part of a battalion, and during the First World War a British company's full strength was around 200 men. There were four companies in a battalion. Commanded by a major.

Battery – For artillery units, there would be several batteries of guns in the brigade, and several artillery brigades would be under command of the division.

Platoon – In the British army, the platoon was a part of an infantry company, and during the First World War was usually about fifty men. It was further subdivided into sections. Commanded by a lieutenant or second lieutenant.

Section – The section was the most basic part of the unit. Platoons tended to be divided into four sections. Commanded by a corporal.

Illustration Credits

p. 4 Douglas Gillespie, newly enlisted in the Argyll and Sutherland Highlanders, 1915
p. 6 The frontispiece of *Letters from Flanders*, with a photo of Douglas Gillespie in 1911
p. 16 'The marker of three states', with a Swiss soldier to the left, and two Frenchmen on the right. *Swiss Federal Archives*
p. 26 Kilometre Zero, Day 1, 9 August 2021
p. 34 *La Tache Noire* (*The Black Spot*) by Albert Bettannier (1877)
p. 37 Sarah in Colmar, helping me plan Day 2
p. 43 My path through Alsace, with the Vosges in the distance
p. 51 The Hartmannswillerkopf battlefield in 1915
p. 58 The memorial at Le Linge, with the stone-supported trenches on either side
p. 111 *Monument aux enfants de Verdun morts pour la France*
p. 130 Poppies by the side of my track through the Champagne battlefield
p. 135 A contemporary map of the Nivelle Offensive
p. 142 Susie marrying Jonny in Saint-Jean-de-Côle
p. 156 The remains of trenches near the Chemin des Dames
p. 161 British and French war graves on the Aisne
p. 166 Soissons in 1919. *US Library of Congress*
p. 174 Anne Morgan. *US Library of Congress*
p. 182 The ruins of Chaulnes in 1918. *National Library of Scotland*
p. 185 R. C. Sherriff in 1918. *Pictorial Press Ltd/Alamy*
p. 201 Prime Minister H. H. Asquith visits the Somme in September 1916. *Imperial War Museum*
p. 204 *The Welsh at Mametz Wood* (1917) by Christopher Williams
p. 226 Walter Tull in 1917. *Hulton Archive/Getty*
p. 232 Field Marshal Montgomery at Vimy Ridge in September 1944. *Imperial War Museum*
p. 249 The damaged cathedral of Armentières in 1918. *US Library National Archives*
p. 255 In search of the track near the Belgian border
p. 270 The ruined Cloth Hall in Ypres during the winter of 1917. *The US National Archives*
p. 273 *The Menin Gate at Midnight* by Will Longstaff
p. 294 The British ambassador and defence attaché on the path beyond Diksmuide
p. 297 The Dodengang or 'Trench of Death'
p. 316 The La Bassée Canal near Cuinchy during the First World War. *Imperial War Museum*
p. 320 My father, Arthur Seldon, outside his stepfather's cobbler shop in approximately 1923

Notes

1. The Silent Witnesses

1 A. D. Gillespie, *Letters from Flanders*, Third Edition, London, Smith, Elder & Co., 1916, p. 324.

2 John Lewis-Stempel, *Where Poppies Blow: The British Soldier, Nature, the Great War*, London, Weidenfeld & Nicolson, 2016, p. xx.

3 Gillespie, op. cit., pp. 311–13.

4 'Killed, Wounded, and Missing', *Encyclopaedia Britannica*, https://www.britannica.com/event/World-War-I/Killed-wounded-and-missing (accessed 14 April 2022).

2. Kilometre Zero

1 David T. Zabecki, 'Kilometer Zero: Western Front Flashpoint', historynet.com, August 2019, https://www.historynet.com/westernfrontflashpoint.htm (accessed 1 December 2021).

2 Sebastian Laudan, 'The Southern Tip of the Western Front', *Stand To!*, no. 89, August–September 2010, https://web.archive.org/web/20140910044147/http://www.westernfrontassociation.com/wfa-publications/118-wfa-stand-to/1420-stand-to-no-89-august-september-2010.html (accessed 1 December 2021).

3 Ian Senior, *Invasion 1914: The Schlieffen Plan to the Battle of the Marne*, Oxford, Osprey, 2012, pp. 336–7.

4 For a good overview of the opening stages of the war on the Western Front, see Holger H. Herwig, *The Marne, 1914: The Opening of World War I and the Battle that Changed the World*, New York, Random House, 2009. For an in-depth look at the Marne, see Senior, op. cit.

5 Gillespie, op. cit, p. 281.

6 Joseph E. Persico, *11th Month, 11th Day, 11th Hour: Armistice Day 1918, World War 1 and its Violent Climax*, London, Arrow Books, 2005, p. 378.

7 Orlando Figes, *A People's Tragedy: The Russian Revolution, 1891–1924*, London, Pimlico, 1996, p. 679.

8 Jonathan Smith, *Wilfred and Eileen*, London, Hutchinson, 1976.

3. Alsace

1 Herwig, op. cit., pp. 74–104.

2 Ibid., pp. 80, 132–158, 217.

3 Elizabeth Vlossak, 'Alsace-Lorraine', 1914–18 Online , 21 October 2016, https://encyclopedia.1914-1918-online.net/article/alsace-lorraine (accessed 1 January 2022).

4 Ibid.

5 Ibid.

6 David O'Mara, 'The First to Fall: Peugeot and Mayer', Western Front Association, 2 August 2014, https://web.archive.org/web/20151118154741/http://www.westernfrontassociation.com/great-war-people/brothers-arms/1515-the-first-to-fall-peugeot-and-mayer-2-august-1914.html#sthash.qTrjk9oN.dpbs (accessed 15 November 2021).

7 'Army Horse Care in the First World War', National Army Museum, https://www.nam.ac.uk/explore/british-army-horses-during-first-world-war (accessed 1 February 2022).

8 Chris Pearson, *Mobilizing Nature: The Environmental History of War and Militarization in Modern France*, Manchester, Manchester University Press, 2012, p. 97.

9 'Army Horse Care in the First World War', op. cit.

10 John Singleton, 'Britain's Military Use of Horses, 1914–1918', *Past and Present*, no. 139, May 1993, https://www.jstor.org/stable/651094 (accessed 20 March 2022); Pearson, op. cit., p. 97.

11 'Horse Power in the First World War', National Army Museum, https://www.nam.ac.uk/explore/horse-power-first-world-war (accessed 1 February 2022).

12 Michael Reeve, 'Smoking and Cigarette Consumption', 1914–1918 Online, 23 May 2018, https://encyclopedia.1914-1918-online.net/article/smoking_and_cigarette_consumption (accessed 4 March 2022).

4. The Vosges

1 Quoted in Herwig, op. cit., pp. 99–100.

2 For further detail, see Herwig, op. cit., pp. 74–104.

3 'The Hartmannswillerkopf', kaiserscross.com, http://www.kaiserscross.com/40047/41321.html (accessed 1 December 2021).

4 Ferdinand Belmont, *A Crusader of France: The Letters of Captain Ferdinand Belmont*, trans. G. Frederic Lees, New York, E. P. Dutton & Co., 1916, pp. 363–4.

5 'Vosges, Battles in the', *Encyclopaedia Britannica*, vol. 32, London, The Encyclopaedia Britannica Company Ltd, 1922, p. 936.

6 Belmont, op. cit., p. 285.

7 'Stages of Decomposition', Australian Museum, 25 June 2020, https://australian.museum/learn/science/stages-of-decomposition (accessed 15 January 2022).

8 'The Reichsackerkopf', kaiserscross.com, http://www.kaiserscross.com/40047/41273.html (accessed 1 December 2021).

9 Frank McLynn, *Carl Gustav Jung: A Biography*, New York, St Martin's Press, 1996, pp. 248–9.

10 Elizabeth Greenhalgh, *The French Army and the First World War*, Cambridge, Cambridge University Press, 2014, pp. 77–8.

11 Belmont, op. cit., p. 323.

12 Ibid., p. 328.

13 Ibid., p. 72.

14 Belmont, op. cit., p. 284.
15 Chris Baker, 'Life in the Trenches of the First World War', Long Long Trail, https://www.longlongtrail.co.uk/soldiers/a-soldiers-life-1914-1918/life-in-the-trenches-of-the-first-world-war (accessed 10 November 2021).
16 Richard Holmes, *Tommy: The British Soldier on the Western Front, 1914–1918*, London, HarperCollins, 2004, p. 302.
17 Gordon Corrigan, *Mud, Blood and Poppycock*, London, Cassell, 2003, p. 230.
18 Holmes, op. cit., pp. 563–70.
19 Anthony Seldon and David Walsh, *Public Schools and the Great War*, Barnsley, Pen & Sword, 2013, pp. 141–2. In 2006, all but the thirty-seven convicted of murder (who would have faced the gallows in civilian law) were pardoned. The pardons no doubt provided some comfort to those who had campaigned for them for so long.

5. Lorraine

1 Herwig, op. cit., p. 157; Stéphanie Trouillard, 'August 22 1914: The Bloodiest Day in French Military History', *France 24*, 22 August 2014, https://www.france24.com/en/20140822-august-22-1914-battle-frontiers-bloodiest-day-french-military-history (accessed 1 November 2021).
2 Herwig, op. cit., pp. 200–203.
3 Ibid., pp. 204–18.
4 Ibid., p. 302.
5 Antoine Prost, 'War Losses', 1914–18 Online, 8 October 2014, https://encyclopedia.1914-1918-online.net/article/war_losses (accessed 19 March 2022); 'Killed, Wounded, and Missing', *Encyclopaedia Britannica*, https://www.britannica.com/event/World-War-I/Killed-wounded-and-missing (accessed 19 March 2022).
6 'Place Stanislas, Place de la Carrière and Place d'Alliance in Nancy', UNESCO, https://whc.unesco.org/en/list/229 (accessed 1 February 2022).
7 'Wartime Leisure and Entertainment', Imperial War Museum, https://www.iwm.org.uk/history/voices-of-the-first-world-war-wartime-leisure-and-entertainment (accessed 1 February 2022).
8 Holmes, op. cit., p. 602.
9 Clare Makepeace, 'Sex and the First World War: The Tommies who visited brothels', *BBC History Magazine*, 13 August 2011, https://www.historyextra.com/period/first-world-war/sex-and-the-first-world-war-the-tommies-who-visited-brothels (accessed 1 February 2022).
10 Ibid.
11 Holmes, op. cit., pp. 595–7.
12 Ibid.
13 Richard Marshall, 'The British Army's Fight Against Venereal Disease in the "Heroic Age of Prostitution"', University of Oxford, http://ww1centenary.oucs.ox.ac.uk/body-and-mind/the-british-army%E2%80%99s-fight-against-venereal-disease-in-the-%E2%80%98heroic-age-of-prostitution%E2%80%99 (accessed 20 February 2022).
14 Ibid.

15 'Proclamation', IWM Archives, https://www.iwm.org.uk/collections/item/object/28569 (accessed 1 February 2022).
16 'The National Necropolis of Friscati', Horizon14–18.org, https://horizon14-18.eu/friscati.html (accessed 10 January 2022).
17 Radhika Singha, 'The Short Career of the Indian Labour Corps in France, 1917–1919', *International Labor and Working-Class History*, no. 87, spring 2015, pp. 27–62.
18 Ernst Jünger, *Storm of Steel*, trans. Michael Hoffmann, London, Penguin, 2004, p. 25.
19 Donald A. Carter, *St Mihiel, 12–16 September 1918*, Washington DC, United States Army, 2018, p. 21.
20 Martin Marix Evans (ed.), *American Voices of World War I: primary source documents, 1917–1920*, Chicago, Fitzroy Dearborn Publishers, 2001, p. 127.
21 Carter, op. cit., pp. 57–61.
22 Carol R. Byerly, 'War Losses (USA)', 1914–1918 Online, October 2014, https://encyclopedia.1914-1918-online.net/article/war_losses_usa (accessed 11 January 2022).
23 Richard S. Faulkner, *Meuse–Argonne, 26 September–11 November 1918*, Washington DC, United States Army, 2018, p. 72; 'Meuse–Argonne Cemetery', American Battle Monuments Commission, https://www.abmc.gov/Meuse-Argonne (accessed 19 April 2022); 'Normandy Cemetery', American Battle Monuments Commission, https://www.abmc.gov/normandy (accessed 19 April 2022).
24 'Civil War Casualties, The Cost of War: Killed, Wounded, Captured, and Missing', American Battlefield Trust, https://www.battlefields.org/learn/articles/civil-war-casualties (accessed 19 April 2022); J. David Hacker, 'Recounting the Dead', *New York Times*, 20 September 2011, https://web.archive.org/web/20110925090025/http://opinionator.blogs.nytimes.com/2011/09/20/recounting-the-dead (accessed 19 April 2022).
25 John Milton Cooper Jr, 'The Great War and American Memory', *VQR*, winter 2003, https://www.vqronline.org/essay/great-war-and-american-memory (accessed 1 November 2021).
26 'Saint-Benoît-en-Woëvre', MortHomme.com, https://www.morthomme.com/saint-benoit.html (accessed 1 February 2022).
27 Maarten Otte, *The St Mihiel Offensive: 12 to 16 September 1918*, Barnsley, Pen & Sword, 2019.
28 Douglas Hill and Robert Cowley, 'A Battle of Presumptions', *Quarterly Journal of Military History*, vol. 6, no. 1, autumn 1993, https://www.historynet.com/a-bundle-of-presumptions (accessed 11 November 2021); Tara Patel, 'Technology: War victims bring archaeology up to date', *New Scientist*, 30 April 1993, https://www.newscientist.com/article/mg13818713-800-technology-war-victims-bring-archaeology-up-to-date (accessed 11 November 2021).

6. Verdun

1 Erich von Falkenhayn, *The German General Staff and its Decisions, 1914–1916*, New York, Dodd, Mead & Company, 1920, pp. 248–50.
2 Alistair Horne, *The Price of Glory: Verdun 1916*, London, Penguin Books, 1993, p. 327.
3 Sylvie Pomiès-Maréchal, '"A white city of desolation": Verdun as seen by three British nurses', *Revue Française de Civilisation Britannique*, XX-1, 2015, https://journals.openedition.org/rfcb/294 (accessed 1 December 2021).
4 David Mason, *Verdun*, Gloucestershire, Windrush Press, 2000, pp. 48–9.
5 Christina Holstein, *Walking Verdun*, Barnsley, Pen & Sword, 2012, pp. 46–63.
6 Alistair Horne, 'The Legend of Verdun', *New Statesman*, 17 February 2016, https://www.newstatesman.com/politics/2016/02/the-legend-of-verdun (accessed 1 December 2021).
7 Allain Bernède, 'Verdun 1916: un choix stratégique, une équation logistique', *Revue historique des armées*, 242, 2006, pp. 48–59, https://journals.openedition.org/rha/4122 (accessed 20 February 2022).
8 Horne, 'The Legend of Verdun', op. cit.
9 Charles Delvert, *From Marne to Verdun: The War Diary of Captain Charles Delvert, 101st Infantry 1914–1916*, trans. Ian Sumner, Barnsley, Pen & Sword, 2016, pp. 175–8.
10 Holstein, op. cit., pp. 92–117.
11 Bernd Ulrich and Benjamin Ziemann, *German Soldiers in the Great War: Letters and Eyewitness*, trans. Christine Brocks, Barnsley, Pen & Sword, 2010, Kindle location 1721–32.
12 'Preußische Groteske', *Der Spiegel*, 25 November 1979, https://www.spiegel.de/politik/preussische-groteske-a-b6dc9a1b-0002-0001-0000-000039867416?context=issue (accessed 3 December 2021).
13 Holstein, op. cit., p. 19.
14 Rod Kedward, *La Vie en Bleu: France and the French Since 1900*, London, Penguin Books, 2005, p. 89.
15 Holstein, op. cit., p. 52.
16 Jay Winter, *Sites of Memory, Sites of Mourning: The Great War in European Cultural History*, Cambridge, Cambridge University Press, 1995, pp. 98–102.
17 Ian Ousby, *The Ordeal of France, 1940–44*, London, Pimlico, 1999, p. 314; 'Pétain Body Recovered by French Police', *New York Times*, 22 February 1973, https://www.nytimes.com/1973/02/22/archives/petain-body-recovered-by-french-police-boast-by-a-rightist-verdun.html (accessed 1 December 2021).
18 'The National Characteristics of Cemeteries', RemembranceTrails-NorthernFrance.com, http://www.remembrancetrails-northernfrance.com/history/great-war-remembrance/the-national-characteristics-of-cemeteries.html (accessed 1 December 2021).

7. Champagne–Argonne

1 'Voices of the First World War: Trench Life', Imperial War Museum, https://www.iwm.org.uk/history/voices-of-the-first-world-war-trench-life (accessed 9 March 2022); 'Sanitary arrangements in the trenches. Trench

latrines', The First World War Poetry Digital Archive, http://ww1lit.nsms.ox.ac.uk/ww1lit/items/show/44 (accessed 9 March 2022).

2 Jack Sheldon, *The German Army on the Western Front 1915*, Barnsley, Pen & Sword, 2012, pp. 41–3.

3 Anthony Clayton, *Paths of Glory: The French Army 1914–18*, London, Cassell, 2003, pp. 68–9; Sebastian Lukasik, 'Champagne Offensives', 1914–1918 Online, 20 January 2020, https://encyclopedia.1914-1918-online.net/article/champagne_offensives (accessed 1 December 2021).

4 Falkenhayn, op. cit., pp. 196–7.

5 In French and British military cartography, hills were named according to their height. Hill 304 was 304 metres above sea level. See British First World War Trench Maps, 1915–1918, National Library of Scotland, https://maps.nls.uk/ww1/trenches/info1.html (accessed 9 May 2022).

6 'History', Butte de Vauquois, https://butte-vauquois.fr/en/history (accessed 1 December 2021).

7 William F. Buckingham, *Verdun 1916: The Deadliest Battle of the First World War*, Stroud, Amberley, 2016, p. 87.

8 'History', Butte de Vauquois, op. cit.

9 'Deminex Terres d'Avant Guerre', deminex.fr, https://www.deminex.fr (accessed 1 February 2022); Donovan Webster, *Aftermath: Remnants of War*, New York, Random House, 1996, p. 19.

10 'An American Hero: Sargent [*sic*] York', *American Heritage*, vol. 63, issue 3, fall 2018, https://www.americanheritage.com/american-hero-sargent-york (accessed 1 December 2021).

11 George Morton-Jack, *The Indian Army on the Western Front*, Cambridge, Cambridge University Press, 2014, p. 156.

12 'War in Winter', Imperial War Museum, https://www.iwm.org.uk/history/voices-of-the-first-world-war-war-in-winter (accessed 21 April 2022).

13 'Northampton shoemaking – the impact of war', Northamptonmuseums.com, https://www.northamptonmuseums.com/info/3/collections/54/shoes-1/6 (accessed 1 December 2021).

14 'Voices of the First World War: War in Winter', Imperial War Museum, https://www.iwm.org.uk/history/voices-of-the-first-world-war-war-in-winter (accessed 1 December 2021).

15 Erich Maria Remarque, *All Quiet on the Western Front*, trans. A. W. Wheen, New York, Ballantine Books, 1996, pp. 20–21.

16 Morton-Jack, op. cit., p. 156.

17 'Boots on the Ground: The History of the Combat Boot', filson.com, https://www.filson.com/blog/field-notes/history-of-combat-boot (accessed 1 December 2021).

18 Jeffrey S. Bush, Trevor Lofgran and Simon Watson, 'Trench Foot', NCBI, 11 August 2021, https://www.ncbi.nlm.nih.gov/books/NBK482364 (accessed 1 February 2022).

19 Shannon Baker Moore, *The Harlem Hellfighters*, Minneapolis, Abdo, 2016, p. 74; 'The Harlem Hellfighters: The most storied Black combat unit of World War I', American Battle Monuments Commission, 9 February 2021, https://www.abmc.gov/news-events/news/harlem-hellfighters-most-storied-african-american-combat-unit-world-war-i (accessed 21 April 2022).

20 'Reporting from a World War I Battlefield: the Champagne, September 1915', *Roads to the Great War*, 22 September 2014, https://roadstothegreatwar-ww1.blogspot.com/2014/09/reporting-from-world-war-i-battlefield.html (accessed 1 December 2021).
21 'Army Dental Corps', National Army Museum, https://www.nam.ac.uk/explore/royal-army-dental-corps (accessed 1 December 2021).
22 'Soldiers' Teeth: Need for Dental Surgeons', British Dental Association, 1914, https://bda.org/library/history/Documents/soldiersteeth-needfordentalsurgeons.pdf (accessed 1 December 2021).
23 'History of Royal Army Dental Corps', Museum of Military Medicine, https://museumofmilitarymedicine.org.uk/about/corps-history/history-of-the-royal-army-dental-corps (accessed 1 December 2021).
24 Maurice Baring, *RFC HQ 1914–1918*, London, G. Bell & Sons Ltd, 1920, pp. 212–13.
25 Lorraine Boissoneault, 'The Debate Over Rebuilding That Ensued When a Beloved French Cathedral Was Shelled During WW1', *Smithsonian Magazine*, 19 April 2019, https://www.smithsonianmag.com/history/debate-over-rebuilding-ensued-when-beloved-french-cathedral-was-shelled-during-wwi-180971999 (accessed 1 February 2022).
26 Chris Mercer, 'Champagne and World War One: "the darkest hour"', Decanter.com, 11 November 2015, https://www.decanter.com/learn/champagne-and-world-war-one-the-darkest-hour-281711 (accessed 1 February 2022).

8. The Aisne and Marne

1 Alexandre Lafon, 'War Losses (France)', 1914–1918 Online, 8 October 2014, https://encyclopedia.1914-1918-online.net/article/war_losses_france (accessed 21 April 2022); 'Killed, Wounded, and Missing', *Encyclopaedia Britannica*, https://www.britannica.com/event/World-War-I/Killed-wounded-and-missing (accessed 21 April 2022).
2 'County 24425 – Saint – Jean-de-Cole – War dead', fr.geneawiki.com, https://fr.geneawiki.com/index.php?title=24425_-_Saint-Jean-de-C%C3%B4le_-_Morts_aux_guerres (accessed 4 January 2022).
3 David Stevenson, *1914–1918: The History of the First World War*, London, Penguin Allen Lane, 2004, p. 60.
4 J. P. Harris, *Douglas Haig and the First World War*, Cambridge, Cambridge University Press, 2008, pp. 279–97.
5 Stevenson, *1914–1918*, op. cit., pp. 174–7.
6 David Stevenson, *With Our Backs to the Wall: Victory and Defeat in 1918*, London, Allen Lane, 2011, pp. 78–88.
7 Ibid., pp. 105–17.
8 Tim Gale, '"Everything in war is very simple…": The Great War French tank regulations and their implementation', *British Journal for Military History*, 5.2, 2019, pp. 100–19.
9 Stevenson, *With Our Backs to the Wall*, op. cit., pp. 216–18.
10 Clayton, op. cit., pp. 145–6; Stevenson, *1914–1918*, op. cit., p. 328.

11 Ian Sumner, *They Shall Not Pass: The French Army on the Western Front, 1914–1918*, Barnsley, Pen & Sword, 2012, p. 184.

12 David Payne, 'Why the British Army did not mutiny en masse on the Western Front during the First World War, Western Front Association, https://www.westernfrontassociation.com/world-war-i-articles/why-the-british-army-did-not-mutiny-en-masse-on-the-western-front-during-the-first-world-war (accessed 15 January 2022); 'Jesse Robert Short', Imperial War Museum, https://livesofthefirstworldwar.iwm.org.uk/lifestory/4021884 (accessed 1 March 2022).

13 Hugh Schofield, 'Discovering WW1 tunnel of death hidden in France for a century', *BBC News*, 15 March 2021, https://www.bbc.co.uk/news/world-europe-56370510 (accessed 1 December 2021).

14 Richard Fogarty, 'Tirailleurs Sénégalais', 1914–1918 Online, 1 April 2016, https://encyclopedia.1914-1918-online.net/article/tirailleurs_senegalais (accessed 1 February 2021).

15 Quoted in Chris Baker, 'The Battle of the Aisne, 1914', Long Long Trail, https://www.longlongtrail.co.uk/battles/battles-of-the-western-front-in-france-and-flanders/the-battle-of-the-aisne-1914 (accessed 1 February 2022).

16 Max Arthur (ed.), *Forgotten Voices of the Great War*, London: Ted Smart, 2002, p. 38.

17 'A Memorial Stone…', Victoriacross.org, 21 August 2003, http://www.victoriacross.org.uk/bbwilson.htm (accessed 1 February 2022).

18 Arthur Anderson Martin, *A Surgeon in Khaki*, London, Edward Arnold, 1915, pp. 87–9.

19 Stevenson, *With Our Backs to the Wall*, op. cit., pp. 113–17.

20 Paul Greenwood, *The Second Battle of the Marne*, Shrewsbury, Airlife, 1998, p. 196. For the American casualties, see Stephen C. McGeorge and Mason W. Watson, *The Marne: 15 July–6 August 1918*, Washington DC, United States Army, 2018, p. 76.

21 'Third Battle of the Aisne', Quierzy Royal Residence (archived), https://web.archive.org/web/20190504042358/http://dvole.free.fr/quierzy/q318.htm (accessed 1 February 2022).

9. Picardy

1 Gillespie, op. cit., p. 287.

2 'Story of Anne Morgan, Founder of the Franco-American Museum of the Château de Blérancourt', The American Friends of Blérancourt, https://www.americanfriendsofblerancourt.org/anne-morgan (accessed 1 February 2022); 'Anne Morgan's War: Rebuilding Devastated France, 1917–1924', The Morgan Library and Museum, https://www.themorgan.org/exhibitions/anne-morgans-war (accessed 2 May 2022).

3 David Abrams et al., *The Rough Guide to France*, London, Rough Guides, 2005, p. 287.

4 'Canada at War', Canadian War Museum, https://www.warmuseum.ca/firstworldwar/history/going-to-war/canada-enters-the-war/?anchor=21 (accessed 2 March

2022); 'The Cost of Canada's War', Canadian War Museum, https://www.warmuseum.ca/firstworldwar/history/after-the-war/legacy/?anchor=475 (accessed 2 March 2022).

5 Michael W. Homer, 'Arthur Conan Doyle's Adventures in Winnipeg', *Manitoba History*, spring 1993, http://www.mhs.mb.ca/docs/mb_history/25/doyleinwinnipeg.shtml (accessed 2 March 2022).

6 Gillespie, op. cit., pp. 293–4.

7 R. C. Sherriff, *Journey's End*, London, Penguin, 1983, p. 58.

8 Stevenson, *With Our Backs to the Wall*, op. cit., pp. 53–68.

9 Ibid., p. 68.

10 Clayton provides a figure of French dead on the Somme as 37,000. It seems sensible to say that including the missing would likely push the figure beyond 50,000. Clayton, op. cit., p. 118.

11 Jack Sheldon, *Fighting the Somme*, Barnsley, Pen & Sword, 2017, p. 90.

10. The Somme

1 Arthur, op. cit., p. 159.

2 Gary Sheffield, *The Somme*, London, Cassell, 2003, pp. 151–2.

3 Max Egremont, *Some Desperate Glory: The First World War the Poets Knew*, London, Picador, 2014, pp. 124–5.

4 Mark Plowman [published as Mark VII], *A Subaltern on the Somme*, New York, E. P. Dutton & Company, 1928, p. 40.

5 Siegfried Sassoon, Journal, 26 June 1916–12 Aug. 1916 (MS Add.9852/1/7), Cambridge University, https://cudl.lib.cam.ac.uk/view/MS-ADD-09852-00001-00007/22 (accessed 2 March 2022).

6 Arthur (ed.), op. cit., p. 161.

7 Peter Hart, *The Somme*, London, Cassell, 2006, pp. 181–2.

8 Holmes, op. cit., p. 47.

9 Jünger, op. cit., p. 102.

10 Roy Jenkins, *Asquith*, London, Collins, 1978, pp. 412–13.

11 Douglas Haig, Gary Sheffield (ed.), John Bourne (ed.), *Douglas Haig: War Diaries and Letters, 1914–1918*, London, Weidenfeld & Nicolson, 2005, p. 228.

12 Simon Heffer, *Staring at God: Britain and the Great War*, London, Random House Books, 2019, p. 447.

13 Frederick Ponsonby, *The Grenadier Guards in the Great War of 1914–1918*, Volume II, London, Macmillan & Co., 1920, pp. 96–7.

14 Holmes, op. cit., p. 45.

15 Quoted in 'Raymond Asquith', Spartacus Educational, https://spartacus-educational.com/FWWasquithR.htm (accessed 4 March 2022).

16 Margot Asquith, *The Autobiography of Margot Asquith: Volume II*, London, Thornton Butterworth Ltd, 1922, pp. 243–4.

17 Alexandra Churchill, 'Captain David Henderson: Labour Party leader's son on the Somme', The History Press, https://www.thehistorypress.co.uk/articles/captain-david-henderson-labour-party-leader-s-son-on-the-somme (accessed 2 March 2022).

18 David Cannadine, 'War and Death, Grief and Mourning in Modern Britain', in Joachim Whaley (ed.), *Mirrors of Mortality*, Abingdon, Routledge, 2011, p. 214.

19 'Future PM lost two sons in six months', Helensburgh Heritage Trust, 3 April 2015, http://www.helensburgh-heritage.co.uk/index.php?option=com_content&view=article&id=1232:future-pm-lost-two-sons-in-six-months&catid=88:military&Itemid=462 (accessed 2 May 2022).
20 Seldon and Walsh, op. cit., 2013, pp. 245–50.
21 Ibid., p. 247.
22 Ibid., pp. 245–50.
23 John Stuart Roberts, *Siegfried Sassoon*, London, Metro Publishing, 2014, p. 85.
24 Robert Graves, *Goodbye to All That*, London, Jonathan Cape, 1929, p. 272.
25 J. R. R. Tolkien, *The Two Towers: The Lord of the Rings, Part II*, London, HarperCollins, 1997, pp. 612–14.
26 The other Commonwealth nations chose to commemorate their dead on their own, national memorials.
27 Jünger, op. cit., pp. 80–81.
28 Joanna Bourke, 'The Emotions in War: fear and the British and American military, 1914–1945', *Historical Research*, vol. 74, issue 185, August 2001, pp. 314–30.
29 Łukasz Kamieński, 'Drugs', 1914–1918 Online, 7 March 2019, https://encyclopedia.1914-1918-online.net/article/drugs (accessed 4 March 2022).
30 Ibid.
31 Sheldon, *Fighting the Somme*, op. cit., p. 137.
32 Anthony Seldon and Jonathan Meakin, *The Cabinet Office 1916–2016*, London, Biteback, 2016, p. 75.
33 Sheffield, op. cit., pp. 94–6.
34 Exact figures of tanks vary; those here are extrapolated from Christy Campbell, *Band of Brigands: The First Men in Tanks*, London, Harper Press, 2007, p. 205. And from Hart, op. cit., p. 377.
35 Hart, op. cit., p. 397.
36 Charles Carrington [published as Charles Edmonds], *A Subaltern's War*, London, Peter Davies Ltd, 1929, p. 117.
37 Hart, op. cit., pp. 497–8.
38 'Casualties of Cambrai: Brigadier General Roland Boys Bradford VC', Commonwealth War Graves Commission, 30 November 2017, https://www.cwgc.org/our-work/news/casualties-of-cambrai-brigadier-general-roland-boys-bradford-vc (accessed 2 March 2022).
39 For a convincing analysis of the impact of the Somme, see the final chapter of Sheldon, *Fighting the Somme*, op. cit., pp. 241–77.
40 A photograph of the sign can be found at 'Q 78871', The German Withdrawal to the Hindenburg Line, March–April 1917, Imperial War Museum Collections, https://www.iwm.org.uk/collections/item/object/205323631 (accessed 2 March 2022).
41 'Last Letter Sent to [Horace Iles] By His Sister – Returned Unopened "Killed in Action"', Imperial War Museum, https://livesofthefirstworldwar.iwm.org.uk/story/11171 (accessed 2 March 2022).
42 'The Story of the Leeds Pals who fought and died in France over 100 years ago', *Leeds Live*, 11 November 2020, https://www.leeds-live.co.uk/news/leeds-news/story-leeds-pals-who-fought-15394955 (accessed 3 May 2022).

11. Artois

1 For an indication of just how valuable this area was to the French economy, see Stevenson, *With Our Backs to the Wall*, op. cit., p. 392.
2 Gillespie, op. cit., p. 296.
3 Archibald Wavell, *Allenby: A Study in Greatness*, London, George G. Harrap & Co. Ltd, 1940, p. 171.
4 'Private 13908 Christopher Augustus COX, V.C.', The Bedfordshire Regiment in the Great War, http://bedfordregiment.org.uk/7thbn/christophercoxvc.html (accessed 3 March 2022).
5 'Conscientious Objectors in Their Own Words', Imperial War Museum, https://www.iwm.org.uk/history/conscientious-objectors-in-their-own-words (accessed 3 March 2022).
6 E. Mayhew, 'Regimental Medical Officer Charles McKerrow: saving lives on the Western Front', *Royal College of Physicians Edinburgh*, 2014, vol. 44, pp. 158–62, https://www.rcpe.ac.uk/sites/default/files/mayhew.pdf (accessed 3 March 2022).
7 Chris Baker, 'The evacuation chain for wounded and sick soldiers', Long Long Trail, https://www.longlongtrail.co.uk/soldiers/a-soldiers-life-1914-1918/the-evacuation-chain-for-wounded-and-sick-soldiers (accessed 3 March 2022); Holmes, op. cit., pp. 470–76.
8 'Hugh McIver, VC, MM', VC GC Association, https://vcgca.org/our-people/profile/760/Hugh--McIVER (accessed 3 March 2022).
9 'Voices of the First World War: Arras and Vimy', Imperial War Museum, https://www.iwm.org.uk/history/voices-of-the-first-world-war-arras-and-vimy (accessed 3 March 2022).
10 Ibid.
11 Brian Gardner, *Allenby of Arabia*, New York, Coward-McCann Inc., 1966, p. 147.
12 Sheffield and Bourne, op. cit., p. 278.
13 Helen Thomas and Myfanwy Thomas, *Under Storm's Wing*, Manchester, Carcanet, 1988, p. 173.
14 Ibid., p. 108.
15 'Voices of the First World War: Arras and Vimy', op. cit.
16 'The war diary of Edward Thomas', National Library of Wales, https://www.library.wales/discover/digital-gallery/manuscripts/modern-period/the-war-diary-of-edward-thomas#?c=&m=&s=&cv=&xywh=-1545%2C0%2C6283%2C4382 (accessed 3 March 2022).
17 'Arras April–May 1917', The Royal Scots, https://www.theroyalscots.co.uk/823-2/ (accessed 1 May 2022).
18 *Manual of Military Law*, War Office, London, HMSO, 1914, pp. 192, 198.
19 Richard Conway and David Lockwood, 'Walter Tull: The incredible story of a football pioneer and war hero', *BBC News*, 23 March 2018, https://www.bbc.co.uk/sport/football/43504448 (accessed 3 March 2022).
20 Richard Elvin, 'Walter Tull: From Cobbler to Soldier', National Archives, 25 March 2015, https://blog.nationalarchives.gov.uk/walter-tull-cobbler-soldier (accessed 5 April 2022).
21 Mike Bechtold, 'Bloody April Revisited: The Royal Flying Corps at the Battle of Arras, 1917', *British Journal of Military History*, vol. 4, issue 2, February 2018, pp. 50–69, https://bjmh.gold.ac.uk/article/view/790 (accessed 3 March 2022).

22 Trevor Royle, *The Flowers of the Forest: Scotland and the First World War*, Edinburgh, Berlinn, 2006, p. 119.
23 Erich von Ludendorff, *My War Memories 1914–1918*, Volume II, London, Hutchinson & Co., 1919, p. 422.
24 Gillespie, op. cit., p. 298.
25 Bourke, op. cit., pp. 314–30.
26 Ibid.
27 A. D. Macleod, 'Shell shock, Gordon Holmes and the Great War', *Journal of the Royal Society of Medicine*, February 2004, pp. 86–9, https://www.ncbi.nlm.nih.gov/pmc/articles/PMC1079301 (accessed 3 February 2022); Joanna Bourke, *Dismembering the Male: Men's Bodies, Britain and the Great War*, London, Reaktion Books, 1996, p. 109; Edgar Jones, 'War of the Mind: Psychiatry and Neurology in the British and French Armies', in Leo Van Bergen and Eric Vermetten, *The First World War and Health: Rethinking Resilience*, Leiden, Brill, 2020, p. 109.
28 'The secret history of the gay soldiers who served in the First World War', *The Week*, 3 August 2018, https://www.theweek.co.uk/history/95476/the-secret-history-of-the-gay-soldiers-who-served-in-the-first-world-war (accessed 3 March 2022).
29 Alan Bishop (ed.) and Mark Bostridge (ed.), *Letters from a Lost Generation: First World War Letters of Vera Brittain and Four Friends*, London, Abacus, 1999, p. 6.
30 'J. R. Ackerley', jrackerley.com, https://www.jrackerley.com/about (accessed 3 March 2022).
31 Holmes, op. cit., p. 362.
32 For a description of a typical day, see Carrington, op. cit., pp. 23–5.
33 Jünger, op. cit., p. 59.
34 Kamieński, op. cit.
35 Ibid.
36 'The Battle of Vimy Ridge, 9–12 April 1917', Canadian War Museum, https://www.warmuseum.ca/the-battle-of-vimy-ridge (accessed 3 March 2022).
37 'Vimy Memorial', Canadian War Museum, https://www.warmuseum.ca/firstworldwar/history/after-the-war/remembrance/vimy-memorial (accessed 3 March 2022).
38 Ibid.
39 'Bernard Law Montgomery: Unbeatable and unbearable', National Army Museum, https://www.nam.ac.uk/explore/bernard-montgomery (accessed 3 March 2022).
40 'Voices of the First World War: Arras and Vimy', op. cit.

12. Forgotten Flanders

1 Letters, 26 April, 4 August, 25 August, Gillespie family archive.
2 Lyn Macdonald, *1915: The Death of Innocence*, London, BCA, 1993.
3 Holmes, op. cit., pp. 138–9.
4 Chris Baker, 'The Battle of Festubert', Long Long Trail, https://www.longlongtrail.co.uk/battles/battles-of-the-western-front-in-france-and-flanders/the-battle-of-festubert (accessed 4 March 2022); Chris Baker, 'The Battle of Aubers', Long Long Trail, https://www.longlongtrail.co.uk/battles/battles-of-the-western-front-in-france-and-flanders/the-battle-of-aubers (accessed 4 March 2022).
5 Chris Baker, 'The Battle of Loos', Long Long Trail, http://www.longlongtrail.co.uk/battles/battles-of-the-western-

front-in-france-and-flanders/the-battle-of-loos (accessed 4 March 2022).

6 Gillespie, op. cit., p. 302.

7 'Solving the mystery of Rudyard Kipling's son', *BBC News*, 18 January 2016, https://www.bbc.co.uk/news/magazine-35321716 (accessed 4 March 2022); 'The Unidentified Irish Guards Lieutenant at Loos', Great War 1914–1918, http://www.greatwar.co.uk/people/john-kipling-grave.htm (accessed 4 March 2022).

8 Robert Sackville-West, *The Searchers: The Quest for the Lost of the First World War*, London, Bloomsbury, 2021, pp. 115–16.

9 James Edmonds, *Military Operations France and Belgium 1915, Volume II: Battles of Aubers Ridge, Festubert and Loos*, London, Macmillan & Co., 1936, p. 388.

10 Baker, 'The Battle of Loos', op. cit.

11 Holmes, op. cit., p. 37; Nick Lloyd, *Loos 1915*, Cheltenham, The History Press, 2008, p. 168.

12 Toni Pascale, 'Hidden Profanity: Language and Identity in the First World War', 3 February 2020, Queen's University, https://www.queensu.ca/strathy/hidden-profanity-language-and-identity-first-world-war (accessed 7 March 2022).

13 Robert Graves, op. cit., pp. 202–3.

14 'Neuve Chapelle Memorial', Commonwealth War Graves Commission, https://www.cwgc.org/visit-us/find-cemeteries-memorials/cemetery-details/144000/neuve-chapelle-memorial (accessed 4 March 2022).

15 Ibid.

16 Roy Jenkins, *Churchill*, London, Macmillan, 2001, p. 302.

17 Andrew Roberts, *Churchill: Walking with Destiny*, London, Penguin, 2019, p. 239.

18 Jenkins, *Churchill*, op. cit., pp. 302, 304–9.

19 'May 30th 1915', Skippers War, 30 May 2015, https://skipperswar.com/tag/william-temple (accessed 4 March 2022).

20 Owen Gibson, 'Sepp Blatter and Michel Platini banned from football for eight years by Fifa', *Guardian*, 21 December 2015, https://www.theguardian.com/football/2015/dec/21/sepp-blatter-michel-platini-banned-from-football-fifa (accessed 4 March 2022).

21 Wilfred Willett, unpublished memoir, Imperial War Museum Archive, Documents.4329 (*c*.1930s), p. 61.

22 Frederick Maurice, *The History of the London Rifle Brigade, 1859–1919*, London, Constable, 1921, p. 79.

23 Bourke, *Dismembering the Male*, op. cit., p. 31.

24 Jonathan Smith, *Wilfred and Eileen*, op. cit.

13. Ypres Salient

1 Paul Reed, *Walking Ypres*, Barnsley, Pen & Sword, 2017, p. 11.

2 'Menin Gate: the History, Design and Unveiling', Commonwealth War Graves Commission, 17 July 2017, https://www.cwgc.org/our-work/news/menin-gate-the-history-design-and-unveiling (accessed 8 March 2022).

3 Chris Baker, 'Ypres: murder, pure and simple. Why hold it?', Long Long Trail, 10 July 2017, https:/

/www.longlongtrail.co.uk/ypres-murder-pure-and-simple-why-hold-it (accessed 4 March 2022).

4 For a good overall history of the Ypres salient, see Alan Palmer, *The Salient: Ypres, 1914–18*, London, Constable, 2007.

5 Thomas Weber, *Hitler's First War*, Oxford, Oxford University Press, 2010, pp. 51–8, 68–76.

6 Ian Passingham, *Pillars of Fire: The Battle of Messines Ridge June 1917*, Stroud, Sutton Publishing, 1998, pp. 68–72 (see footnote 20).

7 Ibid., p. 70; Reed, op. cit., p. 341.

8 Gillespie, op. cit., p. 278.

9 'Samuel Frickleton VC', New Zealand History, https://nzhistory.govt.nz/media/photo/samuel-frickleton (accessed 8 March 2022).

10 Reed, op. cit., p. 337.

11 Chris Baker, 'Actions in the Spring of 1916', Long Long Trail, http://www.longlongtrail.co.uk/battles/battles-of-the-western-front-in-france-and-flanders/actions-in-the-spring-of-1916-western-front (accessed 8 March 2022).

12 Gavin Stamp, 'War Memorials, Belgium: Bedford House Cemetery, Ieper', Twentieth Century Society, https://c20society.org.uk/war-memorials/belgium-bedford-house-cemetery-ieper (accessed 8 March 2022).

13 Palmer, *The Salient*, op. cit., pp. 197–204; Roberts, *Churchill*, op. cit., p. 254.

14 Palmer, *The Salient*, op. cit., p. 204.

15 'Will Longstaff the artist', Australian War Memorial, https://www.awm.gov.au/articles/encyclopedia/menin/notes (accessed 8 March 2022).

16 Rachel Aspden, 'War through women's eyes', *New Statesman*, 12 March 2009.

17 Bruce Cole, 'A Deadly Weapon, a Solemn Memorial', *Wall Street Journal*, 9 November 2012.

18 Meirion Harries and Susie Harries, *The War Artists: British Official War Art of the Twentieth Century*, London, Michael Joseph Ltd, 1983, pp. 1–4, 20–22, 52–9; 'How the British Government Sponsored the Arts in the First World War', Imperial War Museum, https://www.iwm.org.uk/history/how-the-british-government-sponsored-the-arts-in-the-first-world-war (accessed 8 March 2022).

19 'The Archival Trail: Paul Nash the War Artist', Tate, https://www.tate.org.uk/art/artists/paul-nash-1690/paul-nash-war-artist (accessed 8 March 2022).

20 Simon Jones, 'Pure Murder: John Nash's "Over the Top"', simonjoneshistorian.com, https://simonjoneshistorian.com/2017/12/31/over-the-top (accessed 8 March 2022).

21 'Paths of Glory', Imperial War Museum, https://www.iwm.org.uk/collections/item/object/20211 (accessed 8 March 2022).

22 'The Archival Trail: Paul Nash the War Artist', Tate, op. cit.

23 For a look at *The Wipers Times*, see Christopher Westhorp, *The Wipers Times: The Famous First World War Trench Newspaper*, Oxford, Osprey, 2018.

24 J. P. Harris, *Douglas Haig and the First World War*, Cambridge, Cambridge University Press, 2008, p. 381.

25 Robin Prior and Trevor Wilson, *Passchendaele: The Untold Story*, Yale, Yale Nota Bene, 2002, p. 200.

26 Harris, op. cit., p. 382.

27 David Lloyd George, *War Memoirs*, London, Ivor Nicholson & Watson, 1934, p. 2,251.
28 'Met Office forecasts from World War I to Now', Met Office, https://www.metoffice.gov.uk/about-us/who/our-history/met-office-forecasts-is-world-war-i (accessed 8 March 2022).
29 Quoted in Prior and Wilson, *Passchendaele*, op. cit., pp. 177–8.
30 Nick Lloyd, *Passchendaele: A New History*, London, Penguin, 2017, p. 253.
31 Martin Gilbert, *Winston S. Churchill: Volume V, Companion Part 1 Documents*, London, Heinemann, 1979, p. 884.
32 Lloyd, *Passchendaele*, op. cit., p. 107.
33 Ibid., p. 289.
34 Jonathan Boff, *Haig's Enemy: Crown Prince Rupprecht and Germany's War on the Western Front*, Oxford, Oxford University Press, 2018, p. 275.
35 Jonathan Boff, 'Rupprecht, Crown Prince of Bavaria', 1914–1918 Online, https://encyclopedia.1914-1918-online.net/article/rupprecht_crown_prince_of_bavaria (accessed 8 March 2022).
36 Reed, *Walking Ypres*, op. cit., p. 213. See also Robert Cowley, 'Massacre of the Innocents', *Quarterly Journal of Military History*, vol. 10, no. 3, spring 1998, https://www.historynet.com/massacre-of-the-innocents (accessed 8 March 2022).
37 Quoted in Cowley, 'Massacre of the Innocents', op. cit.
38 Ibid.
39 Reed, *Walking Ypres*, op. cit., p. 214. See also Cowley, 'Massacre of the Innocents', op. cit.
40 Reed, *Walking Ypres*, op. cit., p. 216.

14. To the Sea

1 Palmer, op. cit., pp. 145, 193.
2 Ibid., pp. 193–4.
3 Remarque, op. cit., p. 296.
4 Alan Kramer, *Dynamic of Destruction: Culture and Mass Killing in the First World War*, Oxford, Oxford University Press, 2007, p. 314.
5 Tom Simoens, 'Belgian Soldiers', 1914–1918 Online, 11 August 2016, https://encyclopedia.1914-1918-online.net/article/belgian_soldiers (accessed 8 March 2022); Benoît Majerus, 'War Losses (Belgium)', 1914–1918 Online, 25 January 2016, https://encyclopedia.1914-1918-online.net/article/war_losses_belgium (accessed 8 March 2022).
6 Majerus, op. cit.
7 Evan Andrews, 'Why Was It Called the "Spanish Flu"', history.com, 12 January 2016, https://www.history.com/news/why-was-it-called-the-spanish-flu (accessed 8 March 2022).
8 Becky Little, 'As the 1918 Flu Emerged, Cover-up and Denial Helped It Spread', history.com, 26 May 2020, https://www.history.com/news/1918-pandemic-spanish-flu-censorship (accessed 8 March 2022).
9 Dorothea Crewdson and Richard Crewdson (eds), *Dorothea's War: The Diary of a First World War Nurse*, London, Weidenfeld & Nicolson, 2013, pp. 300, 306.
10 In an interview for *The Prime Minister at 300*, Radio 4, April 2021.

11 Neil Prior, 'Coronavirus: Boris Johnson hospital stay and parallels to Lloyd George', *BBC News*, 8 April 2020, https://www.bbc.co.uk/news/uk-wales-52203254 (accessed 8 March 2022).
12 Anthony Seldon, Jonathan Meakin, Illias Thoms, *The Impossible Office?*, Cambridge, Cambridge University Press, 2021, pp. 179–219.
13 Cecil Margolis, unpublished memoirs.
14 Ibid.
15 Ibid.
16 Palmer, op. cit., pp. 209–10, 223–5.
17 Gillespie, op. cit., p. 300.
18 'The Trench of Death and its Myths', Royal Museum of the Armed Forces and Military History, https://www.klm-mra.be/D7t/en/content/trench-death-and-its-myths (accessed 8 March 2022).
19 Robert Cowley, 'Albert and the Yser', *Quarterly Journal of Military History*, vol. 1, no. 4, summer 1989, https://www.historynet.com/albert-and-the-yser (accessed 8 March 2022).
20 Chris Baker, 'Last Stand on the Yser', firstworldwar.com, 22 August 2009, https://www.firstworldwar.com/features/yser.htm (accessed 8 March 2022).
21 Cowley, op. cit.
22 Ibid.
23 Ibid.
24 James Edmonds, *Military Operations France and Belgium 1917, Volume II*, London, His Majesty's Stationery Office, 1948, pp. 16–17.
25 Ibid., p. 116.
26 Harris, op. cit., p. 361; Edmonds, *Military Operations France and Belgium 1917*, op. cit., pp. 118–22.
27 J. F. C. Fuller, *Memoirs of an Unconventional Soldier*, London, Ivor Nicholson and Watson Ltd, 1936, p. 118.
28 Sean McMeekin, *July 1914: Countdown to War*, London, Icon Books, 2014, p. 373.
29 Paul Gallico, *The Snow Goose*, New York, Alfred A. Knopf, 1942, p. 4.
30 Matthew Arnold, 'Dover Beach', Poetry Foundation, https://www.poetryfoundation.org/poems/43588/dover-beach (accessed 20 June 2022).
31 *The Times History of the War, Volume XXI*, London, *The Times*, 1920, pp. 31–2. For an account of the Dover Patrol, see Charles Lightoller, *Titanic and Other Ships*, c.1935, pp. 338–407, https://archive.org/details/lightstitanic/mode/2up (accessed 8 March 2022).
32 Arnold, op. cit.

15. Epilogue

1 Gillespie, op. cit., pp. 311–12.
2 Ibid., p. 313.
3 Edmonds, *Military Operations France and Belgium 1915*, op. cit., pp. 253–4.
4 Andrew Rawson, *Loos – 1915: Hohenzollern Redoubt*, Barnsley, Pen & Sword, 2003, p. 70.
5 Edmonds, *Military Operations France and Belgium 1915*, op. cit..
6 Nick Lloyd, *Loos 1915*, Cheltenham, The History Press, 2008, p. 128.
7 Rawson, op. cit., p. 70.
8 Lloyd, op. cit., p. 128.
9 Rawson, op. cit.
10 Ibid.
11 Gillespie, op. cit., p. 280.
12 Ivor Gurney, 'Laventie', Poetry Foundation, https://www.poetryfoundation.org/poems/57254/laventie (accessed 9 March 2022).
13 Gillespie, op. cit., p. 256.
14 Gillespie, op. cit., p. 281.

15 Graves, op. cit., pp. 137–8.

16 Edmund Blunden, *Undertones of War*, London, Penguin Books, 2000, p. 53.

17 Gillespie, op. cit., p. 318.

18 Letter, Daisy Gillespie to Douglas Gillespie, 5 November 1914, Gillespie Family Archive.

19 Gillespie, op. cit., p. 281.

20 Weber, op. cit., pp. 220–22.

21 Antony Beevor quoted in the *Financial Times*, 28 May 2022.

Acknowledgements

First, especial thanks to Jonathan Meakin, collaborator on many books, who provided high-quality research, historical context and military analysis.

Next, I would like to thank my colleagues on the Western Front Way, above all Rory Forsyth, Kim Hay, Tom Heap, Amanda Carpenter, Lal Mills, Kitty Buchanan-Gregory, Charles Pike, Laura Lestoquoy, Andrew Gillespie and Flora Devillers.

David Walsh, working with Suzanne Foster, the archivist at Winchester College, brought Douglas Gillespie's letter to my attention in 2012, during our work on *Public Schools and the Great War*.

Peggy Heap and Tom Heap, and Douglas Gillespie's descendants at large, have been supportive and eager to help throughout. My thanks to them for the permission to quote from the unpublished family letters.

I would also like to thank those who provided me with their specialist knowledge: Geert Bekaert, Peter Francis, Xavier Puppinck and George Hay of the Commonwealth War Graves Commission, alongside director-general Claire Horton and chair Lieutenant General Sir Bill Rollo; Aaron Brohi of the Wiener Library; John Taylor for his classical knowledge; Dominiek Dendooven of the In Flanders Fields Museum in Ypres; and Professor Sir Simon Wessely of KCL. My thanks to fellow writers and historians including Martin Gayford, Nick Lloyd and Juliet Nicolson.

I am deeply grateful to Sir Anthony Goodenough, Joe Davies, Peter Francis and David Walsh who all read and offered their valuable thoughts on the text. So too did my long-term trenches-trip collaborator and consultant throughout the trip, Philip Stevens, author of *The Great War Explained*. Louise Hayman, close friend of Joanna and me, and Sarah, read the entire book in proofs, and improved it greatly. Edward Twohig read over the art history sections.

Special thanks is due to James Pulford and all the team at Atlantic Books. James and copy-editor Sarah-Jane Forder improved the text immeasurably with their suggestions. The final stages of a book can often be rather treacherous, but I can honestly say that thanks to James and Sarah-Jane, it was plain sailing. My agent, Martin Redfern of Northbank, confirms why he is the most sought-after in the trade.

Thanks to Jess Macaulay for her early work on the maps. She is a superb artist. My thanks to Bell Hutley, an equally fine artist, for producing the maps in the book. It is always a particular joy to work with former students.

Thank you also to ambassador Martin Shearman and Group Captain Justin Fowler (from the British Embassy in Brussels) who walked the final section of the route in September 2021. Thanks also to Manon Stoffen of the British Embassy in Belgium for her photography. My thanks to Ed Llewellyn, British ambassador to France, and his staff, as well as to his successor Menna Rawlings for invaluable support throughout. Members of the diplomatic service were extraordinarily helpful, including Jill Gallard in Germany, Peter Wilson and Joanna Roper in the Netherlands and former FCO permanent undersecretaries Peter Ricketts and Simon McDonald. Huberta von Voss-Wittig, wife of former German ambassador to the UK Peter Wittig, helped open doors in Germany.

Andrew Murrison MP, the Prime Minister's Special Representative for the Centenary of the Great War, and David Thompson in DCMS and Matt Baugh at the UK Mission to the EU were staunch and invaluable supporters throughout. Colleagues on 14-18 NOW were all very helpful, in particular chair Vikki Heywood, Nigel Hinds and director Jenny Waldman.

My trip in the summer of 2016 helped pave the way for this walk, and I would like to thank the many friends and colleagues who accompanied Rory and me, including Rory's late father Jamie, Cherie Lunghi and Dominic West, as well as Andrew Mullen and Simon Collyer who helped facilitate it, and Susanna Spicer and Andy Hill for their forbearance.

I would also like to thank those who offered their encouragement, including Michael Morpurgo, Sebastian Faulks, Rory Stewart, Essie North of Big Change, Clare McKinnel of Windsor Fellowship, Rachel Sylvester, Jonathan Smith (my lifelong inspiration), John James (on nature, especially birds), and Rupert Molloy who showed me how my legs work.

A very special thanks too to the veritable regiment of Airbnb hosts, hoteliers, taxi drivers, medical professionals, and café staff I met along the path. Without their endless patience with my changing schedule and inconstant French I could never have finished the journey. Wikipedia proved a useful source while on the road.

The Times covered the walk and my thanks to Ian Brunskill and Jenny Coad. Nicholas Hellen and the *Sunday Times* were continuous supporters.

Finally, I would like to thank Sarah Sayer for her patience, love and encouragement throughout the whole walking and writing period, and my three children, Jessica, Susie and Adam, and their partners, Alex, Jonny and Steph, who were with me all the way, even though they were not present physically.

Index

Page numbers in *italics* indicate illustrations

About the Author

Sir Anthony Seldon is a former headmaster and vice-chancellor, and a historian, writer and commentator. He helped found the Institute for Contemporary British History and Action for Happiness, was a director of the Royal Shakespeare Company and honorary historical advisor at Number 10, and is chair of the National Archives Trust. He is author or editor of over forty-five books on contemporary history, politics and education, including *The Impossible Office?*, *Johnson at 10* and *Beyond Happiness*.